ADVOCATES FOR
THE HUMAN RIGHT

"There is a lot of talk today about human rights and social justice. Yet few people consider which worldview best accounts for these. In *The Human Right*, Rice Broocks convincingly argues that the Christian worldview makes the most sense of our cry for justice and reconciliation. In other words, the gospel is the only hope we have for human rights and dignity. And this book can help you apply this truth to make a lasting difference."

> —Sean McDowell, PhD
> Biola University apologetics professor,
> international speaker, and bestselling
> coauthor, *Evidence That Demands a Verdict*

"Rice Broocks rightly emphasizes that whether Christ is true is an eternal life-and-death matter—yet people have no opportunity to make a free choice of faith unless we give them the opportunity (Romans 10:14). He also rightly emphasizes the gospel's concern for justice and its power to bring social transformation. May we heed this message because there is no apologetic for the gospel greater than the lives of those transformed by it."

> —Dr. Craig S. Keener
> Asbury Seminary professor and New Testament
> commentary author, *NIV Cultural Backgrounds Study Bible*

"I strongly encourage seekers of truth and followers of Jesus to read *The Human Right*. It's a powerful and readable defense of the validity of the Christian faith. Witnessing involves sharing our faith, but it also involves giving a reason for the hope that we have. *The Human Right* honestly identifies the objections to Christian faith and answers those objections."

> —Dr. George Wood
> Chairman, World Assemblies of God Fellowship

"In a world where everyone is claiming a right to something, Rice Broocks shoots up this literary flare to highlight the most important right every human being has: to hear the gospel of Jesus Christ. In *The Human Right* he shows how you can help solve injustice now and for eternity. There's little more exciting and fulfilling than that!"
— Dr. Frank Turek
Coauthor, *I Don't Have Enough Faith to Be an Atheist*

"I love these books that Rice has written that are helping believers defend their faith in an age of skepticism. *The Human Right* is his best work yet. He puts forth the most compelling case I've ever read that the gospel should be heard by everyone everywhere!"
— Stormie Omartian
Bestselling author, The Power of a Praying series

"If our 'right to life' is critically important, how much more important is our 'right to *eternal* life'? Dr. Rice Broocks addresses this timely issue in *The Human Right: To Know Jesus Christ and to Make Him Known*. In this book, which expresses his heart for evangelism, Rice examines the power of the gospel to explain reality, address our deepest needs, and change the course of human history."
— J. Warner Wallace
Cold-case detective, Colson Center for Christian Worldview senior fellow, Biola University apologetics adjunct professor, and author, *Cold-Case Christianity*

"The infectious enthusiasm for justice and truth in *The Human Right* comes from Rice Broocks's passion for God. Rice is a story-teller, thinker, activist, author, and strategist, but most of all, he is a follower of Jesus with a relentless desire to help people find the grace that he has received. Read this book if you want an accessible, engaging account of the Christian faith and its call to engage with the biggest challenges facing our world."
— Dr. Krish Kandiah
Founder, Home for Good, UK, and author, *God Is Stranger: Finding God in Unexpected Places*

"In our post-truth culture, truth seems evasive or untenable to the masses. However, Rice Broocks, in *The Human Right*, has cleared the fog and brought a clarifying work that points to the only anchor of truth, hope, and justice: the gospel of Jesus Christ. Each chapter brings convincing and compelling truth that was born in real-life conversations Dr. Broocks has had with thousands of students and leaders around the world. It would be difficult to find anyone more gifted or qualified to bring forth these truths in a language that can be understood by all."

—Ron Lewis
Every Nation NYC senior minister

"Justice and compassion are at the forefront of most conversations in society's spheres—especially with students and young adults. The beauty of the gospel is its ability to translate God into the dialect of each sphere. Dr. Broocks is not only a leading expert in this arena but also a close friend. I highly recommend *The Human Right* to anyone who seeks proven language from a proven leader on this timeless subject."

—Heath Adamson
Chairman, World Assemblies of
God Fellowship (Next Gen)

"My friend Rice Broocks shows us that absolute truth is not something to be cast aside and that the prevailing worldview of the age has shaky foundations. He explores philosophy, neuroscience, and theology to show that each human is endowed with soul, conscience, and free will—and it's our opportunity and call to tell each of them of the Christ who gives them purpose."

—Ed Stetzer
Billy Graham Distinguished Chair, Wheaton College

THE
HUMAN
RIGHT

THE HUMAN RIGHT

TO KNOW JESUS CHRIST
& TO MAKE HIM KNOWN

Rice Broocks

W PUBLISHING GROUP

AN IMPRINT OF THOMAS NELSON

Published in Nashville, Tennessee, by W Publishing Group, an imprint of Thomas Nelson.

Thomas Nelson titles may be purchased in bulk for educational, business, fund-raising, or sales promotional use. For information, please e-mail SpecialMarkets@ThomasNelson.com.

ISBN 978-0-7180-9366-2 (eBook)
ISBN 978-0-7852-1623-0 (IE)

Library of Congress Cataloging-in-Publication Data

Names: Broocks, Rice, author.
Title: The human right : to know Jesus Christ and make him known / Rice Broocks.
Description: Nashville, Tennessee : W Publishing Group, an imprint of Thomas
    Nelson, [2018] | Includes bibliographical references.
Identifiers: LCCN 2017037669 | ISBN 9780718093624 (hardcover)
Subjects: LCSH: Witness bearing (Christianity) | Evangelistic work. | Missions. | Mission of
    the church.
Classification: LCC BV4520 .B664 2018 | DDC 269/.2—dc23 LC record available at https://
    lccn.loc.gov/2017037669

That all may know

CONTENTS

CONTENTS

INTRODUCTION

The Revolution We Need

In the summer of 1984, I had a front row seat to an actual revolution taking place in the Philippines. "People Power" was being unleashed against the government's massive corruption and human rights violations. Thousands of students marched in the streets and demanded the president step down. The passion of the protestors felt like one of the typhoons that regularly smash the island-chain nation.

I was in the Philippines to conduct a monthlong Christian outreach to university students. With me were my wife, Jody; our three-month-old child; my friend and former college roommate Steve Murrell and his wife, Deborah; and sixty students from the United States and Canada.

Steve and I sat in a small coffee shop in Manila and drew a five-mile-radius circle on a map of the city where some three hundred thousand students lived. It was called the U-Belt. This would be the target area for our efforts. Our team met daily with the students on campus and in the streets, sharing our testimonies about a personal relationship with God through Jesus Christ; nightly, we hosted larger rallies, where the gospel was presented. At times during our nightly meetings, students could be seen weeping—not because of our powerful speaking ability, but because of the tear gas wafting into the basement auditorium from the riotous street protests right outside our building.

We also received some pushback from people who felt we were trying to distract the protestors from bringing an end to the nation's rampant political and social injustices. After all, they argued, the nation had a very long, deep religious heritage. If religion were an effective agent for justice, it would have succeeded long ago.

Despite the obstacles, the truth we presented slowly sank in. "Political change has its limits," we told them over and over again. If you change only the government and not the hearts of the people, the problems will continue to multiply, and disillusionment and cynicism will surely set in. The idealists who lead the revolution will simply become a new, ossified establishment. By contrast, the gospel of Christ offers a peaceful revolution of the heart. By changing the hearts of people, it deals with injustice at its true source.

Hundreds of students responded to the call to follow Christ that summer. From that larger group, a core of believers was formed and has since grown into a Christian fellowship called Victory, which on any given weekend attracts more than eighty thousand worshippers in more than thirty locations throughout metro Manila.

It is also the flagship church of a global network of churches and ministries called Every Nation—a formidable force for good, helping the needy, reaching out to students with the gospel, building churches, speaking the truth to those in power, and reminding leaders at all levels of society to serve the people and lead with integrity.

Ferdie Cabiling, one of the Filipino students who came to Christ during that original outreach more than thirty years ago, now serves as the senior leader of Victory in Manila. His life was turned around because of the gospel's revolutionary message: radical change happens when you receive Jesus Christ your Lord. Many years later he told me something I'll never forget, which is at the center of this book's message: *"What you were preaching was not the revolution we wanted,"* he said, *"but it was the revolution we needed."*[1]

The News Everyone Deserves to Hear

Hearing and believing the gospel radically changed my own life when I was a third-year student at Mississippi State University. A fellow classmate told me about the God of the universe who became man in Jesus Christ and died on a Roman cross to remove injustice (sin) from the world, including the sin and injustice in my very own heart. I learned the gospel was not a fairy tale. The events in the life and death of Jesus actually happened, and three days after His death, His tomb was found empty. The best explanation of these facts is that Jesus Christ rose from the dead—thus verifying His identity as the Son of God. His resurrection also affirmed the authority of His words in the Bible.

Ultimately these events changed history. Humanity was given the gift of hope, the assurance that evil would not have the last word, that virtually every wrong in the world could be rectified by transforming the human heart.

Given all this, I submit that there can be no greater cause than telling others about these momentous historical events. Indeed, the central thesis of this book is that hearing the gospel is the *ultimate human right* because it alone has the power to destroy injustice at its very root: the human heart. The corollary would also be true. It is a human right to be able to tell others this all-important message.

To say we are in need of a spiritual revolution today is an understatement—particularly in America. Whether it's because of racism, immorality, or terrorism perpetrated by misguided and maniacal religious fanatics, our world seems to be getting closer and closer to self-destructing. Yet, at precisely the time when the Christian church should be having a powerful impact on the culture, it seems to lack confidence in the promise of the gospel to subdue and eventually eradicate injustice and evil. Long forgotten are the past great awakenings, when the gospel produced lasting changes and helped mold our national character. Even the Jesus Movement of the 1960s is a faint memory to most. The challenge to today's believers to share the message of Christ with others to affect the culture seems to fall on deaf ears.

Because of this—because the collective voices of people of faith seem so faint and uncertain—the masses are looking to other sources and agents of change to deal with the problem of human corruption and societal evil. Record numbers of young people under the age of thirty are dropping out of church or giving up their faith altogether. This demographic shows up in surveys as "nones"—people who are not necessarily atheists or agnostics but have no formal religious affiliation.[2] Many nones see religion and other meta-narratives merely as cultural stories that transmit values, not as facts or true knowledge, so they feel completely free to take them or leave them.

Reaching out to nones was one of my primary concerns in

writing the first two books in this series, *God's Not Dead* and *Man, Myth, Messiah*—which inspired a God's Not Dead series of movies. My working assumption has been that many nones do not practice Christianity simply because they doubt its message is really true.

This unbelief in the Bible's veracity is accompanied by record levels of biblical illiteracy. Out of ignorance, nones and other skeptics caricature the Bible as a repressive, out-of-date book that promotes injustices, such as slavery, genocide, and intolerance. To these unbelievers, miracles are nothing more than myths.

These perceptions have contributed to the steady rise in agnosticism, atheism, and antitheism (so much for tolerance)— and to the misguided belief that only science and reason can save humanity. By refusing to take seriously any metaphysical truth beyond the material world, they leave us languishing in uncertainty and relativism.

That is why I've written this third book for those who are following Christ and seeking to share the gospel with others. You have a daunting challenge, given today's record level of skepticism, and my aim is to help you evangelize in a way that is uniquely effective for our times—to help you explain to nonbelievers that the best solutions to our twenty-first-century problems are found in a collection of first-century documents.

The Gospel as Public Truth

In this book we look closely at the evidence for the Bible's truthfulness and credibility. I take on today's popular view that the gospel is merely a private truth—meaningful to our personal spiritual lives but not the kind of objective, factual truth that, say, science or history offers. I argue that the gospel of Jesus Christ is a *public truth*,[3] as factually true as stating 2 x 2 = 4 or that America's Declaration of Independence was adopted in 1776.

Tragically this idea is as foreign to regular churchgoers as to the culture at large. Yet the gospel is rooted in historical claims that can be investigated and evaluated like any other claims. Scripture makes sure we don't miss the importance of this point when it states, "If Christ has not been raised, your faith is futile; you are still in your sins" (1 Corinthians 15:17). Christianity is the only religion that places the entire weight of its truth on one historical event: the resurrection of Christ.

Many unbelievers will recoil at the idea that Christianity is a public truth, solidly based on objective, verifiable facts. The rise of postmodernism is partly a reaction to a lack of faith in the ability to know any real truth—especially in the area of metaphysical claims and belief systems. By suggesting all stories and cultural narratives are essentially equal, it keeps any one of them from gaining an advantage and thus control. The search for truth, therefore, is abandoned for the sake of tolerance.

Being a follower of Christ means not having to choose between the two as if they were mutually exclusive. Christians are instructed to show others genuine respect while defending the things we believe are true (1 Peter 3:15). Remember, God Himself gives every human being the right to make free choices, even the right to be wrong, and Christians are called to respect that.

Indeed, in the process of following Christ, we learn that truth is not just about being or living right; it's about doing everything in the spirit of love—even for those who consider you their enemy. This charitable behavior is critical if we are to reverse the growing flight of young people from the Christian faith, an exodus that happens after high school, when they enroll in a university. The widespread apostasy is the elephant in the room at almost every gathering of concerned Christian leaders these days. Because our Every Nation ministry focuses on university students around the world, we receive calls regularly from Christian leaders, pastors, parents, and even the students themselves looking for some kind of antidote to help reverse this trend.

To everyone who calls or attends one of our meetings, our message is the same. The gospel is a public truth—*the most important of all public truths*, in fact—about which everyone everywhere has the right to know, because Christ Himself boldly stated, "I am the . . . truth" (John 14:6). He came not only to speak the truth but to model what it looks like in flesh and blood.

Truth, in other words, is not an abstract set of logical propositions; it's a living person. *Knowing* Him is the only way an individual or an entire nation is liberated from the bondage of sin, corruption, and injustice.

The Human Right Movement

I learned the phrase *Great Commission* very soon after becoming a Christian. It refers to Jesus commanding us to go into all the world with the gospel (Matthew 28:18–20). I also knew we were to help feed the poor and tend to the needy, to lead the fight against oppression and injustice with all our might. But there was a subtle separation in my mind between our efforts to stand against injustice on the one hand and the power of the gospel to actually end it on the other. Sadly, too many Christians believe they need to choose between fighting injustice and preaching the gospel. The typical thinking goes like this: one mission deals with problems that are of this world, while the other deals with people's eternal destiny. The tension between the two missions has split believers for decades and is often the key demarcation between those who are theologically liberal and those who are conservative.

In this book I explain to you what I now realize: the gospel is the only source of true freedom, and everyone in the world has the right to hear it. *It is the human right above all others.* That's why it is called "the human right." This phrase is intended to capture the heart of a new generation to take the message of Christ to the ends of the earth. I have found that Christians today, especially those under thirty, are moved to action when they understand spreading the gospel as a human right and justice issue.

The human right doesn't see the pair of missions as the horns of a dilemma. Rather, it sees proclaiming the gospel as requiring us to take on *both* missions. We must use words to communicate the good news but also back them up with actions that testify to the gospel's truthfulness and power. It is not a "social gospel"⁴ but a message that has a dramatic impact on society.

At its core *the human right* declares that God not only cares about injustice but came to earth as Jesus Christ to deal with it personally. The death He suffered on the cross atoned for the sins of the world *and* created a new way for us to connect with God and thereby become new people. To be born again, as Jesus told the religious leader Nicodemus, is to receive the promise that the prophets of old had foretold: "I will give you a new heart and put a new spirit in you; I will remove from you your heart of stone and give you a heart of flesh" (Ezekiel 36:26).

The human right gives top priority to the proclamation and practice of the gospel because the good news deals with injustice at its source: the human heart. When we present the gospel, we are calling every person first to repent and turn from evil (injustice) and then to pass the good news on to others. Just as injustice can spread like a virus, justice can spread as well. This change in our hearts produces the needed change in our character. It is impossible to be a follower of Christ and continue practicing injustice (sin) in any area of human activity.

To call Christ "Lord" means believing in His words *and* modeling them to the world around us. Trying to coerce people into believing the gospel is inconsistent with the very nature of the gospel, which offers true freedom. It is a freedom that gives every person the opportunity to reject the truth or embrace it.

In short, our greatest calling in life is to proclaim the truth and to support its claims with our lifestyles. As Jesus said, "Let your light shine before others, that they may see your good deeds and glorify your Father in heaven" (Matthew 5:16).

To lack a sense of urgency in this calling is to evidence some doubt about its truth and therefore its power and primacy. This is why many have opted for social justice campaigns that have no reference to the gospel, substituting God's truth for their own wisdom. Now is no time to perpetuate that catastrophic mistake.

Jesus Ends Injustice

A few months ago I made a return trip to Manila's U-Belt to address a gathering of some five thousand students. Gone were the protestors, tear gas, anger, and hopelessness I had seen in the summer of 1984. Sadly, massive problems, such as poverty and crime, still exist, but something else is also very apparent. There is a rising force for justice and change at work, spearheaded in part by thousands of men and women whom our fledgling ministry reached more than thirty years ago. They've grown up to be authentic world changers, serving their country in almost every facet of society.

This is what the kingdom of God is like. Once planted, it grows up alongside the kingdom of darkness. The contrast is a constant reminder that injustice will not completely end until the final judgment day. It is toward that final reckoning we are all speeding.

Among those whom I addressed during my recent visit were student leaders from the nation's leading colleges and universities. They are well acquainted with corruption, evil, and injustice, as they witness daily the many victims of that sinfulness. I spoke to the student leaders about *the human right* to see if the concept would have the same impact on them as it has had on me.

At the conclusion of my presentation—when I proclaimed, "Jesus ends injustice!"—the students exploded with thunderous applause, and a high-spirited celebration followed. They sang songs they had sung many times before, but with passion and, I believe, a greater sense of confidence and faith than ever before. In the coming months and years, it will be interesting to see if the gospel remains the best remedy for injustice in the minds of these believers in the Philippines. If it does, then there should be a dramatic rise in the number of Filipinos spreading the good news.

The world today seems to be a more dangerous place than ever before. To bring the gospel to every nation is a far riskier mission than it was when I started more than thirty-five years ago. More than sixty nations still have restrictions against anyone openly affirming Christianity. In more than thirty predominantly Muslim nations, an apostate can receive the death penalty for turning from Islam to Christianity. Now more than at any other time in history, Christians are being persecuted and martyred for their faith.

Nevertheless, the need for preaching the gospel to every ethnicity, generation, and gender has never been greater. With the rise of secularism and the spread of Islamic terrorism, I believe there must be a renewed dialogue about what is true. All *people* are created equal, but their *beliefs* and *behaviors* are not. Christ stated that He is the exclusive representative of the Creator (John 14:6). This should be taken seriously and not dismissed in the name of tolerance. Those of us who believe in the truthfulness of the gospel are called to walk in love and service to others, regardless of their own beliefs. Our purpose is to proclaim and practice the truth, not try to subjugate others.

My aim is to help you communicate the gospel with clarity as well as with the conviction of its truth. Above all, I provide you with reliable information and thought-provoking discussions that help drive home my core belief that hearing the gospel is a fundamental human right—arguably the most important right of all. And denying it to anyone is likewise the greatest injustice of all.

CHAPTER 1

THE HUMAN RIGHT

God's Plan to End Injustice

Yet to all who did receive him, to those who
believed in his name, he gave the right to become
children of God.

—JOHN 1:12

The worst oil spill in US history occurred on April 20, 2010, when a drilling platform exploded off the coast of Louisiana. The disaster known as the BP Oil spill resulted in more than two hundred thousand gallons of crude oil pouring into the waters of the Gulf of Mexico for more than eighty-seven straight days. *Scientific American* described the challenge as trying to cap an "oil volcano."[1] The task of stopping this unmitigated calamity was met with one failure after another as every attempt to cap the ongoing spill at its source failed. Even though it was officially stopped on

July 15, 2010, the damage to the environment was catastrophic. The company was ultimately found guilty of multiple charges and cited by the courts with "gross negligence and reckless conduct."[2]

The damage was difficult to tabulate and continues to be felt today. The flow of oil became a river of death that destroyed wildlife and marine life and altered the livelihoods of thousands of people. Its impact was eventually felt around the world. Images of oil-drenched pelicans and schools of dead fish filled the news and print media. The cost of the ecological disaster was estimated in the multiplied billions. Outside of trying to rescue wildlife helplessly struggling in the sludge, there was not much that could be done. The first and only rational response was to stop the flow of oil at its source—the blown-out rig. What a futile effort it would have been to try to clean up the damage from this spill and ignore the ongoing cause of the problem. Common sense tells you that the most important task was to focus on stopping the problem at its source.

Humanity continues to be its own worst enemy. As great as the damage was from this disaster, it is but one on the list of endless examples of loss and pain due to human error and sin. Nothing should be more obvious than that our world is broken and the results of our wayward behavior have been catastrophic in almost every way you can think. Evil and injustice seem to pour continuously into our world from every place, every city, and every nation. The list of atrocities grows daily—from genocide, human trafficking, exploitation of the poor, and oppression of women and children, to poverty and crime. The very thought of ending all the evil in the world is a dream that might happen in a fairy tale but not in real life.

Contrary to skeptical mockery, the existence of evil doesn't point to God's absence from the world. He is not unmoved by our pain or ambiguous in what the remedy for the world's needs is. But like the oil volcano, the problem can't be fully addressed by just trying to manage the damage. In His wisdom, God foresaw the breakdown before the world was even created. His solution to the multifaceted, hydra-headed monster of evil was to come to earth in the form of a man to shut down this deluge at the source: human sinfulness. This is why the message of this great work is called the gospel (good news).

Jesus announced it when he began His earthly ministry: "The Spirit of the Lord is on me, because he has anointed me to proclaim good news to the poor. He has sent me to proclaim freedom for the prisoners and recovery of sight for the blind, to set the oppressed free" (Luke 4:18).

The claim that the gospel is the cure for injustice is certainly a bold one but, in reality, is the essence of Christianity. My hope is to challenge people who claim to be followers of Christ to grasp the far-reaching claims of the gospel message. When this happens, we can never again be ambivalent about its power or priority in our lives. What anchors this truth—that knowing the gospel is the most fundamental human right—is that without God, there is no ultimate source or foundation for any human rights. In defending the thesis of this book, we must begin with answering the important question, *where do human rights come from?*

The Rise of Human Rights

The idea of human rights is the most important, controversial, and compelling issue of our generation. There is no greater label you can attach to a cause or concern than this.

A landmark in the modern-day rise of human rights can be traced to 1948, when the United Nations passed the Universal Declaration of Human Rights in the wake of World War II and the loss of millions of people who were murdered simply because they were Jewish, Polish, or of any ethnicity deemed "undesirable" by the Nazis.[3] In total an estimated 50 million worldwide died because of the conflict.[4] The declaration included thirty basic human rights that more than 190 nations eventually would affirm. The UN hoped to use its authority to ground the rights of all people in this document. (By *right*, I'm referring to a moral or legal entitlement to have or obtain something or to act in a certain way.)[5] The basic rights listed in the UN declaration include the freedom of religion and the freedom of speech. You could conjoin these two rights and say, *the right to believe and the right to voice those beliefs.*

In recent decades the subject of human rights has taken center stage in the public consciousness in the West, as discussed in the UK's *Guardian*: "The use of 'human rights' in English-language books has increased 200-fold since 1940, and is used today 100 times more often than terms such as 'constitutional rights' and 'natural rights.'"[6] While the increased awareness and focus have been enormously needed and important, most have sought to establish these rights without a solid foundation. As we will discuss shortly, if human authority is the source of these rights, then they can be taken away as well as granted. Many human rights advocates seek to establish fundamental rights apart from any recognition of God and His moral standards. This is an attempt to establish a secular, religion-free basis for how humans deserve to be treated. This seems to be the mind-set of philosophers such as Richard Rorty, who dismiss any notion of duty or allegiance to God as the grounding of morals or right human behavior:

I think the answer to the question "Where does our duty lie today?" is "Our only duty is to our fellow citizens." You may conceive your fellow citizens as the other Italians, your fellow Europeans, or your fellow humans. But, whatever the boundaries of one's sense of responsibility, this sense of civic responsibility is possible even if you have never heard either of reason or of religious faith.[7]

Rorty is correct in saying that you know that there are moral duties without hearing about reason or religious faith. But that simply implies that you are ignorant of where they come from, not that they have no ultimate source. Severing morals and human rights from the ground in which they have grown and flourished is like doing the same to a beautiful flower. It's only a matter of time until its beauty fades. So it is with the culture and society that bloomed into the most influential and prosperous in world history because of its roots of faith in God.

The framers of the United States Declaration of Independence understood this principle and clearly stated, "We hold these truths to be self-evident, that all men are endowed by their Creator with certain inalienable rights." This ideal was the result of the influence of John Locke (1632–1704), considered a philosophical father of the Declaration of Independence and the United States Constitution. Historical revisionists seeking to erase the influence of Scripture and theism on the founding of America want to obscure Locke's faith and its influence on his thinking. This is historical revisionism on full display. Locke's belief in the Christian faith clearly motivated his view of human rights. His theory of unalienable rights invokes God, posing a problem for those who seek a moral basis for human rights that does not rest on religious assumptions.[8]

If there is any doubt about his faith in God, his book *The Reasonableness of Christianity as Revealed in the Scriptures* (1695) confirmed his belief in the truthfulness of the Christian faith.

> And that he was the Messiah, was the great truth he took pains to convince his disciples and apostles of; appearing to them after his resurrection: as may be seen, Luke xxiv. which we shall more particularly consider in another place. There we read what gospel our Savior preached to his disciples and apostles; and that as soon as he was risen from the dead, twice, the very day of his resurrection.[9]

The point is, we are products of divine creation; therefore, our rights as humans are grounded in a transcendent moral authority. This connection of God to human rights is foundational in the same way that many philosophers have recognized that without God there are no moral absolutes. If these rights came from humans, then they wouldn't be inalienable; that is, they could be taken away. Vishal Mangalwadi, one of India's leading intellectuals, made the connection between God, the inalienable rights mentioned in the US Declaration, and Locke, adding the word *sacred*: "In his original draft, Thomas Jefferson penned, 'We hold these truths to be *sacred* and *unalienable*.' That was the truth. That's why the Declaration grounded the 'unalienable' rights in the Creator rather than in the state."[10]

As for the assertion of truth being self-evident, it was due to the culture of faith in God that existed at that time. What was self-evident then appears not to be so self-evident today. To take God out of the equation when anchoring human rights is to remove from them the foundation necessary to survive the shifting tides of human opinion. As pastor Tim Keller explained, human rights simply don't make sense in a materialistic, survival-of-the-fittest worldview:

> Historians tell us that the idea of rights grew out of societies that believed in the God of the Bible. That is not a proof of the existence of God. Nevertheless, human rights make more sense in a universe created by God. Without God, it is difficult to explain why or how they exist.[11]

Keller states the obvious: belief in existence of the God of the Bible is the source of our belief in human rights.

The Origin of Human Rights

Can you imagine the Supreme Court of the United States of America declaring a man "not guilty" and then awarding him capital punishment? Two thousand years ago a Roman governor did exactly that: Pilate pronounced the verdict that Jesus' accuser had failed to provide any basis for a charge against Him. This disrespect of human rights on behalf of the powerful typifies the reality of injustice in the ancient world. How could the Chief Justice of Israel kill an innocent Messiah? Didn't he know that he was violating an innocent person's fundamental right to life, as well as undermining the people's trust in the judicial system?[12]

For most of history, governments terrorized people into submission. Ancient Rome recognized no authority greater than Caesar's. Therefore, pre-Christian Europe had no transcendent source of law that could limit the state's power over an individual. As in every pagan or atheistic civilization, the state's power was ultimate and totalitarian. Because of this, no individual could possibly have a secure, inalienable, or fundamental right to life unless there was a God who had declared this. It is vital to understand that the concept of human rights in the way we recognize them today would have made no sense in the classical world of the Greeks or Romans.[13]

This is why the Bible should be viewed as a great gift by God to humankind. It is truly the fountainhead of freedom and human rights. For example, the Ten Commandments given to Moses more than three thousand years ago were actually statements of individual human rights. For instance, the command to not murder delineated the right to life; the command to not steal spoke of the right to personal property. The teachings of Scripture are clear about just and unjust behavior. (We will look at this in greater detail in chapter 3.)

It was the belief in God, who had created mankind for a purpose, that proved human beings had a right to life, liberty, and the pursuit of happiness. The existence of God was as self-evident as the rights that emanated from Him. The point is that the backdrop of Christianity and its principles have shaped Western culture and have provided the moral framework from which human rights could emerge.

This was the significance of the period in history known as the Reformation. More than five hundred years ago (1517), a German monk named Martin Luther changed history by publicly proclaiming that all human authority, particularly ecclesiastical rulers, were subject to the law of God and not above it. To say this was revolutionary is an understatement. Not since the establishment of ancient Israel had there been a recognition of truth and the rule of law taking precedence over human authority.

For approximately the next three hundred years, there would be a flowering of Western civilization due to this worldview. During this period, great strides would be made toward peacefully reforming nations and kingdoms in light of the truth that God had created the world and made us as humans in His image. Furthermore, He had communicated to us in the Bible and given us the moral code that led to life, freedom, and happiness.

The Age of Skepticism

Eventually there would be a concerted attack to disprove the existence of God and discredit the Bible as a reliable source of truth. As King David warned more than three thousand years ago, "If the foundations are destroyed, what can the righteous do?" (Psalm 11:3 ESV). Radical skepticism came of age in the nineteenth century. It was Friedrich Nietzsche who is credited with the statement "God is dead." This phrase appeared in his writings and was placed on the lips of a madman who goes into the center of a village and begins to cry aloud to the people passing by, "Where is God? I am looking for God."

The bystanders begin to mock him and say, "Has he gone on vacation?" and "Is he lost?" Then the madman turns to them and delivers his message: "God is dead."

He goes on to chide the onlookers with this haunting rant:

God is dead. God remains dead. And we have killed him.

How shall we comfort ourselves, the murderers of all murderers? What was holiest and mightiest of all that the world has yet owned has bled to death under our knives: who will wipe this blood off us? What water is there for us to clean ourselves?

What festivals of atonement, what sacred games shall we have to invent? Is not the greatness of this deed too great for us? Must we ourselves not become gods simply to appear worthy of it?[14]

His deluded message was not that God had never existed but that the idea or concept of God had died. Nietzsche understood the implications of what the "death of God" meant. It meant that the rules of morality that civilization assumed were true were dead as well. Without God, the foundation of the morality that had emanated from this belief was dead. Nietzsche also wrote about a "super-man" in the belief that humanity needed to be unshackled from these restrictive beliefs. In the end, life was meaningless. The super-man would, therefore, look into the meaninglessness and assert his or her own meaning.

This is why it has been so important to articulate the evidence for God's existence. Most people who claim to believe in God (or gods)—worldwide, at least eight out of ten people—would simply cite an intuitive belief or a testimony of some type of subjective experience. These reasons are certainly legitimate. But it is vital that we be able to defend the existence of God to those who do not share or understand our personal experiences. This again was my primary motivation in writing the book *God's Not Dead*. In that book I detailed nine key areas of evidence for the existence of God, including the beginning of the universe, the origin of life, the reality of good and evil, and the resurrection of Jesus Christ.

As we learn later in this book, it is important to help unbelievers realize the faith commitments and presuppositions that their worldview assumes. For instance, Penn Jillette, an entertainer as well as an atheist, concedes that certain beliefs he accepts—such as the existence of the external world—cannot be 100 percent proven in a mathematical sense, yet he feels rational in accepting them as true.[15] He then proceeds to accuse believers in God of being irrational, unable to prove God's existence. But just as he accepts the existence of certain things that can't be proven (the existence of minds other than his own and the laws of logic, mathematical truths, and so on), believers are just as rational for assuming a creator and designer of the universe.

Most of the time we are battling insults rather than arguments. Perhaps the world's most famous atheist, Richard Dawkins, wrote in his book *The God Delusion*:

> I am inclined to follow Robert M. Pirsig, author of *Zen and the Art of Motorcycle Maintenance*: "When one person suffers from a delusion, it is called insanity. When many people suffer from a delusion it is called Religion."[16]

Atheists such as Dawkins endlessly repeat slogans like "There is no evidence for God." Yet when you ask them, "What would you accept as evidence?" they pause and either propose some outlandish request for God to write His name (or theirs) in the sky or honestly admit they haven't really considered the question. In the end they are guilty of circular reasoning by concluding there is no evidence for God because God doesn't exist. Should you meet someone who seems merely to echo the standard skeptical slogans, you can respectfully offer them one of your own:

Belief in God is a conclusion, not a delusion.

Why Secularism Can't Establish Human Rights

The alternative to the theistic foundation of human rights is the philosophy of *secularism*. Secularism defines all of life in physical terms, driven by the natural law of cause and effect. Consequently, the authority of Scripture is rejected, and the very possibility that God would reveal Himself or His will to humanity is denied. Man would henceforth look only to himself to reshape society. Secular values attempt to replace moral values rooted in a theistic world-view. The problems with secularism as a foundation for human rights could be summarized as follows:

1. There is no source grounding them objectively. If God does not exist and man is a product of a purely materialistic evolutionary process, then any concept of human rights could only be a product of the same process. Certainly these rights can be asserted, but that doesn't make them really true and morally binding.

Writing from a Christian perspective, Keller agrees with this: "I'm not saying that you can't assert rights from a secular foundation, I'm saying they don't really follow from an evolutionary world view."[17] Friedrich Nietzsche concurs: "Once sin against God was the greatest sin; but God died, and with him these sinners. To sin against the earth is now the most terrible sin, and to revere the entrails of the unknowable higher than the meaning of the earth!"[18]

It must be pointed out that in some countries, a secular government means that there will be a measure of religious liberty (e.g., Turkey). While this is certainly a good thing, I am talking about the very foundation of these secular values. These so-called secular values of liberty and freedom came from the

Judeo-Christian worldview. This doesn't mean that secular values aren't true or that secular people cannot be moral. It means that secularism can't offer a real foundation for the values they espouse.

2. There is no standard of ultimate justice. With secularism, the only basis for societal rules are people's choices to embrace some social contract, so moral standards change according to people's whims. Any desire can be elevated to the status of a right, and any existing right can eventually be denied. Even more problematic, in times of stress people could surrender their fundamental rights to dictators in exchange for the promises of security or prosperity, as was done in Nazi Germany and fascist Italy—to the citizens' dire regret.

Like a restaurant that offers its menu on a chalkboard so the items can be replaced when they are no longer popular, a society can change its values to match the mood and beliefs of the people of that generation. Going even further down the rabbit hole, the secularism that was spawned from the Age of Enlightenment (the seventeenth and eighteenth centuries) dismissed the idea of any overarching purpose in the universe. All that exist are matter and physical energy, governed by the laws of cause and effect guided by the "blind watchmaker" of natural selection. If there is no purpose, then there is no way of knowing what is good or bad in terms of human behavior.

3. There is no solution for the problem of evil. In the end, secularism has no real solution for the problem of evil. If man is an animal or a molecular machine that acts according to genetic programming, then there is little hope for real reform. How do you address a problem you don't really understand? Evil is obvious. As we will look at in detail in the next chapter, it is indisputable

that evil is the scourge of the human race. To ignore it or deny its existence is to simply empower it.

Going a step further, the idea of a secular society is itself a myth. A secular society is not a valueless culture but one where traditional beliefs are exchanged for new gods (idols). Theologian and missiologist Lesslie Newbigin wrote:

> We have learned, I think, that what has come into being is not a secular society but a pagan society, not a society devoid of public images but a society which worships gods which are not God. But the myth of the secular society remains powerful.[19]

We can also dismiss the notion that secular values offer some kind of neutral ground where cultures can find values apart from any reference to God.

Does this mean that secular people can't be concerned with human rights? Of course not. Keller, however, makes the point that secular people fail to acknowledge the religious foundations of their actions: "This in no way means that nonreligious people cannot believe in human dignity and human rights. Millions of them can and do. But any such belief is, in itself, essentially religious in nature."[20]

Even though I will make the case that the gospel is the solution for the problem of evil, people first must hear the message so they can access this incredible promise. You could discover a cure for cancer, but without knowledge about it, people would continue to die. As the prophet Hosea warned, "My people are destroyed from lack of knowledge" (Hosea 4:6).

This fact was dramatically seen in the American civil rights movement in the 1960s. Dr. Martin Luther King Jr., an ordained minister, stated in his "I Have a Dream" speech that the masses had come to Washington, DC, to cash a check that had been written nearly two hundred years before, stating that all men are created equal and have inalienable rights. King said he had come to claim those rights.[21] Reminding the African American community that their rights were being trampled on was a critical step in the process for deliverance and justice. In the same way, when we come to God and hear about His promises for forgiveness of sins, we can claim the right to become a citizen of heaven, no longer hiding in the spiritual shadows, shrinking from divine justice. We can be truly free.

Why Would God Allow Evil?

For many people, the greatest stumbling block to their embracing the Christian faith remains the problem of evil. In spite of the evidence for God's existence and the truth that human rights are dependent on that reality, many default to the age-old question, *why would a loving God allow evil?* The emotional nature of the argument makes it difficult to respond. I'm constantly aware that personal pain can be overwhelming. When people present this objection, I am very slow to react with a philosophical answer. Many times I just listen and try to serve as a comforter as much as possible.

If, however, this is presented as nothing more than an argument against God, I feel compelled to answer head-on that God has given us the tremendous privilege and right to choose. Our moral choices are real and have consequences in this life and the one to come.

Ample facts demonstrate that humans have the power to rid the world of moral evil (the evil due to man's inhumanity to man). Yet time and again we have used our resources and technology to perpetrate the problem of evil. Last year, while addressing a small gathering of students in a classroom at Georgetown University, I was asked the question, how could a loving God allow evil? Turning to the whiteboard, I wrote out the number one trillion. That is the dollar amount nations spend collectively on their national defenses. This number does not include the amounts spent on police, security, and all the related costs from the legal fallout of crime and social evil. It also doesn't factor in the cost of war in terms of the impact on the people and the environment.

I asked the follow-up question: *What could we buy with a trillion dollars?* In other words, if humans were basically good, then we wouldn't need to waste all this money protecting ourselves from one another. The first thing we should do is end world hunger. According to the World Health Organization, we could feed every person on the planet for thirty billion dollars a year—for just a mere 3 percent of the total defense budget.[22] Think about how revolutionary that would be. The headline could finally read, "The End of Hunger." Then what about clean water and sanitation? The lack of these necessities is the cause of so much disease and misery. British comedian Stephen Fry was asked what he would say to God if he met Him face-to-face. He responded with an angry rant about cancer in children and the terrible hardships humanity suffers, and then he mentioned an insect that bores into the eyes of little children.[23] The disease he highlighted would be eliminated if those areas that are afflicted had clean water and adequate sanitation.

The price tag for the monumental task of giving every person on the planet clean water and sanitary living conditions? One hundred billion dollars a year.[24] That's 10 percent of the total yearly defense budget. So let's add this up. For less than 15 percent of the money the world spends on defending themselves from one another, we could give every person in the world clean water and food.

As they say on TV, "But wait! There's more!"

The World Health Organization says that for every one dollar spent on clean water and sanitation, we receive seven dollars back in terms of savings from all the costs surrounding health care and mitigation of this massive evil.[25] So that means if we spent one hundred billion dollars on clean water and sanitation, we would save seven hundred billion dollars.[26] We actually would profit by performing these lifesaving services for our fellow man. We could then devote this money to moving people away from disaster zones or rebuilding cities and villages to withstand earthquakes and other natural disasters. Though we couldn't eliminate all human suffering completely, we could go a long way toward making such tragedies as scarce as polio. These facts demand a response to the question, *why don't we perform these services?*

The reason is, something is broken in the human condition.

Transformation: Inside Out

"Unless you are born again, you cannot enter the kingdom of heaven." (John 3:3, author's paraphrase)

God wants evil to stop happening not just *to* you, but *through* you. This transformation from the inside out has been how God has lifted people and nations for the past two thousand years. As Vishal Mangalwadi observed:

> When the light comes in and begins to dwell in us, our inner darkness will be driven out. In other words, Jesus does what no dictator can do. A dictator could punish me for taking a bribe, but Jesus deals with the greed in my heart that prompts me to covet other people's money. A dictator could punish me for abusing my wife. Jesus, if he dwells in my heart, convicts and asks me to repent. He also gives me his power to love. When I invite Jesus to come into my heart by his Spirit, then I am born again into a new spiritual life.[27]

Like the law of entropy, which states that things will go from order to disorder unless acted on by an outside source, God is the One who raises us up and saves us from the inexorable slide into evil and despair. As the book of Romans states, "The law of the Spirit of life has set you free in Christ Jesus from the law of sin and death" (8:2 ESV). This language of lifting us up or raising us up with Christ is a major theme in the New Testament. Christianity started in the most unlikely place, against all odds. The Roman Empire exerted absolute power over a majority of the world and cared little about human rights. Though Roman citizens had certain civic rights, the idea that slaves could be freed or children had any special protection was, to say the least, not their concern. Jesus entered this hostile milieu with a message of transformation of the heart. He didn't focus on the outward oppression that afflicted the masses; He came to deal with injustice at its source.

After His death and resurrection, He sent His disciples into the world to preach the gospel. "Go therefore and make disciples of all nations" (Matthew 28:19 ESV). They were to announce that a new kingdom was present. To believe meant to enter this kingdom and follow the orders of the King: Jesus Christ. The confession that was made was "Jesus Christ is Lord." This didn't mean rebellion and overthrow of the secular powers, but a recognition that members of this new kingdom had a higher set of laws to obey. The supreme command was to love God and love your neighbor as Christ had done for you.

Jesus called people to love everyone—regardless of ethnicity, class, or religion. He dealt with racism head-on. When asked, "Who is my neighbor?" He answered with a story we have come to call the parable of the good Samaritan. The story centered on a man who was on the road from Jerusalem to Jericho and fell among thieves and was beaten, robbed, and left for dead. I have been on that road many times. Though it is obviously paved today, you can imagine the danger of someone traveling through the hills and winding little roads two millennia ago. Jesus described how two different people passed by who could have helped the man, and both were apparently religiously observant. But they diverted their attention elsewhere and stepped around the dying man.

Then a Samaritan came along and stopped to help. This man of another ethnicity was the hero of the story. Jesus calls us to do the same. Throughout history, this kind of obedience to Christ has raised up people and the societies they live in. Christianity would dramatically affect the Roman Empire and the barbarians who came to invade it. As the gospel spread, it revolutionized nations and grew to more than two billion adherents. The good that came to the world has been too overwhelming to ignore.

To live in opposition to God's Word is to unleash the chaos and turmoil of hell through our very hearts and lives. Christ alone has the power to stop this at its source. This is no time to be uncertain about the truth of the message, unclear about the need to share it, or to lack confidence in its power to transform anything and everything it touches.

Summary

God is the source of human rights. The existence of God points to a solid foundation for these rights that secularism and materialism can't provide. Realizing this gives us confidence to present the gospel as a viable solution for the evil that plagues the human race. We can engage the world around us with compassion and give those who disagree with the message the dignity and respect they deserve because they are created in God's image. Everyone has the right to make real choices about their morals and destiny.

The existence of evil continues to be a stumbling block to many in spite of any of the sound philosophical arguments that might be presented. Nothing is more painful and vexing to overcome. The gospel provides the only real hope for what is called *the problem of evil.* Not only does it deal with injustice at its source; it also provides comfort that justice will ultimately be served to everyone. I have had more conversations than I could count in which this question of evil eventually becomes the focus of the discussion. Many have admitted their attitude of rejecting God because of evil may not be really justified, but it's all they can do to push back against the torment they feel. It is at this point I am so grateful that I can present the fact that God entered history as Jesus Christ. He was called by the prophet Isaiah "a man of suffering, and familiar with pain" (Isaiah 53:3).

The message God brought to humanity was that He cared for us enough to do something about injustice. This isn't what some would call "fake news" or "alternative facts"; it is public truth that can withstand investigation and scrutiny. The billions of people on this planet have the right to know the message and how it impacts their lives.

CHAPTER 2

THE GOSPEL AS PUBLIC TRUTH

Engaging the Public Square

*But the Lord said to Ananias, "Go! This man [Paul]
is my chosen instrument to proclaim my name to
the Gentiles and their kings."*
—Acts 9:15

Lesslie Newbigin was an Anglican missionary-theologian who
served in India for thirty-four years. When he returned home
to England in the 1970s, he was shocked at the spiritual decline of
the nation—particularly the state of the churches and their commitment to the mission to proclaim the gospel. Being a missiologist
(an expert in the area of missions), Newbigin sought to understand
the reasons for this noticeable recession of engagement with the

culture and overall decline in Christianity in the nation. As a missiologist myself, there are few voices that have inspired me as much as his. Most of his significant writing and impact on the global church came after his retirement and his return to England at age sixty-five.[1]

The most glaring problem Newbigin confronted upon his return from India was a dichotomy that had developed in the collective minds of Christians. It relegated the articles of their faith to the domain of private beliefs and not public truth—certainly not the same kind of truth found in science. The general public mirrored this perception by viewing Christianity as a source of values, not of true knowledge or facts. In short, facts belonged to science and history; values emanated from religious faith. According to Newbigin, Christianity was based on facts and truth that shouldn't be ignored because of their religious implications. More than just facts, the gospel was a news story—true news that needed to be told to everyone everywhere. He wrote:

> A serious commitment to evangelism, the telling of the story which the Church is sent to tell, means a radical questioning of the reigning assumptions of public life. It is to affirm the Gospel not only as an invitation to a private and personal decision but as public truth which ought to be acknowledged as true for the whole of the life of the society.[2]

His central contention was that because the gospel is based in history, its claims should be presented like any other claims of truth. Of course, this presentation should be thoroughly examined and debated—but not ignored or sequestered to church meetings. Open dialogue and debate should follow the proclamation of the gospel, yes, but the story must first be told. He would also empha-size that the cultural context greatly impacts the way the gospel is presented and perceived. This was certainly true in Europe, where the wars of the sixteenth and seventeenth centuries fueled the desire to escape the cycle of violent coercion and confusion by building a world based on truth revealed by God and/or discov-ered by reason, not religious dogma:

> The cohesion of European Christendom was shattered by internal dispute erupting into bloody warfare, and that in the seventeenth and eighteenth centuries Europe turned to another vision of public truth, a vision inspired by the achieve-ments of the new science and eventually embodied in the idea of a secular state.[3]

Secularism did win over Christianity, but most historians have so revised the story from a purely secular perspective that most "educated" people are unaware that so-called religious wars were not just about religion. Even though the end result of these conflicts would be religious freedom coming to the West, they would leave a lasting scar on the European continent. The Scripture is clear that God neither uses nor approves of the use of force to convert people.

Anyone who has read John Locke's *Letter Concerning Toleration* (1689) knows that every single argument for institutionalizing tolerance as public policy came from the Bible. Every principle that John Locke put forward had been argued by Christians such as Martin Luther, John Milton, and Oliver Cromwell and in the Westminster Confession. Biblical Christianity brought peace. In contrast, secular political, economic, and ideological interests have produced history's worst wars: World Wars I and II are prime examples, but earlier, "religious wars" were also driven by rival political interests.

It is also critical to point out that violence in the name of God results from disobeying Christ's commands, not following them. Newbigin stressed that while the gospel should be presented as public truth, it should never be forced upon anyone through coercion by any political or religious authorities. When it is, the message is seriously undercut and ultimately discredited.

That people with vested interests have used religion to do bad things doesn't mean God doesn't exist or the Christian faith isn't true; it just demonstrates that division and hatred are a part of human nature and need to be redeemed and transformed. The cross was pagan Rome's symbol of terror. Christ transformed it into a symbol of love and self-sacrifice. It is true that religious leaders demanded that Jesus be crucified. That only shows that being outwardly religious isn't enough; there must be a change of heart. This is the hope the gospel brings and why it should be openly proclaimed.

I have been fascinated with Newbigin's story because of some of the parallels I have seen in my own experience. After twenty-five years of campus ministry and church planting around the world, I entered a doctoral program at Fuller Theological Seminary to formally study the condition of the North American church. I was intrigued by a statistic I came across: only 3 percent of churches were growing through evangelism.[4] I had witnessed spectacular growth of Christianity in places such as Asia, Africa, and Latin America but seen the message in America and especially Europe face strong opposition.

Why does evangelism fail so miserably in North America? What I had found through my research, as well as my years of practical ministry, is that people in this region of the world doubt the truth of the gospel. Reasserting the truth of the message of the gospel must be a primary focus if we are to see a fresh, vibrant spiritual awakening sweep across the West.

Secularism Is Not Neutral

A major factor behind this loss of confidence in the gospel is the effect of secularism on the thinking of the culture at large. Newbigin would make the case that the so-called secular realm was not a neutral place where only objective facts about the world were discussed. To him, this was the real myth. The failure to understand the faulty thinking behind this secular mind-set had allowed assumptions to be smuggled into society's collective consciousness that were simply unchallenged. We all come to any discussion with our set of presuppositions and prior beliefs. In his book *Lesslie Newbigin: Missionary Theologian*, Paul Weston emphasized the challenging of this myth of neutrality of the secular state:

> We have to question the assumption that a secular state is neutral. It does not establish any of the world's religions, but it does establish a world view which embodies truth-claims which Christians cannot accept and which must be brought into the open and challenged.[5]

As we have discussed, secularism has no ultimate source of human rights, nor does it possess objective truth. Without God as the source and foundation of these things, society is unknowingly operating on so-called secular principles that actually stem from a theistic worldview. Even more unsettling to the secularist is the reality that their outlook is based on faith just as much as the theist's is. Dr. John Williams, an Anglican clergyman, makes this point in summing up what should be called the secular secret: "Our most fundamental beliefs cannot be demonstrated but are held by faith."[6]

Getting a secularist or materialist to admit this is not easy. Yet understanding this will help you dismiss the patronizing assertion that they have transcended the need to believe anything. Most honest scholars will freely concede this. Newbigin understood the need to unmask this misunderstanding about the connection between faith and knowledge and stressed the need to recognize that a person's faith in the truth of the gospel was indeed justified. He also labored to demonstrate that secular values were not neutral and that they ultimately would lead to overt paganism—the belief in multiple gods: "England is a pagan society and the development of a truly missionary encounter with this very tough form of paganism is the greatest intellectual and practical task facing the Church."[7]

Though this is a daunting challenge, it is certainly not an unprecedented cultural scenario. Paganism best describes the world the early apostles had to face, and yet they boldly proclaimed the gospel in spite of fierce opposition. They prevailed because the message was true. This means that though the challenge for us today is similar to the one faced by the first-century believers, we can have great confidence that, as it did for them, the word of God will grow mightily and prevail (Acts 19:20).

The Gospel Defined

As we look deeper at the phrase *the gospel as public truth*, we must first be clear about what the gospel message is that we are to proclaim and defend. One of the most important things we must do as believers is to be clear in our presentation. The theological literature that describes the gospel in all its truth and glory fills countless volumes and would take years to read and process. In dealing with all of the dimensions of this message, we could talk about love, grace, truth, justification, sin, redemption, and forgiveness. As Dr. Krish Kandiah, a UK-based theologian and activist, says, "The gospel is bigger than you think."[8] We don't normally have the time to engage everyone we speak to in an evangelistic conversation or dialogue or in a lengthy theological explanation of the gospel, but we can provide a simple and clear summary.

Here is a definition of the gospel that I want you to consider: *The gospel is the good news that God became man in Jesus Christ. He lived the life we should have lived and died the death we should have died—in our place. Three days later He rose from the dead, proving that He is the Son of God and offering the gift of salvation and forgiveness of sins to those who repent and believe in Him.*

Before I explain each part in more detail, let me remind you how important it is to memorize and master this definition (or something similar), as well as understand the meaning and the truth behind it. People can spend years attending religious meetings, Bible studies, and other events and cannot communicate the gospel clearly and succinctly to others, much less explain its significance in the life of an individual, family, city, or nation. Faith in this message is what changed your life if you are a Christian today. It is faith in this message that will bring others into a life-altering relationship with their Creator. Embracing its truth is also the first step in ending the source of injustice resident within us all. Here is a quick summary of each of the truths in the definition.

God became man in Jesus Christ. God stepped into the world by taking on human flesh. Most religions of the world call men to ascend and work their way to God. Christianity explains that God came down to us. In Christianity, we don't have a god who sits detached from the problems in the world, like the gods of the ancient Greeks, or a cosmic watchmaker who wound up the world and turned his back on it. We believe in the God who entered the world to deal with injustice personally.

He lived the life we should have lived. God expects us to keep the moral law. This is the plumb line that sets apart justice from injustice. The life Jesus lived was completely just and merciful. There is no parallel to the life of Christ. Far from some ecstatic mystic or fiery prophet, He was the embodiment of grace and truth.

He died the death we should have died—in our place. Everyone cries out for justice when evil affects them. If there is no consequence for breaking a law, then the law ceases to be a law. Since we have all broken God's law, we all deserve judgment. However, Christ bore our punishment by taking our place through His death on a Roman cross. The harshness and torture of Christ's death was the payment for all injustice and the provision to set us free from the slavery of sin.

Three days later, He rose from the dead. Christ's resurrection from the dead verified His identity and proved that His authority was real. It also gives us hope that there is life after death. This further demonstrates His exclusive claim to be the true path to

God. This event can be examined historically and presented as fact, not merely subjective belief or opinion. Christianity is the only religion that bases the entire weight of its truth on one historical event—the resurrection of Jesus Christ from the dead.

He offers the gift of salvation and forgiveness of sins to those who repent and believe in Him. In God's gift of salvation we not only receive forgiveness of sins but also are delivered from the power of injustice and its consequences—both in this life and the next. To repent means to turn from injustice and from trusting in our own efforts to earn our own salvation. In turning from evil, we turn to Christ and believe. The promise is staggering: "If anyone is in Christ, he is a new creation. The old has passed away; behold, the new has come" (2 Corinthians 5:17 ESV).

This doesn't mean we aren't able to sin or act unjustly. It does mean Christ has taken His rightful place in our hearts and made us new people. We now have a new power at work from within us that is empowering us to live holy lives. This is such a critical truth that we will take an entire chapter to examine this promise of a new self and a new creation. The transformation of our hearts is how the world is changed, one life at a time. With this clarity in the content and meaning of the gospel in mind, let's look deeper at the reasons why we should view this message as public truth.

The Gospel Is Historical Truth

First and foremost, the gospel is news about events that occurred in history. There is no mythological aspect to this story. It is indeed news. Newbigin says, "The Gospel is news about things which have happened. What has happened has happened, and nothing can change it."[9]

In my book *Man, Myth, Messiah*, I gave an extensive defense of the historicity of Jesus Christ. The record of history conclusively affirms that Jesus lived and was eventually crucified at the hands of Pontius Pilate, the Roman procurator. A third historical fact is that His tomb was found empty, three days after His death. Christianity started in the very place (Jerusalem) where it would have been easiest to disprove. Dr. Gary Habermas, one of the foremost scholars on the resurrection, refers to these as "minimal facts" of history.[10] By this he means these are facts that an overwhelming majority of even skeptical scholars acknowledge as true. These facts of history took place within a framework of other factors that point to the reality that Christ was raised from the dead three days after His crucifixion. This event, foretold by prophets hundreds of years in advance and explicitly predicted by Christ Himself, points to the truth that He is who He said He is, the Son of God.

Having written about this in my previous book, I will not repeat the defense I gave for the evidence of the resurrection. A massive amount of misinformation proliferates on the Internet, making foolish and unfounded claims that the story of Jesus was simply a retelling of ancient myths. Those claims are modern myths that have no scholarly backing or historical sources. This is why it is critical to investigate any claim to truth.

Because the gospel is based in history, it allows us to investigate and debate it in the public arena. This is no legendary tale set in a galaxy, far, far away. The gospel is news about what happened, and regardless of how Christianity evolves based on culture or context, nothing can change the fact of those events in Jerusalem two thousand years ago. Dr. Kandiah also confirmed:

> The church needs to humbly yet boldly enter the public sphere with a persuasive retelling of the Christian story—not as personal spirituality, but as public truth. [Newbigin] takes the logic for this public dialogue from the scientific community. A scientist does not present research findings as a personal preference, but with hope for universal agreement if the findings stand up to investigation.[11]

This view of the nature of the gospel is foreign to most Christians in America. We don't just need a spiritual awakening, but an intellectual one as well. Whether we like it or not, we are in the midst of an enormous global conflict about ideas. For the most part, we haven't trained believers to engage successfully in this critical arena.

The most belligerent and aggressive opposition today to the Christian faith comes from the militant factions of Islam and the skeptical ranks of atheism, both of which maintain that their worldview provides the true picture of ultimate reality. Islam makes historical claims that should be and must be challenged. We will talk about these challenges in detail in chapter 7. Atheism gives detailed explanations about the origins, morality, and destiny of humanity that contain many serious logical and philosophical problems. The gospel makes claims that directly contradict both of these belief systems and offers a competing worldview or meta-narrative that better explains our origins and provides solutions for the crisis of the human condition.

The greatest threat to the progress of the Christian faith is *silence.* Newbigin's challenge to us as Christians is to speak up boldly and lovingly in the public arena:

> Christianity has to take its stand among other religions in this pluralistic marketplace. The church is easily misled into presenting the gospel as just such a way to private salvation. This in fact changes the character of the gospel in a fundamental way by giving up the meta-narrative which encompasses the whole human story from creation to new creation.[12]

As we see on a daily basis, a person's beliefs can have a dramatic effect on the world. We must engage in respectful but straightforward debate about any beliefs that affect our world. When we fall into the trap of seeing the Christian faith as simply a private, personal issue, we are lying down in the face of the greatest struggle and most important challenge of our day.

The Gospel Is True Knowledge

The fact that the gospel makes valid historical claims means it should be considered as true knowledge. Predictably, for those who are committed to the notion that only scientific, empirical knowledge is true knowledge, no amount of evidence will be enough. Even philosophical claims to knowledge are dismissed by those who have embraced this kind of "scientism." This is at the heart of the challenge when presenting this message in the public arena.

We must realize the error in the notion that all religious knowledge is subjective—as opposed to objective scientific knowledge.

As we do with knowledge from all other areas of our existence, we use our senses, logic, intuition, reason, as well as a set of assumptions to interpret the data and input we receive. Reason depends on intuition and imagination. It can only work with the data it is given. Reason is not an independent source of information. It is only as reliable as the data it takes in and the truth of the presuppositions it filters the data through. It is not reasonable to dismiss the evidence of the historical claims of the gospel because of a worldview that excludes the existence of God and the possibility of miracles. That's like saying there is no proof that a suspect committed a crime provided you exclude the evidence that points to his or her guilt.

The quality of our decision-making process depends on whether the knowledge we possess is true or false. All knowledge is not equal and should be diligently and carefully evaluated. The more I have done this kind of evaluation with the gospel, the stronger I have become in my conviction that it is true knowledge. Starting with the historicity of the gospel's setting, it then passes the test of logical coherence. The life of Christ and His message to humanity are indeed consistent with the claim of the existence of a loving Creator. Because the universe came into existence out of nothing, it is also logically consistent that miracles are possible. Therefore, the prophetic announcements of Christ's birth, life, death, and resurrection are evidence of this kind of supernatural power at work in our world. The miracles themselves, including His virgin birth and the resurrection, are consistent within the *plausibility structure* the gospel provides.[13] When it comes to reliable knowledge, therefore, we can say that the gospel gives us true knowledge about the most important questions and challenges of our existence. This includes knowledge of our origins, purpose, condition, and God's plan for our salvation.

Origins: That we are created by God with a capacity to reason, love, experience beauty, and even think about these kinds of things demonstrates that life is no accident. The worldview of materialism and naturalism that reduces our existence to chance is directly contradicted by the gospel.

Purpose: The gospel tells us that humans have a purpose. The loss of this belief in human purpose has produced catastrophic results in terms of the inevitable nihilism (meaninglessness to life). If there is no knowledge of what human purpose is, then there is no way to decide what actions are good or bad. Because there is a purpose to life, it has meaning. Our lives matter and our choices are important as well—beyond their mere, albeit important, practical value here on earth.

Condition: The gospel tells us that something is wrong with human nature, that we have a spiritual problem. We are separated from God due to sin and need a Savior. Though we wish to do good, we have a proclivity toward selfishness and evil—the evidence of which is painfully obvious worldwide. (The next chapter gives a more detailed description of this fact of human evil.) We have the ability to do good or commit evil acts. The evidence of the impact of both of these potentials is overwhelmingly obvious. The gospel tells us that something is indeed wrong with human nature and that we need a Savior.

God's plan: The gospel gives us true knowledge to deliver us and help us. The knowledge of salvation is the essence of this story. By accepting this as true, our lives are healed and uplifted. Rejecting this knowledge leads to futility and despair. This is why the gospel should be heard by everyone everywhere.

Grasping the reality of the truth of the gospel provides the anchor and foundation to our faith and our desire to tell the story to others. It offers a new starting point for humanity to trust that this knowledge is indeed true.

A New Starting Point

To speak about a beginning of things is unnerving to a materialist. The discovery in the twentieth century that the universe had a beginning prompted the phrase *the big bang* as a way to mock this notion. The idea that there was an absolute beginning of space and time sounded too much like Genesis. When it comes to the gospel, we encounter another starting point. By God revealing Himself in history through Christ and verifying it by His resurrection from the dead, we have not only a beginning of a new faith, but a new starting point for humanity. This idea that the gospel provided a new starting point was a constant refrain for Newbigin as he made his case for the gospel being public truth:

> The fact that a man that has been dead and buried for three days does not rise from the tomb was well known even before the invention of electric lights. If it is true it has to be a new starting point of a wholly new way of understanding the cosmos and the human situation in the cosmos.[14]

Every belief system—philosophical, scientific, or theological—seeks a secure foundation by discovering a credible, verifiable starting point for its creed. For Descartes in the seventeenth century, his very ability to think was the starting point of his philosophy. His famous statement *"Cogito ergo sum"* (I think, therefore I am) pointed to his own thoughts as the only thing he could not doubt. This exemplifies the tendency to make us humans the ultimate reference point, which leaves us in a continuous cycle of subjectivism and despair. That's why all knowledge rests on presuppositions—a starting point, Newbigin said, that must be believed:

> Every kind of systematic thought has to begin from some starting point. It has to begin by taking some things for granted. In every domain of thought it is always possible to question the starting point, to ask, "Why this rather than another?" or "What grounds are there for starting here?" It is obvious that this kind of questioning has no theoretical limit. One can go on questioning, but then one would never begin to form any clear conception of the truth. No coherent thought is possible without taking some things as given. It is not difficult to show, in respect of every branch of knowledge as it is taught in schools and colleges, that there are things taken for granted and not questioned, things which could be questioned. No coherent thought is possible without presuppositions.[15]

The gospel is indeed good news because it rests on sound epistemological grounds and gives us confidence that we can know what is true. The challenge to demonstrate the validity of our knowledge of God comes along with preaching the gospel as public truth. (We will examine the area of epistemology in detail in chapter 4.) In the resurrection of Christ, we have evidence that God has revealed knowledge to us that we can receive as truth. Jesus was, in fact, called the Word of God—the living message or information from God about the world and about who we are as humans. The Creator gave us a tremendous gift by giving us this epistemological reference point. It provides a firm foundation for truth and knowledge, as well as critical issues such as human rights and justice. We are able to say with the apostle Paul, "I know whom I have believed" (2 Timothy 1:12 KJV).

Using the term *revelation* conjures up mystical esoteric claims that carry little weight beyond the person making the claim. People making claims to having received divine revelation might even gain a following if they articulate these claims to others with enough passion. But the *revelation* we have in Christ is nothing like these other claims (for all the reasons we have mentioned so far).

In our own experience, very few people can know what we are thinking unless we reveal our thoughts and intentions to them. In the same way, the Creator has revealed knowledge to the human race about Him and us. This gives us a true knowledge of our purpose as well as knowledge of good and evil. Newbigin said:

> If I do not know the purpose for which human life was designed,
> I have no basis for saying that any kind of human life-style is good
> or bad. It is simply an example of human life as it is. Judgments
> about what is good or bad can only be personal hunches.[16]

The gospel offers us a new starting point for our own lives as well. As shown in the chapters that follow, we have been given a chance to be born again—a fresh start in life regardless of our past (John 3:3). This regeneration is available for not only individuals but also society as a whole. This is why we must boldly go forth and proclaim the good news to everyone.

The Gospel in a Pluralistic Society

Western culture in the twenty-first century is defined as pluralistic. Practically, we understand that we live in the midst of a variety of ethnicities, cultures, and beliefs and therefore must live in a way that is respectful of others. This means people of all faiths—including secularists—have to learn to get along. What has followed in the wake of this growing pluralism is the pressure to relativize truth. Pluralism is a sociological reality. Relativism is a philosophy that says that no one can know truth. The fact is, we all know some truth for sure, and we reveal it to one another.

As in the Roman era, modern paganism pressures us to treat every belief as equally valid. On the surface, this type of reasoning quickly breaks down. There are erroneous beliefs of all types, especially religious ones that are obviously false and should be challenged. This is the kind of pluralism that we should desire and defend as valid. It is one in which there is an *encounter of commitments*. This means that we bring our firmly held beliefs into the public square and debate their merits or deficiencies openly. Newbigin wrote:

> Pluralism is conceived to be a proper characteristic of the secular society, a society in which there is no officially approved pattern of belief or conduct. It is therefore also conceived to be a free society, a society not controlled by accepted dogma but characterized rather by the critical spirit which is ready to subject all dogmas to critical (and even skeptical) examination.[17]

The gospel message was birthed in the pluralistic culture of Rome. The classical world was filled with the notion of multiple gods and beliefs, held together by the authority of the state, which mandated ultimate allegiance but gave opportunity for private and personal beliefs to be held. Into this milieu the early apostles ventured with their message of Christ crucified and resurrected. They preached there was salvation in no other name but the name of Jesus (Acts 4:12). In many instances, their preaching produced either a revival or a riot. While they spoke of the exclusivity of Christ, they did not seek to legally stop others from practicing their particular beliefs. They relied on the truth of their message and its persuasive power alone.

As Christians living in America in the twenty-first century, we find ourselves in a similar atmosphere in terms of the plethora of beliefs and religions that surround us. It is critical that we rely on the truth of our message, rather than seek to silence other opinions. We should thrive on the challenge presented by every other worldview and ideology. As I say this, we must be mindful that unless our message is clearly stated in terms of its unique and exclusive claims, and boldly proclaimed, it will get lost and ultimately ignored in the midst of the tsunami of information that exists. Newbigin reminded us:

> The Gospel is news of what has happened. The problem of communicating it in a pluralist society is that it simply disappears into the undifferentiated ocean of information. It represents one opinion among millions of others. It cannot be "the truth," since in a pluralist society truth is not one but many.[18]

We must not shrink back from the proclamation of the gospel and the respectful confrontation of other belief systems that seek to define the nature of ultimate reality. We aren't presenting a message that has nothing to say about morality, lifestyle choices, marriage, or personal identity. For some, preaching the gospel means avoiding controversial topics at all costs. When we do this, we abdicate the belief that Jesus is Lord. To say this means that He is the ultimate authority of all of life and its accompanying issues. It means we are to seek His truth through His Word regardless of our feelings or cultural pressures. This must be done in a spirit of humility, as well as boldness. We cannot back away from answering the tough questions with the answers the gospel offers. We must also not shy away from declaring the truth because it might seem unpopular.

Speaking Truth to Power

The gospel is good news for everyone—individuals, families, businesses, sports teams, cities, and nations. Wherever humans are and whatever we do, the gospel has something to say to us. It speaks to every area of life and every issue we face and struggle with in the twenty-first century: race, sexuality, gender identity, political practices, government, economics, you name it. The impact of the privatizing of the Christian faith has left a gap in the public discourse when it comes to truth. Christians have been excluded from any meaningful place at the table of critical dialogue and relegated to being chaplains. They offer vague and ambiguous prayers at the beginning of ceremonies or conferences and then politely and quietly leave the room. This was not the posture of the prophets in the Old Testament or the apostles in the New Testament. The apostle Paul sought earnestly to make his defense of the gospel in front of political leaders—even Caesar himself. His message was not about political reform and the need for social justice but to announce the message Christ had sent him to tell. When anyone receives this message as true knowledge, then a decision must be made about the best way to apply this truth. Though I believe that Christians should be involved in politics and government or any other vocation and calling in life, this is not a call to try and establish a Christian society from the top down. We are to be salt and light and trust that the truth of our beliefs will willingly and freely win hearts and minds.

Proclamation and Dialogue

This brings us to the obvious conclusion that the gospel must be clearly communicated to others. We are, indeed, to engage in respectful dialogue with unbelievers but not at the expense of proclamation. Because the gospel is news about events that have happened, we should be free to present the case for Christ and the evidence for the reality of His life, death, and resurrection. We have news to tell—that's what the gospel means: good news. We are called to proclaim the events that happened and explain their meaning and the implications for all humanity everywhere.

We must also be involved in ongoing dialogue to explain, defend, listen, and respond to the competing and opposing voices against this message. We can't make the mistake of failing to engage in respectful dialogue after the claims of the gospel are presented or simply engage in dialogue without a definitive presentation of the historical events surrounding the life, death, and resurrection of Jesus of Nazareth. This boldness to proclaim and enter into ongoing dialogue about the gospel and its implications on all of life is the ultimate test of whether we really believe it is true. About this, Newbigin said:

> To be willing so to publish them is the test of our real belief.
> In this sense missions are the test of our faith. We believe that

the truth about the human story has been disclosed in the events which form the substance of the gospel. We believe, therefore, that these events are the real clue to the story of every person, for every human life is part of the whole human story and cannot be understood apart from that story. It follows that the test of our real belief is our readiness to share it with all peoples.[19]

I am so grateful for those people who engaged me with the truth of the gospel during my third year of university studies. They were able to communicate truth without pretending to have all the answers. It was clear to me that following Jesus meant a lifetime of learning, growing, and changing. If nothing else, the gospel I heard brought me hope. Hope that life had a purpose—and, therefore, I had one as well. Most of all, I had hope of forgiveness and freedom from the grip of sin: pride, immorality, and fear. The gospel brings these blessings of freedom, forgiveness, and hope that can have a dramatic impact on the lives of those who receive them and their society as well. This is why we must not shrink back from bringing this truth to the public square. To do this we must clearly understand what it means to say "the gospel is public truth."

The Gospel Is a Human Right

The primary thesis of this book is that hearing the gospel is a fundamental human right. In light of this chapter, let me review the reasons for this as succinctly as possible.

The gospel points to the source of human rights. The gospel is the good news that God became man in Jesus Christ. He lived and died for the sins of the world. His resurrection from the dead verified His identity as the Son of God and the truth of His words. This is evidence that God exists and, therefore, the real source of these fundamental human rights. If God does not exist, then these rights are ultimately man-made and arbitrary. Understanding this is the most important step in grasping the immovable, undeniable basis for all human rights.

The gospel gives the reason we are human. We are not just physical beings, animals operating by our genetic proclivities. We each possess a soul. (Evidence for the existence of the soul will be presented in chapter 5.) This means our moral actions are real and therefore free will indeed exists. The naturalistic worldview attempts to reduce everything to matter. If this is true, how can our actions be just or unjust? God exists and has made us in His image. This is the reason that as humans we have value and rights beyond the animals or other living things.

The gospel emphasizes your right to choose. Every person has the God-given right to make choices. Faith can't be coerced. The gospel calls us to respond freely to the evidence for God and the claims of Christ. We can also reject these claims and live in any manner we choose. And while we have the right to make our own decisions, we do not have the right to choose the consequences. Real tolerance is grounded in the fact that God is the source of human freedom. We are called to respect others regardless of their differences in morals or religious views because they have a God-given right to hold those views.

The gospel points to the law of God, which describes rights and responsibilities. The law of God is the standard that judges human behavior. The law gives us the knowledge of God's righteous standards and reveals where we have fallen short. Far from a set of restrictive, overreaching commands, these laws also reveal the essence of human rights. Each of God's laws provides justification of basic human rights that He desires to protect.

The gospel tells us that injustice is sin. The reason for Christ's death is because of humanity's injustice and evil. This is what is meant by sin. There is nothing more empirically verifiable than the reality of the sinfulness of humanity and our need for a Savior.

All nations have laws. Some are good, and some are evil and unjust. God's laws are higher than any national laws and carry a greater weight. This means that regardless of any kind of legalized oppression, judgment will come.

There will be a day of judgment. For there to be justice, there necessarily must be judgment. God has promised not only to remove injustice, by offering mankind a new heart, but, ultimately, to judge all. The resurrection of Christ from the dead points to this day of judgment, in which all of mankind will stand before God and give an account for our actions. This serves as a restraint against evil and the promise of an ultimate reckoning for all humanity.

The gospel deals with injustice at its source. The real source of injustice is the human heart (soul). Jesus spoke of the necessity to be born again. This is fulfillment of the Old Testament prophets' words that the faithful would receive a new spirit and a new heart (Ezekiel 36:26–27). This is obviously a supernatural miracle that can reverse the course of any human life. The plan of God is to change the world by transforming humanity from the inside out. Institutional injustice cannot last if those who participate have experienced this kind of rebirth.

The gospel is true. Because the gospel is true, it should be a basic human right for all to hear it. As Newbigin affirmed, "If it is true, it is true for all and must not be concealed from any."[20] May the same passion for the Christ and His message grip us afresh today and awaken us from the nightmare of our doubt and uncertainty.

The apostle Paul took the gospel into the heart of a pagan society two thousand years ago and proclaimed its truth to a culture that embraced virtually every religious idea. One of the main accounts of his efforts, in Acts 17, reveals three responses. Some scoffed and dismissed what he said, others considered and weighed the truth of his claims, and still others believed. May we be willing to proclaim the truth, be patient and wise in our dialogue, and be brave enough to accept these various responses without losing heart.

Summary

The theme of this chapter is truly the heart and soul of the message of this book. The gospel is public truth. When it is diminished to being presented as merely private beliefs, then Christianity ceases to be the salt and light to the world that it is called to be. Secularism does not offer a neutral space where objective facts from science can guide our actions. In fact, all knowledge has an element of faith at its core. As Augustine said, "Do not seek to understand in order to believe, but believe that thou mayest understand."[21]

The gospel is public truth because it is based on historical claims. Whereas religious beliefs are seen as merely a source of values, the real facts of the gospel can stand up to historical verification. Pluralism states that all values and beliefs should be given equal standing and respect, yet there are no such things as pluralistic facts. While being respectful to all individuals, we must lovingly confront all claims concerning the nature of reality and test them to see if they are true or false. Ultimately the gospel is a source of true knowledge—just as valid as any knowledge from the natural sciences. Because God has revealed Himself in history and verified this through the resurrection of Christ from the dead, we now have a new starting point in human history. This new starting point gives us a solid epistemological foundation as well as a fresh starting point for personal and cultural regeneration.

In light of this, we are to announce the truth of the gospel and the lordship of Christ in every area of life. Speaking truth to power is not to seek political salvation or coerced obedience to mere superficial expressions of faith, but a genuine dialogue that patiently contends for the claims of Christ and how they can be applied in the public arena.

The testimony of history is that the gospel has been a driving force of justice and freedom wherever it has been freely and openly proclaimed.

CHAPTER 3

THE CRY FOR JUSTICE

The Gospel and Social Change

Injustice *anywhere is a threat to justice everywhere.*

—Dr. Martin Luther King Jr.
"Letter from a Birmingham Jail"[1]

The nation of South Africa has been on the center stage of the struggle for human rights. Apartheid (Afrikaans for separation) began in 1948 and was the name of the nation's official policy that separated whites from nonwhites in every area of society. Whites were given the place of power and privilege while nonwhites were relegated and divided into permanent lower classes. It was fewer than thirty years ago that the outcry against this evil and oppressive system became so thunderous that it cascaded over the land like a tsunami, wiping out the structure of institutional injustice and ushering in a new day of change and hope.

Even though racism and apartheid were promoted and perpetuated by many in the name of religion, it was the influence of biblical Christianity and its teaching that helped the nation avoid a bloody revolution and find the grace to forgive and reconcile. This was embodied in the life of Nelson Mandela, who—though imprisoned for twenty-seven years for attempting to subvert an unjust system—emerged to lead the country into the fresh air of freedom.[2]

The euphoria from the newfound freedom soon dissipated as the new struggle of building a just society was embraced. Once again, changing hearts is the most difficult challenge of all. The events of the past two decades have been especially important to me because of my involvement in ministry in South Africa over much of this period. I have observed Christians stepping to the forefront to lead the way in social reform and issues of justice and reconciliation. This special nation is overcoming the enormous odds stacked against it when it comes to achieving peace, freedom, and unity. Much work still remains to stem the tide of corruption that threatens to throw the nation back into turmoil.

South Africa recently played host to our Every Nation conference in Cape Town, which drew delegates from fifty-eight nations and was the ideal backdrop to emphasize the theme that as the gospel is freely shared and widely applied, society is impacted for the better. My message to this audience was similar to the one I gave in Manila: "The Human Right." After I spoke, student leaders pressed around to tell me how important they felt it was for the gospel to be framed in this way.

I repeatedly heard about the ongoing challenge of deconstructing the perception that emphasizing the gospel somehow causes people to ignore the real social issues facing the culture. Again and again I am struck with the reality that the history of Christianity, with its radical impact on culture and its power to deal with injustice, has been obscured.

Following the conference, I stayed over to speak at two colleges, the University of Cape Town and University of Stellenbosch. Both campuses were experiencing protests regarding issues of student fees and a general sense that the rights of many young people were still not respected. I spoke again on the same theme from the conference, and the response was enthusiastic as the students made the connection between the gospel and its power to deal with injustice at its source—the human heart.

Mark Griffiths, the pastor of Every Nation Stellenbosch, asked if I would like to tour the campus and have lunch with a few of the campus leaders the following day before my flight home. I agreed, thinking I would have a nice break from the intense meetings I had been involved in at the conference. As we approached the place where we supposedly were to meet this small group of students, I noticed a flood of college students heading in the same direction. "Looks like something exciting is happening on campus, maybe a protest," I remarked. As we rounded the corner, it began to dawn on me that my supposed small meeting had turned into a flash mob of sorts. More than 250 students had heard I was going to be speaking and jammed into a rather small room.

The reason was simple: they wanted to hear the solutions the gospel could offer to their current student unrest. The majority of those who attended this spontaneous gathering were white.

However, the small minority of black students that came had the most to say once I opened the floor for questions and dialogue.

Several students expressed frustration that Christians didn't seem to be interested in their plight or struggles. My response was to listen and try my best to express the greatest hope of their nation (and any nation, for that matter) was Christ and His message of a transformed heart. I stressed to them that this has been the driving force of any lasting change that has happened around the world. To even define what is just and unjust requires grasping the existence of a moral authority in the universe. I could sense a peace in the room as students considered that Christ gave them the best opportunity to have a truly safe place to openly dialogue about solutions to the problems they faced.

God and Justice

The cry for justice is getting louder and louder from virtually every part of the globe. The more these voices are raised, the more we should be provoked to answer the question, *what can be done to end injustice?*

I'll repeat again what I repeated to those students: justice is at the very heart of the gospel of Jesus Christ. It is because of God's justice that the penalty for sin and injustice could not be ignored or dismissed—so much so that God came to earth as Jesus Christ to personally deal with the problem of evil. For this reason, we must go deeper into understanding what justice is and why it is foundational to our understanding of God and how He expects us to live.

Time and time again throughout history, the prophets of God warned of impending judgment because of systemic injustice. Micah was one of those prophets. He lived and ministered during the reign of Hezekiah and was a contemporary of the prophet Isaiah. He issued warnings that judgment was coming to the land. The reason? Rampant injustice: "Hear this, you heads of the house of Jacob and rulers of the house of Israel, who detest justice and make crooked all that is straight" (Micah 3:9 ESV). Reading this short book in the Old Testament gives you a sense of the nature of injustice. Not only was idolatry practiced but also financial oppression, robbery, bribery, and murder. The rulers were corrupt, and the religious leaders preached "peace" while calling evil good and good evil. Beyond the prophetic warning there was given a pathway to justice and to true peace with God, the ultimate Judge: "He has told you, O man, what is good; and what does the LORD require of you but to do justice, and to love kindness, and to walk humbly with your God?" (Micah 6:8 ESV).

We will tour the moral landscape of our world and survey the atrocities that have deeply scarred it. We will see that all injustice is not equal. Just as there are certain crimes that carry a harsher sentence, there are different levels of injustice as well. It is easy to prioritize the cause or concern whose constituents raise the loudest outcry. The slaughter of innocent people at the hands of cruel dictators or Islamic extremists, the blight of human trafficking, and the innocent lives lost in abortion are among the things that should be our highest concern.

In spite of these major issues, there is an ever-increasing movement that demands tolerance for every belief and behavior. Ironically, there is nothing more *intolerant* than many of these same voices being raised for tolerance. The word *tolerance* might be one of the most misunderstood words and concepts of our age. For example, one of the greatest injustices against our fellow man is to *tolerate* evil. In America, a football coach with an incredible record of winning games and a reputation for leadership and integrity was alledged to have known about children being assaulted by one of his assistant coaches—but he failed to act. Any toleration of this evil behavior injures the lives of young children and erases a lifetime of achievements virtually overnight. We cannot be truly just while looking the other way when evil is practiced.

On the other hand, we must do more than simply *tolerate* those with whom we disagree. As believers, we are called to something greater than tolerance. Jesus commanded us to love our enemies (Matthew 5:43–44; Luke 6:26–27).[3] The apostle Peter instructed us to be ready to give the reason for the hope within us, but to do it with gentleness and respect (1 Peter 3:15). In the end, we can't make every offense and personal preference a justice issue. If we cry foul every time someone disagrees with us, quickly label others intolerant at the first hint they don't agree with what is being culturally promoted as the issue of the day, we are guilty of the very intolerance we are accusing others of practicing. If everyone's preferences and sensitivities are cast as justice issues, our society will eventually be torn apart.

This discussion is so volatile that it has divided communities and families as well as nations. The solutions to this dilemma are not easy to grasp. There are some important things to consider if there is to be any hope of resolving this stalemate. The language of rights, as we have said, is a relatively recent phenomenon. Instead of rights, the discussion historically centered more on moral duties. It was more of an issue of sin and judgment versus a violation of someone's rights. There are two critical thoughts one must consider in order to grasp the depths of this ethical dilemma. Newbigin stated this succinctly: "First, in a society which has no accepted public doctrine about the purpose for which all things and all persons exist, there is no basis for adjudicating between wants and needs."[4]

In a world with no God, man is simply another animal with no real purpose. If there is no purpose, then there is no basis for determining what is good or bad in terms of how you use or abuse something. Newbigin continued:

> Secondly, both parties rely on the concept of the rights of the individual . . . but rights are totally void of meaning unless there are parties who acknowledge the responsibility to meet the claim of right. Since there is no corresponding public doctrine about human responsibility, the multiple and contrary claims to right can only destroy society.[5]

Again, it takes a moral authority to define what our responsibilities are to our fellow man. Jesus Christ gave us our greatest command not only to love God but to love our neighbor as ourselves. Christianity offers the moral foundation for human responsibility as well as human rights. This is why it is so futile to hope for justice while ignoring or denying the rightful place of God and His truth as the ultimate standard and judge—the only one that is both totally righteous and completely just. If there is no judge like this, then the term *justice* is simply what each person decides to define it. Any claims of rights by certain individuals or groups are simply competing conflicts of interest.

I will restate this often so that as we examine the painful horrors of man's inhumanity to man, we do not lose heart. It is the hope of the gospel that compels us forward into the darkest places of our world with a message that has historically made the greatest difference with the promise that we will not be put to shame for declaring it (Romans 10:11).

We must remember that wherever injustice is found, the gospel is needed. This was certainly the motivation of Dr. Martin Luther King Jr. When challenged about coming to the city of Birmingham to stand with those who were facing oppression in the 1960s, he wrote, "I am in Birmingham because injustice is here."[6]

We are in desperate need of a new generation of leaders like this—who stare injustice in the face and dare to speak God's truth into every area of human need regardless of opposition.

The Outcry of Injustice

The late Christopher Hitchens was regarded as atheism's most eloquent voice. His book *God Is Not Great: How Religion Poisons Everything* was a global bestseller. His attacks against religion were rehearsed and repeated as often as a politician's favorite cliché. One of his favorites was to liken a world in which God existed and issued commands to humanity from what he called "a kind of divine North Korea."[7] He proposed that such a universe would be as repressive a regime as exists there today. But if God were anything like the dictator in North Korea, Hitchens would never have had the chance to utter those opinions or live in the manner he chose. God created a world in which humans have real choices. Evil is a choice, though it is a wrong choice. *The existence of evil doesn't point to the absence of God from the world but His absence from our lives.*

The reality is that *sin ruins everything*. All of humanity has been affected by the "virus" of evil. It affects not only individuals and families but also governments, religion—everything. In his song "Imagine," John Lennon attempted to sell this notion that if belief in God and religion disappeared, all the world would live in harmony. Is that really true? If all religion disappeared overnight, would crime end? Would murders cease? Would the prisons become empty? Could we unlock our doors, dismiss our police forces, and abolish our armies? Would racism, sexism, classism finally end? We all know this is absurd. A world without God is the best description of hell.

The carnage due to man's flight away from God is almost too much to bear and can be traced back to the beginning of human history. Evil and injustice have been around since the beginning of humankind. Almost four thousand years ago, the volume of this kind of injustice was so great that it produced an uproar: "The outcry against Sodom and Gomorrah is great and their sin is very grave" (Genesis 18:20 ESV).

In fact, the first recorded murder produced a similar phenomenon. When Cain killed his brother Abel, the Scripture says, God told Cain, "The voice of your brother's blood is crying to me from the ground" (Genesis 4:10 ESV). If the blood of one murder and the sin of one city produced an outcry that reached heaven itself, imagine the sound that is being produced today.

Here is a brief overview of the devastating human condition:

Human trafficking: Few realize that more human slaves exist in the world today than ever in history. And human trafficking will soon surpass drug and weapons trafficking in terms of frequency, finances, and personal impact.

The number of victims is estimated around the world at 27 million adults and 13 million children.[8] Some young children are kidnapped or sold to traffickers by their families to become prostitutes, laborers, child soldiers, or even suicide bombers.

Oppression of women: The oppression of women, particularly in countries with minimal historic Christian influence, is still an epidemic. Millions of civilian women experience torture and other abuse during armed conflicts.[9] Millions are married against their will in exchange for property and livestock. Countless girls have little access to education, and their nations' laws do not protect them from domestic violence. As many as twenty thousand women in the Middle East and Southwest Asia die every year as a result of so-called honor killings.

Murder: The United Nations reports that roughly half a million people die each year due to homicide.[10] The highest rates are in Central America and southern Africa, due to political unrest. Other nations see large percentages resulting from the prevalence of alcohol and drug abuse. This statistic does not include the one hundred thousand to two hundred thousand people who die each year from armed conflicts.[11] The total cost of global violence is a staggering $13.6 trillion.[12]

Abortion: You can't fail to mention that an estimated 1.5 billion babies have been aborted worldwide.[13] The fact that a beating heart has been stopped in a majority of cases should make us mourn this catastrophe. While the rights of women should be respected, the rights of the unborn child should be protected as well. That the child has his or her own DNA should be evidence enough that he or she is not an appendage or an extension of the mother's body.

Crime: Throughout the world, nations are overwhelmed as they address the proliferation of such crimes as drug trafficking, money laundering, Internet crime, organized crime, intellectual property piracy, and endangered species trade. The costs of cybercrime alone could be more than $500 billion, which is greater than many nations' entire GDP.[14] The United States alone sees more than 1 million violent crimes in a year.[15]

Terrorism: In 2015, nations around the world experienced 11,774 terrorist attacks. The impact included 35,000 injuries, 12,000 kidnappings, and more than 28,000 deaths.[16] (The death toll today is ten times greater than fifteen years ago, and the economic costs are more than $50 billion.)[17]

Poverty and Hunger: The challenge of poverty around the world is completely staggering. More than 80 percent of the world's population lives on less than ten dollars a day. More than twenty thousand children die each day from living in poverty. Nearly 1 billion people entering the twenty-first century cannot read. An estimated 40 million have HIV, and an estimated 1 million die from malaria. More than 1 billion people have inadequate access to water, and 2.6 billion lack basic sanitation. More than 1 billion live without electricity. And nearly 800 million are chronically undernourished.[18] Many of these problems could only worsen over the next few decades due to continued political unrest, population growth, and limited access to food, water, and fuel.

Racism: I've mentioned racism throughout this book as a prime example of the injustice the gospel of Christ can address. In the United States this seems to be the wound that will not heal. Just when it seems real progress is being made, an incident takes place, such as an African American being shot by police, and the wound is torn open afresh. This is often followed by protests, more violence, and speeches. No lasting change or peace is ultimately attained. The African American community is left with the sense it is expected to suffer in silence.

There are so many other things I could have mentioned that demonstrate the enormous tragedy of the human condition. It's almost humorous that the song playing in the background while I am writing this is "Waiting on the World to Change." Left to ourselves, we are in for a long wait. We are in desperate need of a Savior. This is what the gospel offers. We now turn to the question, *what can be done to end injustice?*

It's a massive understatement to say that the impact of this giant of injustice affects everyone. In one of the oldest books in the Bible, Job cried out in despair to the Lord because there seemed to be no relief from this plague of evil: "Though I cry, 'Violence!' I get no response; though I call for help, there is no justice" (Job 19:7). In light of this mountain of injustice, it is a curious and perplexing tendency among many people to focus on issues afflicting—the symptoms, so to speak—while ignoring the root causes of the problems. Maybe it's because there is uncertainty about what justice is.

What Is Justice?

It's much easier to point out injustice than to define what justice is exactly. I guess you could say that justice means stopping the injustices we've just discussed. The underlying theme in many movies today revolves around the bad guys getting the justice they deserve for their evil deeds. The word *karma* has made its way into Western vocabulary from Hinduism and Buddhism, which teach a principle of "reaping what you sow." You are rewarded or punished based on whether your actions are good or bad.

One basic meaning of *justice* concerns what is morally right and wrong. Another is associated with upholding and defending the laws of a particular government. As you look deeper into the many ways the word *justice* is defined, you begin to see terms such as *fairness* and *equity*. It becomes apparent that how you define justice will be the way you also view injustice. Far from merely quibbling over definitions, the debate about what justice is has become one of the most important philosophical and practical discussions of our day. Moral philosophers may argue about these important concepts in the academic arena, but individuals, governments, and cultures are judged by how they define and defend their view of justice.

Justice Versus Social Justice

Theoretically, justice deals with what is legal, moral, and ethical. Yet the term *social justice* has emerged almost in contrast with the idea of justice. To most people, justice represents convicting people of breaking laws and the consequent punishment involved. Much of what is called *social justice*, however, involves a code of conduct that society views as moral and fair, rather than being strictly legal or illegal. Those who are involved in activities involving social justice would describe themselves as being devoted to correcting the inequities in the justice system that would allow something unfair or immoral to go unpunished.

Social justice movements on campus have little to do with breaking laws in the traditional sense. The phrase has come to describe the front line of cultural wars, where terms such as *microaggressions* and *safe places* are also chief concerns. The safety that is sought is more of a respite from the speech or actions of others. These actions need only make someone feel uncomfortable to qualify as off-limits. Sadly, facts don't matter as much as perceptions and feelings. The freedom *of* speech is being replaced by freedom *from* speech that someone might feel is offensive. The right to disagree is fundamental to the idea of democracy, and a denial of that right is, in fact, a growing injustice that has hijacked a large segment of the social justice movement. If others view what you say or do as judgmental in any way, the social justice police will find its way to your door.

I'm in no way dismissing the entirety of the social justice movement. Many use the terms *justice* and *social justice* interchangeably. But it's important as well to point out that many elements of the social justice movement have been co-opted by political forces that seek to promote their causes and agendas. While the symbol of justice is a blindfolded statue, many social justice warriors take off the blindfold and treat people differently whether they agree or disagree with their underlying worldviews. This bias undermines the credibility of anyone promoting or denouncing something in the name of social justice. Like the events taking place in a sporting match, the actions of the players on the field are viewed as just and fair depending on which team you are supporting.

No God, No Justice

During times of civil unrest, the chants are heard in the streets: *No justice, no peace.* Peace seems to be the elusive goal of all parties involved. Peace is not just the absence of conflict but the presence of something else. When the protests stop, it doesn't mean real peace has been achieved; it just means that the problems have submerged, waiting to resurface at the next flash point of injustice.

The real issue is this: if there is no God, then justice and morality are merely one group's opinions pitted against another's. Atheists such as Sam Harris and Michael Shermer talk about a *moral arc* of history, echoing the words of Dr. Martin Luther King Jr., to try to establish a secular, naturalistic explanation of morality.

Yet as I mentioned in chapter 1, neither human rights nor justice logically proceed from an evolutionary (nontheistic or non-directed) worldview. When the religious implications of morality are not ignored, this connection is obvious. In the movie *Man of Steel*, Superman is battling an invasion of rebels from the planet Krypton. They possess the same superpowers he has. As he struggles to protect the people of Earth from the impending annihilation, he is told by a Kryptonian, Faora, "The fact that you have a sense of morality and we do not gives us an evolutionary advantage."[19]

These were the real-life sentiments of the Nazis in World War II. The fruit of this philosophy was millions of deaths at the hands of those who had shed the shackles of conscience and fully embraced the Nietzschean philosophy that "our so-called human nature is precisely what we should do well to overcome."[20] He meant that the current version of humanity would be superseded by the next step in evolution; just as modern man had overcome his apelike ancestry, the next generation of humanity would overcome what we are today. Nietzsche's disdain for the moral restraints of Christianity came to its full expression in the minds of the instigators of the Third Reich.

On the other hand, there is no question that belief in God and the teachings of Christ have impacted the world for good. The commands of Scripture to love your enemies and help the weak stand in stark contrast to the evolutionary tenet of the survival of the fittest. Let's take a closer look at the incredibly positive impact this set of values has had on the world.

The Bible and Justice

First, we must look at the Bible directly to grasp the depth and breadth of God's love for humanity and His call for justice. As I show in greater detail in chapter 6, the Bible has been the source of much of what we enjoy that is good and honorable.

Old Testament

The beginning of Genesis describes the source of social injustice as the corruption of the human heart, which resulted from people's separation from their Creator. The remaining Old Testament scriptures describe how God responded to humanity's rebellion by staging a rescue operation to bring all people back to Him.

As one of the most notable events, the book of Exodus begins with the Hebrews being forced into brutal slavery by the Egyptians. God hears the cries of His oppressed people and then calls Moses to rescue them out of slavery to bring them into a land in which they could find peace. God also gave the Israelites laws, which defined how, in their context, a just society should function. Skeptics often discount God's laws as antiquated or even oppressive. A closer look reveals that these laws protect us from behavior and practices that will destroy us. God's laws are boundary markers and warning labels to keep us from destroying ourselves.

A classic example is the command for a punishment to be given, which is an "eye for eye, tooth for tooth" (Exodus 21:24). Today this command draws criticism as being harsh and judgmental. The truth is the exact opposite. Most legal codes at the time allocated harsher judgments for the poor than for the rich. In contrast, the Mosaic law prescribes punishment that fits the crime, regardless of the instigator's social status.

The Law also differed from the laws of Israel's neighbors in how it speaks of the most vulnerable in society. Most ancient legal codes favored the social elite, but the Old Testament edicts always emphasize protecting the widow, the orphan, and the foreigner. These groups were at the very bottom of the social ladder, so they could face devastating consequences from any social unrest or economic misfortune. God's law declared that He would be their defender: "You shall not wrong a sojourner or oppress him, for you were sojourners in the land of Egypt. You shall not mistreat any widow or fatherless child. If you do mistreat them, and they cry out to me, I will surely hear their cry" (Exodus 22:21–23 ESV).

Similarly the Mosaic law provides numerous protections for the poor. The statutes provide protection from intrusion, and they prevent the poor from losing their cloaks at night when they are needed for warmth. They also ensure that wages are paid promptly:

When you make your neighbor a loan of any sort, you shall not go into his house to collect his pledge. You shall stand outside, and the man to whom you make the loan shall bring the pledge out to you. And if he is a poor man, you shall not sleep in his pledge. You shall restore to him the pledge as the sun sets, that he may sleep in his cloak and bless you. And it shall be righteousness for you before the LORD your God. (Deuteronomy 24:10–13 ESV)

The Israelites are also commanded to lend freely to the poor (Deuteronomy 15:7–8) and to leave some crops behind after the harvest so the poor could glean them for sustenance (24:19–22). In addition, the poor would have their debts canceled every seven years (15:1–2). If followed, the Law would ultimately end poverty (vv. 4–5). Unfortunately Israel did not follow God's law, so poverty and injustice flourished. However, God did not let these transgressions go unnoticed. He spoke to prophets for hundreds of years to warn Israel that His anger was aroused at such social injustices as taking advantage of the poor and mistreating the marginalized:

The people of the land have practiced extortion and committed robbery. They have oppressed the poor and needy, and have extorted from the sojourner without justice. And I sought for a man among them who should build up the wall and stand in the breach before me for the land, that I should not destroy it, but I found none. Therefore I have poured out my indignation upon them. I have consumed them with the fire of my wrath. I have returned their way upon their heads, declares the Lord GOD. (Ezekiel 22:29–31 ESV)

The prophets also promised that one day a Savior would come who would complete Israel's mission to promote justice, deliverance, and restoration throughout the whole world.

New Testament

In the New Testament, Jesus reiterates many of the justice themes from the Old Testament and takes them to new heights. The first proclamation mentioned in the gospel of Mark calls people to repent (turn from their old path in life) and become part of God's kingdom, which is at hand (Mark 1:15). God's kingdom represents His rule and authority breaking into the earth through people turning to Jesus, receiving forgiveness for their sins, and becoming adopted as God's children.

The ethic of the kingdom was further outlined in Jesus' teaching known as the Sermon on the Mount (Matthew 5–7). It includes commands to forgive one's enemies, show radical generosity, avoid sexual immorality and all violations of God's commands, serve God over possessions, and live free from worry. Keeping with these themes, Jesus in other instances taught His followers not to invite people of influence into their homes for personal gain but to invite the outcasts and marginalized (Luke 14:11–14). He summarized the law as loving God with one's whole being and loving one's neighbor as oneself (Mark 12:30–31).

Jesus also modeled His teaching about compassion and service throughout His ministry. He fed the multitudes, healed the sick, and cast out demons. Matthew, the gospel writer, would interpret these kinds of actions as the fulfillment of the prophecies of Isaiah concerning the Messiah:

> Aware of this, Jesus withdrew from that place. A large crowd followed him, and he healed all who were ill. He warned them not to tell others about him. This was to fulfill what was spoken through the prophet Isaiah:

"Here is my servant whom I have chosen,
    the one I love, in whom I delight;
I will put my Spirit on him,
    and he will proclaim justice to the nations.
He will not quarrel or cry out;
    no one will hear his voice in the streets.
A bruised reed he will not break,
    and a smoldering wick he will not snuff out,
till he has brought justice through to victory.
    In his name the nations will put their hope."

(Matthew 12:15–21)

Christ came to proclaim justice to nations. The impact of this would be so great that He would have to momentarily restrain people from spreading the news about Him in order to first fulfill His mission to die on the cross. His sacrifice for the sins of the world would produce the true freedom that the nations needed. That's why Isaiah the prophet foretold that the nations would put their hope in this Messiah.

In summation, Jesus' teachings modeled the greatest social justice ethic ever devised. He reached out to tax collectors, lepers, Samaritans, and Gentiles. Many of these people were broadly classified by the religious leaders of his day as sinners. No other figure in history has ever taught such a noble ethic, nor has any modeled such teaching so perfectly. When His followers likewise model His teaching and example, the results are the removal of poverty, discrimination, and conflict. And the disenfranchised are elevated both materially and socially. The early church did not follow these ideals perfectly, but even in their imperfect attempts, they transformed the world.

The disciples of Christ, such as Paul, Peter, and James, would live out this call not only to preach the gospel but to care for the needy and fight against the forces of wickedness. They would also make sure people realized that the struggle wasn't just against human evil, but there was a spiritual battle raging behind the scenes. It was this realization that gave the early believers the insight and motivation to help the oppressed and to love and pray for the oppressors as well. There had never been a revolution like this in history. That's why two thousand years later, the gospel of Jesus Christ remains mankind's greatest hope.

Christianity and Social Change

In my book *God's Not Dead*, I devoted an entire chapter to the impact the Christian faith has had on the world. In this chapter I want to highlight a couple of examples that reinforce the thesis that being a follower of Christ necessarily means being committed to confronting injustice with the transforming truth and power of the gospel.

The Writings of Charles Dickens

Charles Dickens is arguably the greatest novelist in history. His works, such as *A Tale of Two Cities*, *A Christmas Carol*, *Oliver Twist*, and many more, are all living classics. Dickens's stories emanated from his own deprived childhood. His father, John, was sent to debtors' prison when Charles was only ten. Charles was forced to find work on the streets of London, which were filthy and treacherous beyond belief. The hunger, danger, and mistreatment he experienced as a child fueled his writings later in life.

Through his books he would bring to life the struggle and plight of the poor—especially children.

Dickens portrayed the struggles of the poor in such a way that the wealthy upper class of England were moved into action to help right the wrongs. In a biography of his life, called *Charles Dickens and the Street Children of London*, Andrea Warren wrote, "All in all, Charles Dickens was a more powerful catalyst for change than any queen, prime minister, or politician. He is known as one of history's greatest reformers."[21]

Dickens's writings had a theme of redemption, epitomized in one of the most iconic figures in all of fiction, Ebenezer Scrooge. This miserly old man came face-to-face with his own selfishness and depravity and was transformed through divine intervention into a new man, all on Christmas Eve. Though Dickens's faith in God comes through in his writings, the depth of this motivation is often missed as people downplay the role this played in his novels. G. K. Chesterton wrote:

> If ever there was a message full of what modern people call true Christianity, the direct appeal to the common heart, a faith that was simple, a hope that was infinite, and a charity that was omnivorous, if ever there came among men what they call the Christianity of Christ, it was in the message of Dickens.[22]

Dickens would respond to those who questioned his portrayal of Christians in his writings:

> With a deep sense of my great responsibility always upon me when I exercise my art, one of my most constant and most earnest endeavors has been to exhibit in all my good people

some faint reflections of the teachings of our great Master, and unostentatiously to lead the reader up to those teachings as the great source of all moral goodness. All my strongest illustrations are derived from the New Testament; all my social abuses are shown as departures from its spirit; all my good people are humble, charitable, faithful, and forgiving.[23]

Dickens would criticize empty religion as much as he would showcase the arrogance of the rich and powerful. He saw through the vanity of mere tradition and sought to place the focus on Jesus Christ and the example of His life. Dickens detested empty piety, which lacked a compassion for the poor, and an overall lack of justice and integrity that he felt was befitting the name of Christianity. His work *The Life of Our Lord*, which was written initially for his children, was the last work of his life. In this simple but beautiful book, he gave an overview of the Gospels and the impact of Jesus' life on the world. He concluded the short book with this admonition:

Remember! It is Christianity to do good always—even to those who do evil to us. It is Christianity to love our neighbor as ourselves, and to do to all men as we would have them do to us. It is Christianity to be gentle, merciful, and forgiving, and to keep those qualities quiet in our own hearts, and never make a boast of them, or of our prayers or of our love of God, but always to show that we love Him by humbly trying to do right in everything.[24]

Harriet Beecher Stowe and Slavery

The scourge of slavery was wrongly tolerated in early America. In England the practice of slavery was abolished in 1833 through the efforts of William Wilberforce, a member of Parliament and a man who was dramatically transformed by Christ. His faith led him to tirelessly work to overturn this injustice and to banish it forever from most of the British Empire. In America, this evil would not be dismantled without a civil war.

At the heart of the story of how American slavery was ended is Harriet Beecher Stowe. The wife of a minister and the daughter of a minister, Stowe had a faith that gave her the mandate to fight injustice. And there was nothing more glaringly wrong than this institution, which reduced people to mere chattel, treated worse than animals. After Congress passed the Fugitive Slave Act of 1850, forbidding any assistance to a runaway slave seeking help, Stowe decided to write something that would change the way people saw this evil practice. On March 9, 1850, Stowe wrote to Gamaliel Bailey, editor of the abolitionist publication *National Era*, of her plans to write about the evils of slavery: "I feel now that the time is come when even a woman or a child who can speak a word for freedom and humanity is bound to speak. . . . I hope every woman who can write will not be silent."[25]

The book was published in 1852, and within a year three hundred thousand copies were sold. In 1862, after the start of the Civil War, Harriet Beecher Stowe met President Lincoln, who, according to legend, greeted her with the words, "So you're the little woman who wrote the book that made this great war!"[26]

These are just two examples of individuals who changed the world because their faith motivated them to fight injustice. We have already mentioned Dr. Martin Luther King Jr. and his efforts to fight institutional racism and discrimination almost a hundred years after the Civil War and the Emancipation Proclamation that freed the slaves. Time doesn't allow us to go into the details of the universities that were founded (106 out of the first 108 in America[27]) to educate young people in response to Jesus' command to make disciples and teach all nations; the hospitals that have been built; the charities that have been launched; disaster relief organizations that have been instrumental in being first responders whenever tragedy strikes. How could we overlook the efforts of the Red Cross or the Salvation Army? Clara Barton, the founder of the Red Cross, was raised as a Universalist yet lived her faith in God in service to her fellow humanity. The Salvation Army, founded by William and Catherine Booth, did not neglect the preaching of the gospel or the good works of helping those in need. Taking a closer look in chapter 6, we discover the Scripture replete with commands to love our neighbor as ourselves, as well as feed the hungry, care for the sick, and help orphans and widows.

Summary

The cry for justice is being heard around the world. Virtually every aspect of life on this planet has been affected by the devastating nature of sin and injustice. The scope of the problem is staggering. For centuries there have been countless failed efforts to right the wrongs committed by humanity merely through political or social reform. Something greater is needed. Humankind first needs an inner transformation that the gospel of Jesus Christ offers to all who believe.

We must understand that the rational conclusion for anyone

seeking lasting change is this: God is the definer of what is just and unjust. To ignore this is to ignore the testimony of history and to be doomed to repeat the futile secular efforts that have attempted to alter society and rectify injustice.

Christianity has demonstrated the power to transform individual lives as well as society. The Bible tells the story of God's dealing with the nations based on whether they are righteous or unjust. This unequivocal call to righteousness and justice based on God's command has been the driving force of real social reform throughout the ages. Individuals moved to action by the sight of injustice have made remarkable changes, demonstrating the awesome power of those who fight for justice and truth.

A truly just society is a tolerant and respectful one as well. Everyone should have the freedom to believe and to express their beliefs, especially if they are in the minority. There are obvious limits to what should be considered free speech. No one has the right to threaten another person or to attack him or her physically. Yet we must not allow our quest for social justice to mutate into a different kind of intolerance, in which those who simply disagree with others are accused of hate speech. We are called as believers to give the reason for our hope with gentleness and respect; we should be respected in return.

We turn now to the subject of truth. When we lose the truth, justice is lost as well. Jesus promised that if we know the truth, we will be truly free. It is *this* freedom that we all desire—specifically, the freedom to pursue our God-given potential and dreams, free from the tyranny of unjust assaults against us. This is the freedom that we are to experience and proclaim to others as followers of Christ. As we walk in this freedom, we possess greater conviction and confidence of the truth of the message we are called to proclaim. This requires that we look closer at the very idea of truth and grasp its implications—as well as the price society pays when truth is lost.

CHAPTER 4

THE SEARCH FOR TRUTH

The Foundation of Reality

So justice is driven back,
and righteousness stands at a distance;
truth has stumbled *in the streets,*
honesty cannot enter.
—Isaiah 59:14

I t's almost humorous that the *Oxford Dictionary* announced the 2016 word of the year was *post-truth*. It is defined as "relating to or denoting circumstances in which objective facts are less influential in shaping public opinion than appeals to emotion and personal belief."[1]

It is no exaggeration to say that the most difficult challenge you will face in life is to know what is really true, whether it is the truth about God, politics, history, or even your own identity. Regardless of the issue, truth is the most valuable thing that exists and is, therefore, under constant assault. For a multitude of reasons, many have simply given up on knowing what is true. The place where this type of thinking is most prevalent is the university campus. Ironically, the first college in America, Harvard, chose as its motto *Veritas,* which is Latin for *truth.* Many of the most prominent universities were founded to fulfill Christ's command to teach His followers. You would think an academic environment would be marked by students and faculty all engaged in a relentless pursuit of truth, regardless of its implications. Nothing could be further from reality. Instead, the average secular university today is a breeding ground of bias and special interest. Hypersensitivity and intolerance are the norm.

In spite of the challenges I've described, there are signs of hope that truth could be making a comeback on university campuses. Ministries such as Every Nation Campus, along with many others, are engaging students and faculty around the world.[2] I have the privilege of speaking regularly on campuses, presenting the evidence for the truth of the Christian faith. Many have recognized the importance of reaching the university campus and are helping to make a difference.

One of the clearest voices for the cause of truth on campuses is Dr. Frank Turek; you will rarely meet a more direct, no-nonsense speaker addressing issues of truth, faith, atheism, and morality. A former naval officer born in New Jersey, Turek is best known for his book *I Don't Have Enough Faith to Be an Atheist,* coauthored with apologist Dr. Norman L. Geisler. Turek asks students the question, "Does truth exist?" He stresses that you need to deal with the existence of truth before you can adequately discuss the existence of God. "Students need to realize truth exists before I can reason with them that God exists," he explains.[3] Turek speaks on campuses around the world and labors tirelessly with audiences in the aftermath of his speeches with Q & A. These encounters can be seen on his website (crossexamined.org) and are must-see TV for anyone interested in issues surrounding the defense of the faith.

Invariably a student will make the claim that "there is no such thing as absolute truth." Frank will pause and then deliver his signature response, "Is that true?" In case you missed the punch line, the statement "There is no absolute truth" is, in fact, self-defeating. This means that if the statement is true, then it is false.

Many other statements fail the truth test when examined closely. Take, for instance, the claim that "only science can give us real knowledge." Science can't prove that statement; it is a philosophical statement, not a scientific one. Logical fallacies abound when it comes to the debate about the existence of God and the search for ultimate reality. Postmodernism and skepticism have tried to dismiss truth or reduce it to statements made about the physical world without acknowledgment of any metaphysical categories.

To become an effective defender of the faith, you must have a firm grasp on the nature of truth and what should be counted as true knowledge. When it comes to sharing the gospel, you must be able to help others grasp that truth is a gift from God, not an invention of the human mind. Human rights for all people are anchored, therefore, in the bedrock of truth. To be effective communicators about these critical issues, we must be able to give a reasonable response to this fundamental question:

What Is Truth?

The question, *what is truth?* was posed by Pontius Pilate to Jesus during His trial before His crucifixion (John 18:38). Two thousand years later, the answer remains a mystery to many. The answer shouldn't be so elusive. We are taught from an early age to "tell the truth." Somehow as children we know the difference between what is true and false without any classes on moral philosophy. Intuitively we humans grasp how important truth is and recognize that if it is not valued and practiced, society would quickly devolve into chaos. We all depend on truth in virtually every aspect of life without really understanding how to technically define it or philosophically grasp it. Even so, because there is so much confusion swirling around the concept of truth, we are compelled to look into the *truth about truth*.

Let me give you a spoiler alert: truth is not just a set of logical propositions but is actually embodied in the person of Jesus Christ, who proclaimed, "I am the . . . truth" (John 14:6). As Lesslie Newbigin put it, "Truth is not a doctrine or a worldview or even a religious experience; it is certainly not to be found by repeating abstract nouns like justice and love; it is the man Jesus Christ in whom God was reconciling the world. The truth is personal, concrete, historical."[4]

While keeping in mind that Christ is the embodiment of truth, we must also remember that there are rules to logic and tests for truth that stem from the recognition of a rational Mind who created the universe. The best place to start answering the what-is-truth question is with a basic definition. To put it as simply as possible, truth is that which *corresponds* to reality. In academic terms it is called the correspondence theory of truth.[5]

As we embark on this all-important discussion about truth, it is necessary to alert the casual reader that some of this might seem a little technical. Pondering these definitions and descriptions of the tests for truth, however, will greatly enhance your confidence in the truth of the gospel and the Christian faith. Consider this definition:

> Truth is defined as "the true or actual state of a matter." It is generally considered to be the same as fact or reality. Truth is something that can't be disputed, it is generally considered as fact, which is verifiable. Truth is something that is real, genuine and authentic. It is not something that can be false or deceitful.[6]

Along with this definition there are several tests for truth. These include (1) coherence, that is, logical consistency; (2) empirical adequacy; and (3) experiential relevance.[7]

Coherence means that a statement is logically consistent—not absurd or riddled with logical fallacies (which we will discuss shortly)—and coheres to the known facts. When I was in high school and would come in late on a Saturday night, my parents would question me about where I had been—searching for any inconsistencies in my story compared to the facts they knew to be true (based on their "sources"). This is how crime detectives, like my friend J. Warner Wallace, author of *Cold-Case Christianity,* examine the testimony of murder suspects to test the coherence or consistency of their statements with the known facts.

The test of *empirical adequacy* refers to having the backing of empirical data whenever possible. If we say, "The patient has a high temperature," then there is data that is available to verify the claim. Empirical adequacy would not be relevant, however, on a statement such as "I love you."

A third test is *experiential relevance*. If you say, "It's cold outside," then someone would be able to verify this through his or her own experience.

Laws of Logic

A basic course in logic will introduce you to three traditional laws of logic: (1) the law of noncontradiction, (2) the law of the excluded middle, and (3) the law of identity. Understanding these laws will be vital as we contend for the existence of truth, as well as the truth of the Christian faith. Skeptics claim their system of thought is logical and rational simply because they frame their beliefs within these rules of logic, yet, as I have stated, the Christian faith should also be framed and presented within these parameters.

Briefly, the law of *noncontradiction* states that contradictory statements cannot be true in the same sense at the same time; for example, the two propositions "A is B" and "A is not B" are mutually exclusive. There is nothing in the message of the gospel or the orthodox Christian faith that violates this law.

The law of the *excluded middle* states that for any proposition, either that proposition is true or its negation is true. This law guards against language being equivocal, which would render most statements meaningless if it was disregarded.

The law of *identity* states that each thing is the same as itself and different from another. This law will be important in the next chapter when we discuss the question of whether the mind is different from the brain. The law of identity will help us answer that question logically and philosophically.

Logical Fallacies

Undoubtedly you have had a dialogue in which logical fallacies were introduced. These are statements that, by their very nature, attempt to gain the status of truth despite their falsifying deficiencies. The complete list of logical fallacies is too long to mention here.[8] But following are some of the most common fallacies you will confront.

Begging the question. This means you are guilty of circular reasoning; that is, restating a premise as a conclusion: "God does not exist because God does not exist." Christians are guilty of circular reasoning if they argue, "The Bible declares it is the Word of God; therefore, the Bible is the Word of God." (We will look at a linear argument for the claim regarding the truth of Scripture in chapter 6.)

Ad hominem. This states that an argument is wrong because of the person making the claim. This usually takes the form of personal attacks instead of debating the truth or falseness of the claim: "Susie is religious; she obviously isn't willing to admit she's wrong." Abusive personal attacks have become so frequent in the age of social media that it has caused genuine debate and respectful dialogue to virtually vanish.

Genetic fallacy. The statement or belief is false because of how it originated. "You have faith in God because you were born in America in a Christian home." The same could be said of an atheist, "You don't believe in God because your parents didn't believe." The origin of a person's beliefs doesn't make them necessarily true or false.

Straw man. This takes place when you misrepresent someone's argument and then attack it as false. Christians and non-Christians are often guilty of this fallacy. Skeptics fall into this when they try to generalize claims about religion. They take the worst elements of every religion and piece together a monstrous straw man that is simply not true. Believers can do the same by painting the picture of atheists as totally evil and sinister.

Finally, we should remember the "argument from fallacy." According to it, we are wrong to believe that just because an argument contains a fallacy, the conclusion is wrong; it might be correct!

Truth Is Exclusive

Another example of flawed reasoning is when the claim is made that all religions are the same. By its very nature truth is exclusive. To say something is true means you exclude everything that contradicts it as false. This applies to religious beliefs. In fact, the major religions all claim to possess exclusive truths. (I compare Christianity to the major religions in chapter 7.)

Buddha was an Indian, raised in a Hindu culture, who rejected the authority of the Vedas (primary Hindu scriptures) as well as the caste system. Islam makes claims in the Quran that directly contradict Christianity. The most glaring example is the statement that Jesus was not crucified (Sura 4:157). This is a false statement. It is a historical fact that Jesus was crucified at the hands of Pontius Pilate. Therefore, if this is true, the Quran has made a false statement. This doesn't mean we communicate this in an arrogant way but do so with the respect the Bible commands.

It should be our quest to know the truth, regardless of its implications on our existing beliefs or cultural narratives. In our search for truth we must ask the question, *how can we come to know what is true?* But first, in order to answer that question, we have to deal with one of the most popular and prevalent myths of our day: *science is the sole source of true knowledge.* Once this obstruction is removed, we will have a clearer picture of how truth is glaring, obvious, and immovable.

Can Science Answer Everything?

David Hume, an eighteenth-century Scottish philosopher, is most famous for advocating the philosophy of empiricism. According to it, only statements that can be backed by empirical data can qualify to be true. Like the movie title *Die Hard*, this faulty idea lives on and on in the collective academic and scientific mind-set. Hume wrote:

> If we take in our hand any volume; of divinity or school metaphysics, for instance; let us ask, Does it contain any abstract reasoning concerning quantity or number? No. Does it contain any experimental reasoning concerning matter of fact and existence? No. Commit it then to the flames: for it can contain nothing but sophistry and illusion.[9]

According to Hume's own standard, we should commit his statements to the flames! This is because his statements fail the very tests he proposes. As a side note, Hume never married. If he'd had a wife, he would have quickly learned that advising her that all statements to him must have empirical proof would not have produced a happy marriage.

The prevalence of Hume's biased thinking reminds us that science rests on unprovable philosophical foundations. As NYU philosopher Thomas Nagel, a self-described atheist, admitted, "The intelligibility (to us) that makes science possible is one of the things that stand in need of explanation."[10]

The statement "Only science can give us true knowledge" is self-defeating—that is, it is not provable scientifically. These are the kinds of philosophical missteps that many people—especially atheists—tend to ignore.

Philosophical Foundations of Science

Bertrand Russell, an analytical philosopher and atheist who is best remembered for his book *Why I'm Not a Christian*, said, "What science can not tell us, mankind can not know."[11] Again, this bold assertion cannot be demonstrated scientifically. Dr. Michael Guillen, a theoretical physicist who taught physics at Harvard and served as the science editor for ABC News for fourteen years, wrote, "I've always chuckled at this remark from Russell. It is a meaningless, circular statement."[12] This belief amounts to *scientism*, not science. Science is based on philosophical foundations consisting of metaphysical truths. By *metaphysics* I mean the nonphysical realities that must necessarily exist in order to do science. These include the laws of logic, morality, mathematics, purpose, causality, and even truth itself.

As far as other sources of knowledge outside of science, we can certainly gain knowledge through history. Though we can't prove history by use of the scientific method and its principle of experimental repeatability, we can come to the knowledge of what happened in the past by following the guidelines of sound historiography. By consulting multiple independent sources, eyewitness accounts, and forensic evidence when available, we can arrive at the truth about the past. We also gain knowledge through our reason and our experience of the world we interact with. The vast knowledge available through the study of literature, law, journalism, poetry, art, music, and the wide variety of subjects outside the natural sciences makes any claim that science is the sole source of true knowledge truly ridiculous.

A few years ago Ball State physicist Dr. Eric Hedin taught a class called The Boundaries of Science. In it he explained that science depended on philosophical assumptions. After six years of teaching the class, he found himself in a media storm due to the complaints from the Freedom from Religion organization and its spokesperson, Jerry Coyne. Coyne's efforts were aimed at pressuring the university to prevent Hedin from teaching the class due to the importance of maintaining the separation of church and state. Of course, Coyne had little firsthand knowledge of what was taught in the class. In fact, all Hedin did was put science under the same microscope it claims to use on everything else. Though Hedin kept his job, the class was canceled. Today he is a tenured professor and is writing a book called *The Boundaries of Science*, which covers the essence of what he taught in the class. The book includes theological implications not discussed in the class and makes it very clear that science cannot explain itself without philosophy: "Perhaps you maintain that only science can or will provide answers to every meaningful question. But holding this position implies that you have already departed from science into the realm of metaphysics. Statements about science are not statements of science."[13]

Hedin's ordeal is by no means an isolated incident. The commitment to naturalism and materialism is so unwavering in the corridors of academia that any departure from them is treated with the same intolerance that skeptics claim religion has demonstrated in the past.

Reductive Materialism

The ruling philosophy we are speaking of reduces all of life—everything—down to matter and physical energy. Whether describing consciousness, the sense of self, mind, or simply the experience of love and beauty, all can be reduced to physics and chemistry. To suggest the existence of anything beyond the physical is viewed as introducing religion. There is no middle ground. Nagel confirmed, "Among the scientists and philosophers who do express views about the natural order as a whole, reductive materialism is widely assumed to be the only serious possibility."[14] (This is discussed in greater detail in the next chapter when we look at the evidence for the soul.)

We can't ignore the truth that everyone makes statements from a set of philosophical presuppositions. "Science doesn't say anything, scientists do," Frank Turek continually reminds his audiences.[15] The commitment to the philosophy of naturalism keeps you from opening every door available in the search for knowledge and truth. To be told that our search should be limited to the natural sciences is almost silly. An honest inquiry into life's biggest questions must include truth from every source of knowledge possible. Imagine trying to solve a murder case and being told you can only examine DNA evidence and not all the other areas of circumstantial evidence that could provide the clues to the mystery. We must dismiss the voices that tell us only one type of knowledge is legitimate. To do this, we must gain an understanding of *epistemology*, the study of knowledge and how we know what we claim to know. Far from an obscure topic, it is the location of the actual battlefield where the struggle for truth takes place.

Epistemology: How Do We Know What Is True?

We come to this question: *How can we know what is true?* Does truth exist objectively, or are we relegated to what is described on Oprah.com as "speaking your own truth"?[16] Answering these questions will be the most indispensable intellectual task of your life. Much of postmodernist thought rejects the possibility of knowing truth and seeks to find meaning instead of truth through shared stories. In *The Future of Religion* by Richard Rorty and Gianni Vattimo, it is suggested we are living "in the Age of Interpretation. What is our duty today? What are the 'positive' and the 'negative' senses of the deconstruction of the history of ontology regarding faith and belief?"[17]

Rorty underscores that what has been lost is the belief in the ability to find ultimate reality or truth. All we can do is sift through the rubble of human expression and try to extract meaning by interpreting the past through the grid of our own culture and feelings. This stands in stark contradiction of reason as well as Scripture. No one can really live his or her life without being able to sufficiently know things—whether it's a bank balance, the results of an MRI, or the score of a game, there are things we believe we can know.

In philosophy, the study of how we know things is called epistemology, and it is the ground zero where skeptics and religious believers are engaged in the struggle to define and delimit what counts as knowledge. *Epistemology* is defined as "the theory of knowledge, especially with regard to its methods, validity, and scope, and the distinction between justified belief and opinion."[18]

Remember that as a follower of Christ, you are battling the false perception that Christianity is based on blind faith, not reason or evidence. You are seen by most skeptics as merely having beliefs about what you *assume* to be true—not *real* truth. The more firmly you hold to these beliefs, the more you are viewed as unwilling to hear any competing objections. It should be obvious that this is a fallacious argument that doesn't represent how the Bible describes we are to arrive at faith in God. Of course, there are many religions and religious people who base their beliefs on a subjective experience or a supposed unsubstantiated revelation from God. It's understandable why critics might be unnerved by this kind of faith. Just because some people arrive at beliefs through a faulty process does not logically negate all their beliefs—especially ones arrived at through reason and evidence, not against it. (Remember the fallacy of "argument from fallacy.")

It's almost comical to listen to professional skeptics, such as Richard Dawkins and Lawrence Krauss, trying to avoid the word *belief* as if they have transcended the need to use such a term. The great knowledge they possess in their fields of expertise hasn't translated into a sound knowledge of philosophy. As we will further discuss, all beliefs are not equal. This misunderstanding of what belief is has shown up in some dictionaries that define a belief as "an acceptance that something exists or is true, especially one without proof."[19] The *Merriam-Webster Dictionary*, however, defines belief as "conviction of the truth of some statement or the reality of some being or phenomenon especially when *based on examination of evidence.*"[20]

Peter Boghossian, an atheist who teaches philosophy at Portland State University, perpetuates the misunderstanding of what faith is in his book *A Manual for Creating Atheists*. Boghossian asserted that "faith is believing without evidence" and "pretending to know things you don't know."[21] It's actually shocking that he would put such palaver into print. It underscores the irrational, emotional side of atheism that causes educated people to say absurd things. The volumes that have been written detailing the evidence for God from a vast array of believing scientists, philosophers, and theologians (as well as the founders of modern science who were virtually all people of faith) makes such comments inexcusable. Thomas Nagel made a plea to end this nonsense:

> Even if one is not drawn to the alternative of an explanation by the actions of a designer, the problems that these iconoclasts pose for the orthodox scientific consensus should be taken seriously. They do not deserve the scorn with which they are commonly met. It is manifestly unfair.[22]

Boghossian went on to say that "faith is a faulty epistemology."[23] What he means is that believers say that they know things because they simply choose to blindly believe them. My friend Tom Gilson points out that a majority of Christians would agree that you shouldn't claim to know things in this way:

> I do not disagree that faith is sometimes treated as an epistemology. For example: "I know it's true because I have faith!" This

is fideism in its rawest form, and if Lindsay and Boghossian want to complain that it's a poor way to think about life and reality, they'll have loads of company from within the ranks of thoughtful Christians. Let's just stipulate, then, that we agree that this happens. But let's not suppose that fideism comprises all that can be said of faith![24]

Faith is the end result of a process that starts with knowledge, proceeds to truth, and then formulates beliefs—based on evidence and reason. Here is a brief summary of each step in this process:

Knowledge. As previously mentioned, knowledge is not limited to the natural sciences. Through the use of reason and logic, we gather and consider evidence from history, philosophy, literature, art, and our own experience, as well as the testimony of others, including authorities and tradition. As Christians, we do believe that the Holy Spirit can give us knowledge through the truth of Scripture. As I show in chapter 6, accepting the things written in the Bible is not due to circular reasoning (i.e., the Bible is true because the Bible say it's true).

There are good reasons to believe that the Scripture provides us with true knowledge. There is also knowledge that philosophers such as Alvin Plantinga call "properly basic."[25] This means that we all assume certain things in order to formulate beliefs. This would include the belief in the external world and its rational intelligibility.

Truth. Not all knowledge is true knowledge. After considering the evidence, we make decisions about what is true and what is not. This is the critical step in arriving at beliefs that are justified. The gist of this chapter has been about understanding what truth is and how it can be verified. As we have seen, truth is testable and knowable. I have listened to countless testimonies of people around the world who have told me that their journey to the Christian faith started with a desire to know the truth. I've never heard anyone say, "I really don't care whether Christianity is really true. I just like the way it makes me feel." While there are millions of believers who may not be able to defend the rationality of their faith or comprehend all the evidence that exists for its credibility, it doesn't logically follow that Christianity itself is not based on reason and evidence.

Belief. Everyone believes. This includes atheists. It is dishonest and equivocal to pretend not to need to use the word *belief,* as Richard Dawkins and Lawrence Krauss insist. These individuals have done us all a service, however, by demanding a rational explanation of why our beliefs are true. There is, indeed, rampant nonsense fostered in the name of religious faith. We must all test what is said and decide whether it is true or false. Our beliefs should be based on true knowledge. Feelings or subjective experiences are perfectly acceptable as contributing factors that aid us in our efforts to confirm the truth of our beliefs, but they are not the foundation of biblical faith.

For more than thirty-five years, my Christian beliefs have been challenged in every way imaginable. Many of them have changed or evolved through this process. My core beliefs about the existence of God and the truth of the Christian faith have only grown stronger through this journey. This is not because I have refused to listen to any opposing views. I have spent countless hours listening to lectures and reading books by a variety of skeptics from a wide range of disciplines. I've attended gatherings such as the Global Atheist Convention in 2012 in Australia. The more I've listened to the other side of the "God debate," the more convinced I am that faith in God is a *conclusion*, not a *delusion*.

Why Truth Matters

Walking through the death camp at Auschwitz, Poland, where more than a million people (mostly Jewish) were murdered in the gas chambers, is a brutal reminder that ideas have consequences. The twisted logic of those who perpetrated the most horrendous acts of history was fueled by the belief that there was no transcendent truth other than their own Nietzschean will to power. I've made several journeys through the barracks of the infamous death camp; the evidence of man's inhumanity to man is captured in the rooms filled with the personal belongings of those who died. Room after room bears witness to the heartbreaking testimony of the torture and degradation that happened to millions.

Truth matters. The recognition of the reality of objective truth and the existence of a moral Creator of the universe acts as a restraint against evil. The perpetrators of these crimes either thought that there was no God watching them or that those they murdered were less than human. The Scripture warns of the spiral downward into depravity if the light of truth is lost:

The wrath of God is being revealed from heaven against all the godlessness and wickedness of people, who suppress the truth by their wickedness, since what may be known about God is plain to them, because God has made it plain to them. For since the creation of the world God's invisible qualities—his eternal power and divine nature—have been clearly seen, being understood from what has been made, so that people are without excuse.

For although they knew God, they neither glorified him as God nor gave thanks to him, but their thinking became futile and their foolish hearts were darkened. (Romans 1:18–21)

Though truth is evident through the world God created and the moral law He placed inside of all people, it can be suppressed. Once you turn away from truth, your mind and heart become darkened. It is in the darkness of the human soul that evil can grow from a small seed of corruption to an uncontrollable monster. The radiant light of truth, however, can destroy this cancer before it can fully manifest its destructive power. I have watched the power of the truth of God's Word arrest people and extract the deception before it takes root in their hearts and minds. One of the most quoted phrases Jesus ever spoke was, "You will know the truth, and the truth will set you free" (John 8:32).

It is easy to see why the Bible, which contains the words of God, has been the center of this spiritual conflict. From the beginning of humanity, the Devil has challenged God's Word and has worked to deceive us into the same folly. He is called the "father of lies" (v. 44). The contrast between good and evil is actually the conflict between the truth and lies. The Bible is filled with the detailed description of truth and the call for believers to be transformed by it: "This is good, and pleases God our Savior, who wants all people to be saved and to come to a knowledge of the truth" (1 Timothy 2:3–4).

When we lose the truth, we have lost the ability to know God. He cannot be understood apart from truth. Jesus boldly declared, "I am the way and the truth and the life. No one comes to the Father except through me" (John 14:6). This startling claim means that Jesus not only spoke truth; He is the truth. God sent His Son to earth as the living Word to unequivocally demonstrate His nature and character. The impact of truth was felt everywhere He went. Even His enemies had no response to the power of the truth He spoke and represented.

The Roman governor Pilate was shocked to hear Jesus say that He had come into the world to "bear witness to the truth" (18:37 NKJV). Vishal Mangalwadi wrote:

> Pilate could have said to his accusers: "I have never met anyone who knew truth. Now that you have brought him to me, I will keep him at least for a while to learn all about truth." But Pilate had no patience for "nonsense." How could this carpenter know truth when the greatest Greek philosophers and Latin poets were clueless? By Pilate's time, Europe had lost hope of knowing truth and even interest in seeking it. Like the postmodern West today, Pilate believed that no one knows truth—not in any rational sense that could be explained in words.[26]

The world that Jesus came into was ignorant of truth. Nevertheless, there were still plenty of philosophers claiming to peddle it. From Pilate's Roman perspective, Jesus, with His kingdom of truth, was just another harmless sage—no more of a threat to Rome than were street-corner Cynic sages.

On the other hand, the nation of Israel had been commissioned to be a place where the nations could come and learn God's law. They had digressed into an empty shell of what they were intended to be. Jesus came into the world and brought truth. The impact is still being felt two thousand years later. Yet we seem intent on going backward, intentionally expunging truth from our culture and our daily lives. If the light of truth goes out or merely grows dim, we run the risk of the world plunging into a new dark age.

Scoffers suggest that we believe in values and principles simply because they are written in a book. This is one of those insults intended to get people to dismiss their confidence in Scripture without it getting a fair trial. In the United States, the Constitution is respected as the foundation and basis for our laws as a nation. It is widely viewed as a true and historically trustworthy document. Its truth has passed the tests of logical, consistent, and experiential relevance. That simply means that the Constitution works in a pragmatic sense. How much more does the Bible qualify as truth in light of these tests? (This is covered in greater detail in chapter 6.)

Yet we can know truth apart from reading the Bible. I mentioned earlier that the Bible teaches in Romans 1 that creation itself reveals truth about the Creator. And Romans 2 shows that the conscience is marked by the reality of the moral law. How could truth arise from a meaningless past of chance and mutation to become the guiding principle of life? If survival is the driving force of history, how can a truth greater than that exist? The evidence is overwhelming that truth is a gift from God. By recognizing its source, we can confidently look to the future with a well-founded hope that real justice and peace are possible.

Truth Matters

We must fully grasp that truth, indeed, matters. It touches every part of our existence and is the real debate in every question that dominates our cultural dialogue.

Truth matters when it comes to morality. If humans are the authors of morals, we are doomed to slide back into the swamp from which we crawled. (Note: I don't believe humanity came out of the swamp—that is a touch of satire on the evolutionary view of our "lowly origins.")

Truth matters when it comes to justice. Truth and justice are inseparable. If you give up on knowing objective truth, you are sentencing society to a future of injustice.

Truth matters when it comes to the metaphysical categories of purpose and meaning. If there is no such thing as objective truth, then purpose and meaning disappear like a mirage.

The big questions of our day concern morality and sexuality. Is marriage intended to be between one man and one woman? A generation ago, an overwhelming majority of people would have said yes without hesitation. Times have changed. In many settings, you can now lose your job for affirming that simple truth. Social engineers explain this sudden change in our societal beliefs as the evolution of common sense. A quick look in the rearview mirror of history will show you that common sense isn't what it used to be. Certainly the current definition is vastly different from that of our parents or grandparents.

Common sense is merely the collective concepts of the "beliefs du jour."[27] It's typical to call something common sense and not bother asking where it came from or whether it is really true and just. If secular thinkers refuse to be bothered with the "why" question concerning our existence, how much more do they avoid the "why" question when it comes to issues of morality?

Understanding what is true can save us from our proclivity as humans to self-destruct. A critical step in coming to our senses is to regain a firm grip on the existence of truth and the desire to discover it and hold fast to it at all costs.

Truth Is a Human Right

The thesis of this book is that hearing the gospel is a fundamental human right. Ultimately this is because the gospel is true. Everyone should have the right to freely pursue truth and make the case for what they have discovered, as Newbigin has affirmed:

> I believe that every human being has a responsibility to seek to grasp the truth about the reality that meets us and encompasses us and to state the results of that search, knowing that full comprehension is always beyond us. For this Christian this search is sustained by the promise that, while now we only know in part, a day will come when we shall know as we are known.[28]

As humans, we will never know everything there is to know in this life, but that doesn't mean we are left in uncertainty. It means that we should devote ourselves to seeking to know what is true and then living our lives in the reality of the truth. As Jesus promised, "You will know the truth, and the truth will set you free." This freedom, or liberty, points to the vital importance of the opportunity all humanity should have to hear the message that has the power to bestow that gift upon the human mind and heart.

Summary

The greatest challenge of this generation concerns the existence and nature of truth. The question asked by Pilate to Jesus Christ—"What is truth?"—remains elusive for most. Our culture is confused about not only understanding the concept of truth but grasping what is specifically true and false. The term *post-truth* describes a society that bases its beliefs more on feelings than on facts. Truth is a gift from God. It doesn't arise from an evolutionary paradigm. God is the source of truth, and, therefore, there are objective facts about our world both scientifically and philosophically. A basic definition of truth is that it corresponds to reality. This is testable in a number of ways. It must be logically coherent, empirically adequate, and experientially relevant.

Modern science has brought the world many technological and medical advances, but the idea that science is the only source of knowledge is simply false. When it comes to the area of epistemology—which is the study of how we come to know things—science is but one source of knowledge. We can gain knowledge from history, philosophy, art, and literature, as well as our subjective experiences of the world we live in. Contrary to the skeptical charge, Christians are not called to have blind faith as the foundation of our epistemology. Our beliefs are based on knowledge, truth, and reason. Science doesn't make claims; scientists do. Scientists possess beliefs like everyone else. We should all be willing to adjust our beliefs and follow the evidence wherever it leads.

When we abandon truth as objective knowable reality, we base our lives on delusion and wishful thinking. Truth matters when it comes to every area of our existence. In the end it is the truth that will set us free. The message of the gospel is true and points to Christ as the living Truth. Truth isn't just a philosophical concept but a living person.

With this in mind, it is imperative that we come to the truth about ourselves as humans. Are we animals, consisting of physical matter only, or is there a nonphysical or spiritual dimension? We now look into one of the great mysteries of our human existence—the reality of the soul.

CHAPTER 5

THE REALITY OF THE SOUL

We Are More Than Animals

I only note that if Jesus was raised from the dead, He has been to the afterlife and is qualified to tell us about it.

—J. P. MORELAND
THE GOD QUESTION [1]

The image was one of the most terrifying any parent could imagine: a small child in the grasp of a silverback gorilla named Harambe at the Cincinnati Zoo on May 28, 2016. The gorilla had the child for approximately ten minutes, dragging him around like a rag doll, all the while the boy staring calmly yet bewilderedly at the animal as if it were a character at a Disney World ride.

The three-year-old boy had inexplicably crawled through the protective fencing around the gorilla habitat and plunged into its moat. There was nothing the bystanders or zoo officials could do as they watched the child in the clutches of this enormous beast. The video footage on YouTube is agonizing to watch. Harambe finally was shot and killed to save the child's life. The public, as well as animal rights activists, were outraged: "Many are angry the endangered gorilla was put down. Others want the boy's mother to face child endangerment charges, CBS News' Jamie Yuccas reported. Facebook pages like 'Justice for Harambe' are quickly spreading."[2] (Using this as an example is in no way a dismissal of this incident as tragic in many ways.)

While most of the debate centered on the issues of whether Harambe would have harmed the child or why this or any other animal should be in captivity, there was a more disturbing discussion under the surface about why the child was chosen to live over the gorilla. The question of why human life is more valuable than animal life is hotly debated in many intellectual circles. In particular, this is indeed an actual ethical issue for materialists such as Richard Dawkins, who is on the record as saying that humans are not morally superior to animals. In an op-ed in the *Guardian*, a conversation was recounted where Dawkins explicitly made this point:

> You are on a deserted beach with a rifle, an elephant and a baby. This is the last elephant on earth and it is charging the baby. Do you shoot the elephant, knowing the species would become extinct?
>
> This was the dilemma Richard Dawkins put to me during a weekend in the country. Our host, publisher Anthony

Cheetham, had mischievously placed us next to each other at table. I thought the dilemma was a no-brainer—my only doubt was whether I would shoot straight enough to kill the beast.

He was outraged by my answer: man, beast, they were all the same to him and the priority must be to protect the endangered species. He berated me for my foolish belief in the specialness of humanity for its soul.[3]

Though this reason sounds shocking to many, it is the position of those who are committed to the philosophy of naturalism, who insist that human life is no more valuable than any other animal life. I give them this much: at least they are being intellectually and philosophically consistent. If there is no God and man is, therefore, just another animal, then there really isn't much difference. But if humans are truly no different from other animals, then the concept of human rights falls apart as well. The gospel points out that God has created us in His image and we are fundamentally different from anything else in His creation. The existence of the human soul is inextricably linked to the reality of *human rights* as well as *human responsibility*. If we are just animals whose actions are programmed by our DNA, then our actions have no moral consequences. *Animals killing other animals are not crime scenes.* As we look at the evidence for the reality of the soul in this chapter, the resounding conclusion should be apparent that *if the soul does not exist, then there can be no real moral actions, and, thus, injustice is merely an illusion.*

In the past decade there has been a rise in the number of books written not only to promote atheism as the only true worldview of the rational and scientifically literate mind but also to discredit the alleged arrogance of humans who believe we have some special place in the world. One of the most vocal authors is Sam Harris, whose books and speeches have gained him quite a following. He scoffs at the notion that humans have any greater worth than even a fly:

> A three-day-old human embryo is a collection of 150 cells called a blastocyst. There are, for the sake of comparison, more than 100,000 cells in the brain of a fly. . . . If you are concerned about suffering in this universe, killing a fly should present you with greater moral difficulties than killing a human blastocyst.[4]

This position should sound like utter nonsense to most in the twenty-first century; however, what is considered common sense is changing dramatically. What would have been obviously common sense in other generations is now in doubt, so we find ourselves debating whether human life is special compared to animal life. If so, why?

Comments from atheist writers such as Dawkins and Harris demonstrate the logical conclusion of atheism and materialism. If there is no God, then we humans are soulless collections of chemicals, and, as William Lane Craig put it, "We have no more rights than a swarm of mosquitoes or a barnyard of pigs."[5]

The belief that humans are special is not a result of Darwinian thought. It is the result of the influence of Scripture, which explains that men and women are created in the image of God. This fact brings humans a dignity and priority to which no other animal can come close. Christian philosopher J. P. Moreland gave this affirmation:

It is in virtue of the type of soul humans have, reflecting as it does the image of God, that humans have such high, intrinsic value. . . . If it is true that we are merely physical objects, we are of little value, or so it seems to me.[6]

It's not difficult to trace where the view of humans being special and worthy of protection over the animals was challenged. In 1859, when Charles Darwin wrote *On the Origin of Species*, he not only dismissed God as the designer of life but devalued humans as merely an evolutionary curiosity. It is difficult to calculate the effects of this derogatory belief on human behavior—a belief that says that in spite of our achievements in science, the beauty expressed in art and poetry, the magnificence of our heroic efforts in medicine, and the depth of our compassion in our efforts to aid our fellow man, we are still simply animals. As Darwin would write, "We must, however, acknowledge, as it seems to me, that man with all his noble qualities . . . still bears in his bodily frame the indelible stamp of his lowly origin."[7]

If Darwin was mistaken, then believing him anyway is utterly wrong and destructive. The truth is that we are more than physical beings, more than the result of an unguided process called natural selection. We possess an eternal dimension. The most common name given to this aspect of our existence is the *soul*. In this chapter we look at the history of this belief and the evidence for its reality. One caveat worth mentioning: I am not distinguishing between spirit and soul from a theological standpoint. This discussion is simply an attempt to demonstrate that humans possess a nonphysical dimension.

A Brief History of the Soul

From the beginning of recorded history, humans have expressed a belief that there is life after death. The pharaohs of Egypt and their pyramids stand as testaments to this conviction and hope. The biblical patriarchs Abraham and Moses grasped the truth that the existence of an eternal God means there is life beyond the grave, there is a nonphysical dimension of our existence that lives on after the death of the body. This belief in the soul shows up simultaneously with the birth of philosophy.

From the beginning of philosophy on the Ionian coast, with thinkers such as Thales (seventh century BC) to the writings of Homer, the idea that there is a soul that survives the death of the body was believed. The soul was viewed to be synonymous with being alive, as well as the dimension of our existence that experienced and displayed joy, sadness, and courage. Confucius and Buddha were contemplating ideas in the sixth and fifth centuries BC that pointed to the existence of the soul. Generations before them, the prophet Daniel wrote, "Multitudes who sleep in the dust of the earth will awake: some to everlasting life, others to shame and everlasting contempt" (Daniel 12:2).

The three great thinkers, Socrates, Plato, and Aristotle (fifth and fourth centuries BC), all believed in the soul, though their ideas differ slightly. Socrates is considered one of the founders of Western philosophy. (He was sentenced to death for corrupting the youth of Athens and forced to drink poison.) Though none of his writings have survived, we know about him primarily through the work of his student Plato and others. His influence is still felt today through what is called the Socratic method of investigation and inquiry through asking questions. He expressed a belief in life after death and in the existence of the soul. In Plato's work *Phaedo*, this belief is explicit:

> Then tell me, what must be present in a body to make it alive?
>> Soul.
>
> Is this always so?
>> Of course.
>
> So whenever soul takes possession of a body, it always brings life with it?
>> Yes, it does.
>
> Is there an opposite to life, or not?
>> Yes, there is.
>
> What?
>> Death.[8]

Socrates claimed that life's most important project is care of one's own soul. Plato believed in the immortality of the soul and described it in more detail in the *Republic* as possessing three parts: reason, spirit, and appetite.[9]

To Plato, the highest ideal of the soul was the attaining of knowledge. This is expressed in his belief that the soul existed before a person's physical body was created and, therefore, carried with it innate ideas as well as knowledge. In *A Brief History of the Soul*, Stuart Goetz and Charles Taliaferro confirmed Plato's conviction about the ultimate purpose of the soul: "Plato seems to regard reason/intellect as that which alone constitutes the essence of soul, and tells his readers that the soul is nourished by reason and knowledge."[10]

Aristotle was a student who joined Plato's academy at age eighteen. Aristotle rejected the world of the form (that is, the true essence of things occurs in ideas, not reality) and proposed a meta-physical outlook grounded in causality. His introduction of the four causes would provide categories that pointed to the practical reality of the existence of metaphysical truth, such as meaning and purpose. Things consist of a *material cause* (what it is made of; for instance, a rubber ball consists of matter); a *formal cause* (the form it takes that makes it a ball, i.e., roundness); an *efficient cause* (the agent that brought it into existence); and a *final cause* (the purpose of the object).

These categories are vital truths that have been erroneously dismissed through the radical doubt of Descartes and many Enlightenment thinkers. The rejection of Aristotle's metaphysical categories is called by American philosopher Edward Feser "the single greatest mistake ever made in the entire history of Western thought."[11]

For Aristotle, a soul is the form or essence of a living thing, and its final cause (purpose) is to know truth. Feser explained that for Aristotle, a good soul is one that seeks truth and knowledge. Likewise, we are good if our actions correspond to the final ends or purposes for which we were created:

> So, a good human being will be, among many other things, someone who pursues truth and avoids error. And this becomes moral goodness insofar as we can choose whether or not to fulfill our natures in this way. To choose in line with the final causes or purposes that are ours by nature is morally good; to choose against them is morally bad.[12]

Let me take a brief excursus from our discussion of the evidence for the soul and make a connection to this discussion on final causes and the contemporary debates surrounding morality. There is a mistaken notion that Christians derive what is good and evil solely from the Bible at the expense of reason. Scripture calls us to discern the nature and attributes of God through the things God has made (Romans 1:20). It goes on to say that even without knowing the law of God, our consciences are speaking to us about good and evil (2:4–15).

This means that good and evil, as well as meaning and purpose (metaphysical categories), can be discerned through nature. If nothing has a real objective purpose, then is it possible to say what is truly good or bad? The argument that states there is evidence for genetic predisposition for certain behaviors is misguided. Even if you could claim there was a gene that made someone prone to certain behavior or desires, it wouldn't mean that acting on that proclivity should be considered good for that person's well-being. For instance, a genetic proclivity for alcoholism has been established. This doesn't mean that a person is doing what is right by drinking alcohol. It means he or she will have to be more diligent to avoid even the slightest exposure to alcohol. You can make the same connection to any type of moral behavior that is being justified in the name of genetics.[13]

Our Moral Actions Affect Our Souls

Biblical writers certainly taught the existence of soul and that there would be not only life after death but also judgment for all the actions committed in this life. The soul will survive the death of the body and act as the black box (flight recorder) that is recovered after an airplane crash. The existence of the soul means that our actions in this life matter. That is why the debate about what is good and evil cannot be left as attitudes of the culture and what it deems fashionable versus what is ultimately right and wrong. What is good, therefore, is what is best for the well-being of our souls. Evil, conversely, is what degrades or destroys it. We will talk more about this when we outline the evidence for the soul.

One of the most memorable and quoted statements from Jesus Christ recorded by the gospel writer Matthew was, "What good will it be for someone to gain the whole world, yet forfeit their soul? Or what can anyone give in exchange for their soul?" (Matthew 16:26). The writings of the early church leader Augustine of Hippo are often cited in the historical understanding of the existence and nature of the soul. Augustine believed that each of us knows what a soul is from the simple fact that each of us is one. He maintains that nothing is more intimately known and aware of its own existence than a soul, because nothing can be more present to the soul than itself.[14]

Augustine speaks to us today because of the inner struggle he wrote about concerning moral values and objective truth. There were many popular philosophical schools of thought in his day. According to one of them, *Manichaeism* (fourth century), he should go ahead and satisfy his sensual appetites without suffering any pangs of conscience. He bought into this nonbiblical worldview for a while but eventually saw through the vanity of such empty reasoning. He wrote in his *Confessions*:

> Vain trifles and the triviality of the empty-headed, my old loves, held me back. They tugged at the garment of my flesh and whispered: "Are you getting rid of us?" And "from this moment we shall never be with you again, not for ever and ever." And "from this moment this and that are forbidden to

you for ever and ever." What they were suggesting in what I have called "this and that"—what they were suggesting, my God, may your mercy avert from the soul of your servant! What filth, what disgraceful things they were suggesting![15]

Sadly in this generation those filthy and disgraceful things are deemed normal and acceptable.

Several hundred years later Thomas Aquinas (1225–74) embraced the metaphysical truths presented by Aristotle and integrated them with the Augustinian framework that leaned more toward a Platonic view of the world. This provided a rational defense of the Christian faith, the immortality of the soul, and the reality of natural law (the idea that good and evil are knowable through the things that are made). The influence of Aquinas is still felt today due to the force of the truths presented in his arguments.

Belief in the soul continued through the seventeenth and eighteenth centuries and was not be called into serious question until the middle of the nineteenth century with the writings of Darwin and the idea that humans were created not by God but by a long, slow process of random mutation and natural selection. Since then the commitment to materialism and naturalism has become, for the most part, the creed of the scientific, philosophical, and psychological communities.

This is seen in the writings of Sigmund Freud (1856–1939), which still dominate most of the thinking in twenty-first-century psychology and psychiatry. The belief that we are physical creatures leads to the practical notion that all our behaviors are simply a result of cause and effect. Freud's theory of the id, ego, and superego described a mechanistic process that tries to uncover unknown influences from the subconscious (id) and how the resultant desires of the ego are modified and regulated by the superego, which is conditioned by cultural and societal norms.

Like many leading thinkers today, Freud was a determinist who saw free will as an illusion (more on this in a moment). The debate today about the existence of the soul is being waged within the arena of neuroscience—the field of study that skeptics reference most to dismiss the notion of the soul. There are phrases that attempt to give a caricature of this belief, like "the ghost in the machine" or "belief in ectoplasm" (think *Ghostbusters*), not only to mock the belief in the soul but to assert, therefore, that no evidence exists for either of these caricatures. This typifies the fallacy of presenting an argument that frames what you think the evidence should look like and then triumphantly announcing that no such evidence exists. This is why it is important to realize that materialism (the belief that all of our existence can be reduced to a physical, natural explanation) is held as dogmatically by atheists as they claim religious people hold their beliefs. This is because the alternative (the existence of a spiritual world) is unthinkable. Feser calls this belief "the last superstition."[16]

Sam Harris, like other atheists, insists there is no evidence from neuroscience that the soul exists. He cites the ability to correlate, with various stimuli, regions of the brain where memories, emotions, and areas of functionality are located. This doesn't explain critical aspects of our existence, such as consciousness, free will, and the sense of self that we all possess. The fact that damaging the brain impairs the memory or reasoning abilities is the ultimate smoking gun for Harris that the soul doesn't exist.

His favorite quip, which gets a guaranteed chuckle from his skeptical following, goes like this:

> You damage one part of the brain and the mind; something about the mind and subjectivity is lost. You damage another and yet more is lost. And yet if you damage *the whole thing* at death, we can rise off the brain, with all our faculties intact, recognizing Grandma, and speaking English.[17]

In answering people such as Harris, we will look at evidence that demonstrates that our minds are different from our brains. If our brains are damaged or impaired, we aren't doomed to an eternity of disability. The example that is often used is that of a driver in an automobile that is involved in a devastating accident. If the car is crashed, the driver can still be intact and uninjured though the car is of no use. So it is with the brain.

If there is this spiritual essence to our existence that survives our physical death, then humans will be accountable for their actions in the next life, not just this one. This is a frightening proposition for those who seek earnestly to dismiss the existence of the soul because of the inevitable conclusion that God therefore exists also. Just think of the resistance to the discovery that the universe had a beginning at the start of the twentieth century. The term *the big bang* was coined by an atheist as a derisive term because he knew the implications of this cosmic beginning. He said this would "let the divine foot in the door." If this analogy were applied to the existence of the soul, it would be the equivalent to the whole Divine Being moving in the house, not just having a foot in the door!

Evidence for the Soul

We now take a look at the evidence for the existence of the soul. Again, my aim is to demonstrate that there is more to our human existence than merely the physical dimension. Each of these areas is a part of a cumulative case that there is a nonmaterial aspect to our humanity.

The Self

Many times when talking to skeptics who want to debate the existence of God, I will say, "We can talk about God's existence in a moment; my question is, do you exist?" The answer to this question may seem obvious. But prominent atheists actually question whether we truly exist in any ultimate sense. For instance, philosopher Daniel Dennett describes people more as robots programmed by their environment and genetics: "Your consciousness, your sense of yourself, is 'like a benign "user-illusion."'"[18]

Sam Harris boldly asserts "the self is an illusion."[19] The evidence for the existence of the self points to the existence of the soul. If there is a self, then you and I are more than just chemicals and neural connections. As a person, we each have an identity that is no illusion. We can look at our loved ones and friends as well as any other human and detect that they have a real identity—they exist!

Christian thinkers such as Augustine and C. S. Lewis felt that this was the easiest question to verify. As a person, you are obviously aware of yourself. As discussed in the previous chapter, the French mathematician and philosopher René Descartes could doubt everything except the fact that he was doubting. He minimally knew he existed. In his book *The Soul*, Christian philosopher J. P. Moreland wrote that the advances in neuro-science cannot explain the reality of "identity" or "the self":

> In general, neuroscience is wonderful for providing informa-tion about the neurological aspects of mental functioning and the self's actions, but it is of no help whatsoever in telling us what mental states and the self are. Correlation, dependence, and causal relations are not identity.[20]

Christianity and Judaism teach that you and I have this per-sonal identity we call *the self.* The apostle Paul explained that as a follower of Christ, you were given a *new* self. Therefore, being true to yourself means being true to the new identity you have in Christ. Again, we are just getting started in giving the abundant evidence that each individual has a self and a real identity. We con-clude with this simple statement: *if the self exists—the soul exists.*

Consciousness

Closely associated with the reality of the self is *consciousness.* There is no area of human existence that has been studied more, and yet it remains a complete mystery. Consciousness has been described as the first-person subjective experience that we have as humans. The technical term for this is *qualia.* David Chalmers is a cognitive scientist and considered one of the foremost experts in the world in the area of consciousness. He calls this experience "the hard problem of consciousness."[21] In other words, there is no natu-ralistic explanation for why an objectively observable brain with all its capacities can have this sense of subjective experience.

The problem of consciousness would be easy, not hard, if neuroscientists could detect it simply by placing electrodes on the human brain. There is no way that any of those objective measures can tell you what the person is experiencing. You could do a sleep study, for instance, and see what areas of a person's brain are lighting up while he or she is dreaming, but you have to wake the sleeper up to find out what he or she is dreaming about. That's what Chalmers means by the hard problem of consciousness. I am reminded of the scripture, "For who knows a person's thoughts except their own spirit within them? In the same way no one knows the thoughts of God except the Spirit of God" (1 Corinthians 2:11).

Chalmers is a legend in the field of consciousness studies. He is famous for his lecture on zombies, which, he means, are humans functioning physically yet without conscious experience. The question he poses is this: If we humans are merely physical, then why aren't we zombies? "Look, I'm not a zombie, and I pray that you're not a zombie," Chalmers said, "but the point is that evolution could have produced zombies instead of conscious creatures—and it didn't!"[22]

Chalmers explained the challenge of trying to explain consciousness with purely physical, scientific concepts in a TED talk in 2014: "Physics explains chemistry, chemistry explains biology, biology explains parts of psychology. But consciousness doesn't seem to fit into this picture."[23]

Consciousness is the experience of being you. It is both frustrating and comical listening to the leading experts on consciousness trying to speculate where it came from and what it is. They use phrases such as "consciousness is an emergent property," meaning that it is like oxygen emitted by plants. They also conjecture that it is simply a fundamental property, meaning that it is simply there and needs no explanation. Some go as far as speculating that if it is an emergent property of matter, then it's possible everything is conscious in some form or another (from rocks to your iPhone). This is called *panpsychism*. If nothing else, these experts show that in spite of the tsunami of information available, stemming from countless studies of the brain, they don't have a clue about what consciousness is.

Dr. Susan Greenfield, a neuroscientist with an impressive résumé of thirty honorary degrees, stated, "Not only do we not know what it is . . . we have no idea what a solution to demonstrate it would look like."[24] She referred to consciousness as "the miracle":

> Whilst neuroscience can really deliver on understanding psychiatric conditions, mental conditions, the human brain in general, it can help us look at correlations and appreciate the processes. What we cannot as yet do is answer the miracle. But I think we could write science fiction novels if we wished as to what kind of answer we might one day expect.[25]

In a scientific article, Christof Koch, of the Allen Institute for Brain Science in Seattle, talked about how "the water of integrated information turned into the wine of experience."[26] It is, indeed, a miracle. Just like the miraculous beginning of the universe and the origin of life, consciousness points to a conscious Creator that made us in His image and made us living souls.

The Mind Is Not the Brain

One of the classical problems in philosophy has been termed the "mind-body problem," but you could also call it the "mind-brain problem." If materialists are right, the mind is simply a part of the brain and, therefore, a purely physical entity or property. Moreland wrote, "Substance dualism is the belief that a human person has both a brain that is a physical thing with physical properties and a mind or soul that is a mental substance and has mental properties."[27]

It's important to review a dimension of truth we covered in the last chapter, called the law of identity. This law of logic states that if A is identical to B, then there is no difference between A and B. In applying this to the question of whether the mind is the brain, then every trait of the mind would be the same as the brain. If there is any difference, then the mind is not the brain. Materialists are firm in their denunciation of the possibility of any distinction of any kind between the mind and the brain because of enormous implications.

Daniel Dennett offers this summary of the current materialist view of the natural world and the mind:

The prevailing wisdom, variously expressed and argued for, is *materialism*: there is only one sort of stuff, namely *matter*—the physical stuff of physics, chemistry, and physiology—and the mind is somehow nothing but a physical phenomenon. In short, the mind is the brain. According to materialists, we can (in principle!) account for every mental phenomenon using the same physical principles, laws and raw materials that suffice to explain radioactivity, continental drift, photosynthesis, reproduction, nutrition, and growth.[28]

But this is not true. For one thing, brain states and mental states are different, as Moreland explained:

Mental states are characterized by their intrinsic, subjective, inner, private, qualitative feel, made present to a subject by first-person introspection. For example, a pain is a certain felt hurtfulness. The intrinsic nature of mental states cannot be described by physical language, even if, through study of the brain, one can discover the causal/functional relations between mental and brain states.[29]

Just because there is a *correlation* between mental states and brain states doesn't mean they are identical. It just points to a cause-and-effect connection. For example, even though there is a correlation between smoke and fire, it doesn't mean they are identical.

It may be that for every mental activity, a neurophysiologist can find a physical activity in the brain with which it is correlated. But just because A causes B (or vice versa), or just because A and B are constantly correlated with each other, that does not mean that A is identical to B. Sunlight may cause me to sneeze, but it's clear that the sunlight is not the same thing as my sneezing.[30]

C. S. Lewis stated that it was much more logical to believe that mind created matter and not matter produced mind.[31] God's existence means that there is a fundamental aspect to mind in the universe. Specifically, the evidence points to an intelligent mind behind all of life. Because the brain is physical, that would mean that it is different from mind in its most fundamental makeup. To say it plainly, *mental is not physical.*

Other areas demonstrate that the mind and the brain are not

the same. In fact, evidence shows that the mind can change the brain. Studies confirm that cognitive therapy can help to literally rewire the brain and create new neural pathways. The frontier of *neural plasticity*, as it is called, is revolutionizing treatment for those with brain injuries. (More on this a little later.) This is yet another piece of evidence suggesting that, based on the law of identity, the mind is not the brain.

Metacognition: Thinking About Thinking

Animals of all kinds have some level of cognitive ability. Rats have the ability to find their way through a maze. Dogs and horses can clearly identify and relate to humans. A huge distinction exists, though, between the thinking of animals and the thinking of humans—namely, humans are able to think about their thinking. This is called *metacognition*. Being aware of our situation is another aspect of our conscious experience that points to a mental state and not a purely physical process. To be aware of our situation as people is a miraculous thing when you think about it. For the materialist, the universe is created out of nothing for no reason. The laws of physics then come into existence and order the universe in an astonishingly fine-tuned manner. Then chemistry appears, followed by biology, and then conscious life emerges by chance to think about the entire process. The very existence of this kind of reasoning and self-awareness is beyond baffling from an evolutionary point of view.

If you postulate the existence of the soul that is fashioned by God and endowed with reason and cognitive capacity, then it makes sense that we would be able to comprehend our human condition and be able to respond to a hostile world with potential solutions and remedies. The ability to think strategically and apply what we learn from one field of study to another is what distinguishes us as humans. Attributing this astounding trait to natural selection alone would be virtually impossible. Again, all thinking utilizes the brain, but there is something that this type of thinking points to in terms of comprehending abstract concepts as well as connecting those abstractions together to create art and music and to engage in the scientific process. The developers of graduate programs in brain-based teaching at Nova Southeastern University noted the following:

> Although educational research on the power of metacogni-
> tion for increasing student learning and achievement has been
> amassing for several decades, scientists have only recently
> begun to pinpoint the physical center of metacognition in
> the brain. Researchers at the University College London have
> discovered that subjects with better metacognition had more
> gray matter in the anterior (front) prefrontal cortex. Studies
> are ongoing to determine just how this brain area contributes
> to the critically important skill of metacognition.[32]

As discussed in the last section, just because there is a correlation between the location in the brain and a stimulus doesn't mean they are the same thing. Our ability to think abstractly, transcending our own physical existence, points to a nonphysical dimension that would be classified as mind or the soul.

Near-Death Experiences

A fifth area of evidence for the soul is *near-death experiences* (NDEs). With the huge success of books such as *Heaven Is for Real*, about a young boy's experience of life after death, and two other books, written by doctors, *Proof of Heaven* and *To Heaven and Back*, it is obvious that people want to have the comfort and assurance that they will see their deceased friends and loved ones again. For skeptics, this is simply wishful thinking. Yet what was once scoffed at as mere delusions of the dying are now being treated seriously as sources of empirical data.

Newsweek magazine featured a story in 2012 by Dr. Eben Alexander, author of *Proof of Heaven: A Neurosurgeon's Journey into the Afterlife*:

> As a neurosurgeon, I did not believe in the phenomenon of near-death experiences. I grew up in a scientific world, the son of a neurosurgeon. I followed my father's path and became an academic neurosurgeon, teaching at Harvard Medical School and other universities. I understand what happens to the brain when people are near death, and I had always believed there were good scientific explanations for the heavenly out-of-body journeys described by those who narrowly escaped death.[33]

Though his heart never stopped, Dr. Alexander's cortex became completely inactive in an occurrence of bacterial meningitis that thrust him into a coma. Brain activity stopped. He described what happened:

> There is no scientific explanation for the fact that while my body lay in coma, my mind—my conscious, inner self—was alive and well. While the neurons of my cortex were stunned to complete inactivity by the bacteria that had attacked them, my brain-free consciousness journeyed to another, larger

dimension of the universe: a dimension I'd never dreamed existed and which the old, pre-coma me would have been more than happy to explain was a simple impossibility.[34]

Dr. Gary Habermas of Liberty University cites more than three hundred cases in which many of those who were close to death described things about which they could not have possibly known. As he told me in an interview about his forthcoming essay on the topic, "The evidence of the reality of NDEs has changed the notion that there is no scientific evidence for such occurrences."[35]

Neuroplasticity

While skeptics commandeer neuroscience for their own purposes, this field of study does offer evidence that indicates the existence of a soul, a mind that is distinct from the brain. It is similar to the scientific evidence that points to the existence of God, in terms of how you interpret the data—whether from a naturalistic or theistic worldview. When presenting evidence for God's existence from the big bang or the fine-tuning of the laws of physics for intelligent life, the data can be interpreted by both dualist (one who believes there is both body and soul) and physicalist (one who believes that everything is ultimately physical). According to Moreland, "dualism and physicalism are empirically equivalent views consistent with all and only the same scientific data. Thus, the authority of empirical data in science cannot be claimed on either side."[36]

Worth mentioning also is neural plasticity, a frontier gaining ground in the treatment of people who have suffered brain damage. In a 2007 *Scientific American* interview, Sharon Begley, then the senior science writer at *Newsweek* and author of *Train Your Mind,*

Change Your Brain, mentioned both neurogenesis (production of new neurons) and neuroplasticity—both of which were thought impossible. Experiments were conducted with people sitting at a piano for extended periods of time just thinking about playing notes, and regions of the brain expanded even though they did not actually touch the keys with their fingers. Begley concluded, "That was a very striking example of how thinking, how just something happening inside the brain itself with no input from the outside world can change the physical structure of the brain."[37]

A simple search online of the words *neuroplasticity* or *cognitive behavioral therapy* will yield an abundance of information about understanding how to improve brain health through the recognition that the brain can be rewired and, in essence, rejuvenated through deliberate activities. What is not always recognized are the implications, both philosophically and spiritually. The bottom line: *If the mind can change the brain, then based on the law of identity, the mind is not the brain.* This points to the existence of the self, as well as an immaterial mind and, thus, the existence of the soul. C. S. Lewis believed that our actions are not all mere instincts or brain functions. There is something else at work beyond these physical forces:

> Supposing you hear a cry for help from a man in danger. You will probably feel two desires—one a desire to give help (due to your herd instinct), the other a desire to keep out of danger (due to the instinct for self-preservation). But you will find inside you, in addition to these two impulses, a third thing which tells you that you ought to follow the impulse to help, and suppress the impulse to run away. Now this thing that judges between two instincts, that decides which should be encouraged, cannot itself be either of them.[38]

This signals another area that suggests we are more than a collection of physical processes: the reality of free will.

Free Will

If we are merely physical beings, then a logical conclusion is our actions are determined and free will is just an illusion. If, on the other hand, free will exists, then there is a self or a soul that is able to make choices against our very instincts or genetic proclivities. This has enormous implications in the area of justice. If we aren't truly free to make real choices, then are we really responsible for any negative actions we take? As I said before, *animals killing other animals are not crime scenes*. Determinism logically follows the materialistic worldview. As Stephen Hawking confirmed, "It is hard to imagine how free will can operate if our behavior is determined by physical law, so it seems that we are no more than biological machines and that free will is just an illusion."[39]

Sam Harris wrote in his book *Free Will*:

> Our sense of our own freedom results from our not paying close attention to what it is like to be us. The moment we pay attention, it is possible to see that free will is nowhere to be found, and our experience is perfectly compatible with this truth. Thoughts and intentions simply arise in the mind. What else could they do? The truth about us is stranger than many suppose: The illusion of free will is itself an illusion.[40]

Philosopher John Searle spoke about the "problem of free will" as an unyielding philosophical problem. Searle stated that on one hand we have firsthand, daily experiences of consciousness and free will. Yet it is inconsistent with our knowledge of how the natural world works. Free will is the compelling evidence in the world that there is something about us as humans (and only us) that is not physical and subject to causal forces:

> The implications of this conclusion for human rights are daunting. If our actions are simply the products of our genes and external experiences or stimuli then we have no free will. All our actions therefore are determined by forces beyond our control. Such a position undercuts any basis for preferring human life or rights over those of animals, bacteria, or rocks.[41]

Searle, a self-described atheist, candidly draws the logical conclusion of the implications of dismissing free will: human rights disappear. There is nothing more foundational to our human experience than our ability to make choices. Rejecting this truth demonstrates how far someone is willing to go to escape true reason.

The Testimony of Scripture

A final area of evidence for the soul comes from the Bible. It could be called the *owner's manual for the human soul*. Undoubtedly you have bought a car or a computer that comes with an owner's manual that explains how it works as well as how it can be optimally operated. In chapter 6 we examine the Bible as truth and its authority regarding our lives. It is important to remember that Christ calls us to follow and submit to Him by choice, not through coercion. When we recognize the character of the Creator and His perfect love for us, we can trust that He wants nothing more from us or for us than our good. He is worthy of our trust.

The existence of the soul is presented from Genesis to

Revelation. In the New Testament it is clear that Jesus taught that the soul existed. Perhaps the most significant reference is when Jesus was asked about the greatest commandment:

> One of them, an expert in the law, tested him with this question: "Teacher, which is the greatest commandment in the Law?"
>
> Jesus replied: "'Love the Lord your God with all your heart and with all your soul and with all your mind.' This is the first and greatest commandment. And the second is like it: 'Love your neighbor as yourself.' All the Law and the Prophets hang on these two commandments." (Matthew 22:35–40)

This verse gives insight into several dimensions of what we simply call the "soul" in referencing the heart and mind as well as the soul. The self is inferred as well, in the injunction for us as individuals to direct our entire inner affections in this manner. Jesus referred to His own soul in the moments before His suffering on the cross: "Then he said to them, 'My soul is overwhelmed with sorrow to the point of death. Stay here and keep watch with me'" (Matthew 26:38).

Jesus' resurrection three days after His death gives us the ultimate evidence of life after death and, therefore, existence of the soul. Upon the authority of Christ Himself, we can trust not only that the soul is real but also that the wisest decision we could make is to place the well-being of our souls in His care. He promised:

> Come to me, all you who are weary and burdened, and I will give you rest. Take my yoke upon you and learn from me, for I am gentle and humble in heart, and you will find rest for your

souls. For my yoke is easy and my burden is light. (Matthew 11:28–30)

As the Creator of the soul, God desires its well-being and protection. His commandments were given to guide us on the path of life and to help us find the healing and restoration we so desperately need. This is why understanding the gospel is the most important human right. It contains the only real cure for the spiritual disease called *sin* that seeks to destroy us from the inside out.

Summary

For the materialist, there is no evidence for the soul because there can't be any evidence for it—a classic example of circular reasoning. Yet as we have seen, the cumulative case for the soul is substantial. The soul is a nonphysical dimension of our existence. Belief in the soul is as pervasive around the world as the belief in the existence of God. The evidence for the soul's existence comes from philosophy, science, history, and theology. Some current beliefs in the area of neuroscience have attempted to dismiss the reality of the soul due to the mistaken notion that identifying areas of correlation and causality makes the mind and the brain the same thing. The evidence confirms that the mind is not the brain. There is a difference between a mental state and a brain state, though there are correlations between the two. Remarkably, research shows that the mind can change the brain, offering further evidence that they are not the same.

God created us in His image and gave us the capacity to know and seek truth. Because the soul exists, we can have confidence that life has purpose and meaning. We also have knowledge of good and evil as well as the awesome responsibility to make choices. Unlike the animals', our actions aren't determined by our genetics or our instincts. In the end, because the soul exists, justice is possible. Jesus Christ and the truth of Scripture ultimately provide evidence for the reality of the soul and the instructions for how to see our souls prosper in this life and the one to come.

CHAPTER 6

GOD HAS SPOKEN TO US

The Authority of Scripture

All Scripture is God-breathed.
—2 Timothy 3:16

B art Ehrman entered Princeton Seminary in New Jersey as a Bible-believing Christian. He is now one of the world's most recognized skeptics and critics of the Christian faith. This outcome was the last thing the young Ehrman would have thought possible. He first attended Moody Bible College, "where 'Bible' is our middle name," he quips. Then he studied at Wheaton College in Chicago, one of the nation's most respected evangelical schools and Billy Graham's alma mater. He began his doctoral work at Princeton Seminary, which is theologically liberal, to study under the tutelage of Dr. Bruce Metzger, perhaps the most preeminent Bible scholar of his generation. But something happened there that disrupted Ehrman's belief that the Bible was true and trustworthy, causing his faith completely to unravel:

> And it became clear to me over a long period of time that my former views of the Bible as the inerrant revelation from God were flat-out wrong. My choice was either to hold on to views that I had come to realize were in error or to follow where I believed the truth was leading me. In the end, it was no choice. If something was true, it was true; if not, not.[1]

Ehrman eventually would reject the Christian faith and become one of the world's foremost skeptics. He now teaches at the University of North Carolina in Chapel Hill and has become a prolific writer with many bestsellers that dismiss the inspiration of Scripture. The freshmen who enroll in his class on the New Testament quickly realize it isn't a Sunday school. He asks them at the beginning of the semester if they believe the Bible is the Word of God. Reports are that a majority of students raise their hands to acknowledge that they do, indeed, believe this to be true. As you might expect, by the end of the semester a significant majority have abandoned this belief. Parents have been known to receive phone calls from their children within a few weeks of taking his class and saying, "Dad, I don't believe in God anymore."[2]

This sad scenario is happening over and over across America as Christian youth leave their churches and youth groups to attend universities. For some—as in Ehrman's case—a religious institution can contribute to their unbelief. Looking back on his story, he claims that when he came to the conclusion that the

Bible and the truth were at odds with each other, he decided to follow what he believed to be true.

It is my sense that the decision-making process is flawed in terms of how many evaluate the Bible as being true or false. The fundamentalist Christian background stresses an inerrant Bible, which means that the translated English text is completely without any possible errors or unresolved conflicts. Unfortunately, holding such a narrow test for the truth can set up many for a fall. Ehrman's testimony reveals something similar to this happening to him. Once he found the first unresolvable problem in the text, his entire belief system came crashing down like a house of cards. Here is how he described that fateful moment: "I finally concluded, 'Hmm . . . maybe Mark *did* make a mistake.' Once I made that admission, the floodgates opened. For if there could be one little, picayune mistake in Mark 2, maybe there could be mistakes in other places as well."[3]

Like many of the passages in the Bible that have an apparent difficulty, Ehrman's issue with Mark 2 has a reasonable resolution.[4] But even if there were not, that wouldn't discredit the validity and truth of the Scripture. Obviously, no one would apply such a criterion to any other realm of knowledge. Imagine throwing out an entire history book by a preeminent historian because one detail could not be reconciled with other historical records.

One of the leading Bible scholars in America, Dr. Dan Wallace, has known Ehrman for thirty-five years and debated him publicly three times. He concluded, "Bart Ehrman merely exchanged one form of fundamentalism for another."[5] My contention is that people like Ehrman have missed the forest for the trees. There are reasons to believe that the Bible is a gift from God to man. Even though it has come to us through fallible humans, it bears the marks of divine authorship. In this chapter I make the case for the authority of Scripture and the reasons it should be given the highest respect in our lives. This is also crucial when it comes to the issue of human rights in general, as well as for making the case for the gospel being *the human right*. As Vishal Mangalwadi said, "I call the Bible the soul of Western Civilization because it propelled the development of everything good in the West: its notion of human dignity, human rights, human equality, justice, optimism, heroism, rationality, family, education, universities, technology, science, culture of compassion, great literature, economic progress, political freedom."[6]

The key question we will examine in this chapter is whether God has spoken to humanity. It is what is meant by *revelation*. "In the past God spoke to our ancestors through the prophets at many times and in various ways, but in these last days he has spoken to us by his Son, whom he appointed heir of all things, and through whom also he made the universe" (Hebrews 1:1–2).

Because of the evidence that God exists and has revealed Himself in Christ, then it follows logically that He is able to communicate with His creation. It is my hope to demonstrate that this has in fact happened in Scripture.

How the Bible Came to Us

In establishing the truth of Scripture, I believe it is important to understand the backdrop of how the Bible came to us. The dismissive claims by skeptics that it is merely a collection of fables passed down by "Bronze Age illiterate peasants"[7] is indeed an accusation that can be easily refuted with a little research and a measure of objectivity. In the book *God's Not Dead*, I devoted a chapter to the reliability of Scripture. From the number of early manuscripts that exist (compared to other ancient literature) to the testimony of the Dead Sea Scrolls, we have abundant evidence that, as Dr. Dan Wallace says, "what we have now is what they wrote then."[8]

The Bible came to us through a diversity of authors in a variety of cultural settings. It is actually not one book but a collection of sixty-six books, written by more than forty different authors over a period of fourteen hundred years. It is a book of books. The Scriptures we have today have been faithfully preserved over the centuries and have passed the tests of time, persecution, and opposition. The collection of the thirty-nine Old Testament books were gathered together by 500 BC and were translated from Hebrew to Greek starting in the third century BC in what is called the Septuagint. The title alludes to an account describing seventy scholars who gathered in Alexandria, Egypt, to initiate the translation.[9] All twenty-seven New Testament books were written within the first century, and they were recognized as authentic and authoritative almost immediately. Lists of most of these books appeared in the second century. Other, spurious gospels and supposed letters with the names of prominent personalities were written well after the first century, and they were rejected for not being authentic or accurate.

The Christian faith began in Jerusalem after the crucifixion and subsequent resurrection of Christ. The first twenty-five years (AD 30–55) witnessed the church growing explosively in a very hostile environment due to Roman persecution and religious opposition. The first written gospel (Mark) was penned in the 50s. Luke and Matthew were written in the 60s, and the gospel of John in the 90s (before the end of the first century). Paul started writing his letters (epistles) in the 40s and continued to do so until his death at the hands of the emperor Nero in AD 67.

For the first seventy years of the church's existence, it functioned and grew without the Bible we hold in our hands today. The twenty-seven books of the New Testament were first acknowledged as a collection in AD 315 by Athanasius, though most of the books, including the Gospels, were recognized as authoritative much earlier.[10] They were eventually translated from Greek into Latin in the fourth century by Jerome, since Latin was the common language at that time. Other Latin translations existed, but Jerome's version, known as the Vulgate, became the primary translation for more than one thousand years. Latin eventually fell out of use, but few translations were made into the common languages of the people. The reluctance to produce new translations was due to wide-scale illiteracy and concern over the distribution of unauthorized versions by church leaders.[11] Without the knowledge of the truth in the Bible, the masses were often ignorant of the many corrupt religious practices taking place, such as the sale of indulgences (in essence, paying money for forgiveness of sins).

John Wycliffe was called the "Morningstar of the Reformation" because he translated the Bible into English during the 1380s. The hatred for and opposition to Wycliffe from ecclesiastical authorities were so severe that forty-three years after his death, his opponents dug up his bones, burned them, and scattered the remains in the Swift River. In 1526, William Tyndale released the first complete New Testament in English that was a translation of the original Greek. (Earlier versions were translated from the Vulgate.) Tyndale was also the first to use the recently invented printing press to more widely distribute his translation. For doing so, he was strangled and his corpse burned at the stake.

Fueled by the recent development of Gutenberg's printing press, an exponential distribution effort in Europe, circa 1450, placed Bibles in the hands of the masses. Many more translations were eventually distributed in different languages so the masses could have direct access to Scripture. The access to Bibles, which began in the early 1500s, coupled with a rise in literacy, helped drive the Protestant Reformation. Anyone could now directly access and apply the Bible's teaching to his life, as well as compare what Scripture said to what the ecclesiastical authorities taught. In England, any house or pub could turn into a debating center, where people discussed whether official political decrees or claims made by other authorities agreed with Scripture. As a result, some historians have concluded, "The Bible is what made western civilization a thinking civilization."[12]

The Authority of Christ Comes from His Resurrection

Looking back to the sudden expansion of the early church, it is obvious that a momentous event was the reason for its existence: the resurrection of Jesus Christ from the dead. By the end of the fourth century, the church had grown despite several major periods of devastating and cruel persecution. Christians had been thrown to the lions in the Roman Coliseum, burned at the stake, and crucified. They gave up their lives rather than deny Jesus

Christ was the risen Lord. They recognized the essential role of the Old Testament and the eventual New Testament writings, but the driving force for their faith was the unshakable foundation of the resurrection. As Tim Keller posted on Facebook, "The issue on which everything hangs is not whether or not you like his teaching but whether or not he rose from the dead."[13]

Once that fact is established, we have a key building block in place that affirms that the Bible is true. Because of Jesus' resurrection from the dead, we can have the assurance that He is the Son of God and that His words are true and should be the ultimate authority in our lives. As Jesus said, "Heaven and earth will pass away, but my words will not pass away" (Matthew 24:35 ESV).

Jesus' words not only deserve to have the ultimate place of authority over our lives, but He also verified that the Old Testament Scriptures were authentic as well: "Everything . . . in the Law of Moses and the Prophets and the Psalms must be fulfilled" (Luke 24:44 ESV).

On the surface the Christian faith is obviously not based on any one error-free or discrepancy-free translation of the text. If that requirement were true, then we would not have such a variety of translations of the Bible in use today. In contrast, Islam claims the Quran was given in Arabic to an illiterate Muhammad, who simply dictated what he heard to others. They believe it has no flaws. This is demonstrably false. In light of this, Muslims believe it should not be translated from its original language lest the text be corrupted. Christianity, instead, believes the gospel should be heard by everyone and encourages the text of Scripture to be faithfully translated into all languages. While maintaining the integrity of every translation, the truth of the message can be understood by all.

How the Bible Shaped Our World

One of the most important things to recognize is how the Bible shaped the modern world, particularly in the recognition of human rights and the need for justice. It amazes me how anyone could dismiss the grandeur, complexity, and sheer wonder of our planet teeming with life as simply a product of blind processes, with no recognition of a Creator. I have the same astonishment for anyone who dismisses the Bible as merely a human book. Such skeptics must close their eyes to the grandeur and magnificence of its words and deliberately ignore its impact on the world we live in. If the Bible had not been written, the world would be a darker place, almost unrecognizable compared to what we enjoy today. Countless modern benefits can be traced back to something the Bible inspired.

Vishal Mangalwadi wrote *The Book That Made Your World*, detailing the impact of the Scriptures on modern society. He gave many examples—some of which I describe in the pages that follow—but one of the most significant is in the area of science:

> The Bible created the modern world of science and learning because it gave us the Creator's vision of what reality is all about. That is what made the modern West a reading and thinking civilization. Postmodern people see little point in reading books that do not contribute directly to their career or pleasure. This is a logical outcome of atheism, which has now realized that the human mind cannot possibly know what is true and right.[14]

Such statements sound strange to many modern ears, having been inundated with revisionist history for the last one hundred years, telling us that religion in general and the Bible in particular have been the source of oppression. With a little effort and even a small measure of objectivity, the true story will emerge.

The Impact of the Bible

The Bible and its teaching have made an incomparable and irreplaceable impact on the modern world—not just the West. Here is a brief overview of some of the key areas it has affected:

> **Human Rights/Justice.** One of the major contentions of this book is that human rights are real because they are grounded in a transcendent moral authority—God. I hope the preceding chapters have made it clear that the Scriptures delineate these rights and give them the ultimate source of legitimacy.
>
> In Genesis, the right to life is underscored with murder being a capital offense: "Whoever sheds human blood, by humans shall their blood be shed; for in the image of God has God made mankind" (Genesis 9:6).
>
> As mentioned earlier, the command not to steal recognizes the right to personal ownership. God is the giver of life, and He has granted humans liberty to make real choices—even wrong ones.
>
> **Government.** The Bible revolutionized the way leaders and rulers viewed their roles and responsibilities. Kings, presidents, and prime ministers around the world were no longer seen as possessing ultimate authority. While Scripture endorsed the authority of political leadership, it also gave limits and responsibilities. Presidents of the United States since George Washington have been

sworn into office with their left hands on the Bible. This act acknowledges the Bible as the ultimate source of truth, and it reminds new leaders that they are under its authority. The very term *prime minister* comes from "first servant," which alludes to the example of Jesus Christ washing His disciples' feet and calling them to be servants (John 13:1–17), an act that changed the paradigm for leaders forever.

Science. Modern science arose because the Bible revealed the universe was created by an intelligent designer and was, therefore, rationally understandable. It was not the result of a pantheon of gods with competing interests and agendas, but it was intentionally created, permeating with purpose. The founders of modern science were virtually all people of faith, such as Francis Bacon, Johannes Kepler, and Isaac Newton, just to mention a few.

Education. The very idea of the university emerged in Europe in response to the Bible's command to teach the Word of God to your children (Deuteronomy 6:6–7; 11:19). This commission meant children needed to be taught to read and think, since the God of the Bible had communicated His will to humanity with words. Revelation (God's Word) and reason were joined together, not pitted against each other.

This high value on education derived from the Bible has been a driving force to build schools, colleges, and universities around the world. It has produced profound scholarship in the Jewish community. An astounding 22 percent of the Nobel Prize winners have come from a people comprising .02 percent of the world's population.

Medicine and Hygiene. Hospitals had earlier origins but were made pervasive by Christians in the Middle Ages in response to Jesus' teaching to care for the sick and the needy. In addition the book of Leviticus gave instructions on dealing with disease and quarantining infected individuals. These and other laws of cleanliness stopped the spread of disease, and the dietary restrictions protected adherents from foods with greater poison levels. The laws promoted health and longevity in general, and their medical insights were not matched until modern times. Because the mission of Jesus included the healing of the sick, Christianity has started hospitals and clinics around the world, as well as starting churches.

Marriage. The traditional Western concept of marriage being between a man and a woman was clearly a result of the teaching of Genesis (1:27) and emphasized by Jesus Christ (Matthew 19:4–6). God created male and female and blessed them and told them to be fruitful and multiply. You don't have to be a medical expert to acknowledge the design of the male and female anatomy for the purpose of reproduction. Though examples of polygamy exist in the Old Testament, it was not in God's plan. Both Jesus and Paul (Ephesians 5:21–32) spoke of marriage as a covenant between a man and a woman. Their teaching dismisses the delusion of so-called gender fluidity. Male and female distinctions are dependent not on feelings but on facts.

Morality. While many try to dismiss the Bible as a moral book because of its laws and harsh penalties (which we will discuss in more detail momentarily)—it was the belief that there was a moral lawgiver who cared about the details of our lives that promoted a self-governing accountability. Mangalwadi said, "Moral integrity is a huge factor behind the unique socioeconomic/socio-political success of the West."[15]

The Bible taught that there was someone watching our actions. It's easy to credit the laws of physics or grav-ity as the reason we are here—they don't really care how we live or treat one another. The Bible taught that God judges sin. If it is true, then we should not rebel and shake our fists at God but look at what He is asking us to do. Yes, there were strict laws in the Old Testament. These showed that our actions mattered and our behavior would be judged. Mercy was always in the background of every law. God gave laws and also gave ways to be forgiven so we could try again. It's hard to imagine the cruelty and barbarism that would be normal if God had not spoken so specifically to us in the law.

Biblical Teaching Touches Everything. There is no area of life that the Bible has not impacted or addressed explic-itly or its principles have not affected indirectly. The idea that all people are created equal before God—with the right to pursue truth as well as to actualize their potential—are hallmarks of the message of Scripture. We are not to allow the fear of man or the oppression of unjust laws to hinder us from pursuing these God-given rights. In fact, we will be judged one day for how we uti-lized our gifts and talents.

The final topic worth mentioning is that the Bible revealed to humanity the power and glory of faith, hope, and love. These three things are what make life worth living. Without faith, our world would dissolve quickly into mistrust and treachery. Hope in our souls keeps us from sinking into the quicksand of despair. And love is the force that binds us together into families and friendships and allows us to experience something beyond mere existence. Love allows us to participate in the very life of God, who is love.

Handling Objections

There are many books written by Christian theologians and philosophers that thoroughly discuss the objections skeptics raise against the validity of the Bible. My goal is to give a brief introduction to some of the important issues you will most likely encounter in a dialogue with someone trying to discredit the Christian faith. Many skeptics echo the words of the renowned atheist Richard Dawkins, who summed up the collective sentiments of the skeptical world by framing God as a moral monster:

> The God of the Old Testament is arguably the most unpleasant character in all fiction: jealous and proud of it; a petty, unjust, unforgiving control-freak; a vindictive, bloodthirsty ethnic cleanser; a misogynistic, homophobic, racist, infanticidal, genocidal, filicidal, pestilential, megalomaniacal, sado-masochistic capriciously malevolent bully.[16]

These words, being beyond inflammatory and blasphemous, are simply false. They stem from the confused and twisted logic that refuses to acknowledge God's right to judge His creation. As the Creator and source of justice, God cannot be reduced to

146

the level of a human and then accused of arbitrary baseless acts of judgment. God is the only being with the true objective vantage point and complete knowledge of all the facts. I will give an overview of two of the critical areas alluded to by Dawkins's blasphemous rant that deserve a much fairer analysis than he and his skeptical cohorts offer.

Genocide and Violence in the Old Testament

The fiercest criticism centers on the command God gave to the Israelites to destroy the nations that occupied the land pledged by covenant to Abraham in Genesis 12. More than four hundred years after that promise, Moses led the children of Israel out of the bondage of slavery in Egypt to this land of promise. One of the chief obstacles before them was the nations living there. The command issued to destroy them was, indeed, severe.

The Israelites were commanded to utterly destroy the inhabitants of Jericho as well, which would have included women and children. Many facts must be considered in understanding the context of this command. For the sake of clarity and brevity, I will list some of the primary responses I share with others when this charge against God is raised.

This period of judgment covered a forty-year span of biblical history that was unique (in terms of God issuing such a sweeping decree of military action on the part of the ancient nation of Israel). The use of violence from a military standpoint in Scripture was always a last resort for the Israelites, as well as a defensive response to the aggressive threats and immoral actions of their enemies.

The nations mentioned in the Bible had four hundred years to change before judgment came. God gave enough warning for the people to simply flee and not be killed. The crushing defeat of the Egyptian army at the Red Sea followed by the defeat of Kings Og and Sihon were forty years before the Israelites entered the promised land (Joshua 2:9–11). The nations occupying the land God promised to the Jewish people all knew that God was with the Israelites and was providing supernatural assistance.

The abominable practices of these nations should be seen as reprehensible according to standards of any generation. Child sacrifice was commonplace. It is impossible for God to be just and not judge wickedness. These nations were not judged because of their ethnicity but because of their iniquity. God was not an ethnic cleanser but an iniquity cleanser. Though God has judged nations and people by taking their lives, He is much more known for His mercy. The laws of the book of Leviticus with their harsh penalties are preceded by instructions on how to be forgiven and receive mercy. Another example of this pattern is from the book of Jonah. Even though the people of Nineveh were told the city was to be destroyed, they received a divine reprieve because of their repentance. Jonah, however, was angry with God for not destroying the Ninevites and giving them mercy instead:

> But to Jonah this seemed very wrong, and he became angry. He prayed to the LORD, "Isn't this what I said, LORD, when I was still at home? That is what I tried to forestall by fleeing to Tarshish. I knew that you are a gracious and compassionate God, slow to anger and abounding in love, a God who relents from sending calamity. (Jonah 4:1–2)

The Israelites were never instructed to conquer any other people once they took possession of the promised land.

(Remember, the total amount of land they were promised was about the size of the state of New Jersey.) They were simply to obey God and not learn the idolatrous practices of those before them. Israel was to live in the land prescribed for them and not advance aggressively to conquer other nations. In fact, they were constantly commanded to deal kindly and justly with the foreigners among them.

The Israelites would ultimately lose the land by committing the same sins as the nations they vanquished and refusing to change. God is the ruler and judge of the nations. His instruction to evict the nations from the land of Canaan was due to their sinful behavior. Just as the sin cost the original couple their place in Eden, the sins of the people of Israel would cost them their right to live in the land.

God has the ultimate say about the world He created. Because the world belongs to Him, He decides who lives here. Many balk at the stories of God destroying the world through a flood or having a final judgment for all of humanity. The thought of the existence of a place called hell causes many to accuse God, as Dawkins and his cohorts have done. Yet not to judge injustice would make God unjust. Hell is a place of separation from God—a condition that many have chosen to embrace here on earth. As Dr. Frank Turek often says, "God will not force you into His presence against your will."[17] Heaven would be hell for those who are living in darkness to be exposed to such intense light and purity.

Slavery

Dealing with the institution of slavery puts the spotlight on the worst part of human nature. The very thought of such a practice is abhorrent to the human mind. Tragically slavery still exists in the twenty-first century, primarily in countries that reject the Christian faith, which should immediately indicate that the teaching of Jesus Christ is, indeed, the source of true freedom.

Critics of the Bible point to passages in both the Old and New Testaments that mention slavery as evidence that the Bible endorsed and thus perpetuated this repugnant practice. On the surface, the instructions given in Scripture about dealing with slaves or how they should respect their masters appear problematic. A deeper look at what the Bible teaches, as well as the important aspect of the historical context and backdrop of the biblical commentary, is indispensable for making a fair and equitable judgment. It is also important to note the references that forbid slave trading and paint the practice as evil:

> We know that the law is good if one uses it properly. We also know that the law is made not for the righteous but for lawbreakers and rebels, the ungodly and sinful, the unholy and irreligious, for those who kill their fathers or mothers, for murderers, for the sexually immoral, for those practicing homosexuality, for slave traders and liars and perjurers—and for whatever else is contrary to the sound doctrine that conforms to the gospel concerning the glory of the blessed God, which he entrusted to me. (1 Timothy 1:8–11)

In engaging with others who need an explanation of what the Bible has to say about slavery, the acronym DELIVER should help you remember and communicate some of the salient points about this very sensitive and important issue.

Different: To begin with we must recognize that the Old Testament passages where slavery is mentioned were written 3,400 years ago. It was only 100 years ago that women got the right to vote in the United States and a little more than 150 years ago that slavery was abolished. Slavery was a part of the ancient world and not seen as the scourge that it is seen as today. It was not an institution ordained by God but a product of a fallen world. The initial biblical response was to provide boundaries but then to ultimately eradicate it. It was not only a vastly different world at that time, but the slavery was different, too, as the following points demonstrate.

Economics: The slavery referred to in the Bible was driven by economics, not ethnicity. Unlike the trans-Atlantic slave trade between 1600 and 1856, which entrapped black Africans, the Scriptures describe people who became slaves either voluntarily (as indentured servants) or due to debts they owed. Others became slaves after being captured in war. They could not be kidnapped, as was practiced in more recent times.

Limited: The Bible gave slaves or servants various rights. It also gave a time limit for the Israelites to keep slaves in their custody (seven years). Though these rights extended primarily to fellow Israelites, they offered the first limits to a person's control of others. The freedom provided for the Jewish people would foreshadow the freedom offered to all people in Christ.

Internal: God's plan for deliverance from slavery followed a pattern of *internal to external*. Slavery was the picture of the spiritual bondage that resulted from sin. Two thousand years ago, the hope was that the Messiah would end the Roman occupation and enslavement of the Jewish people as Moses had done fourteen hundred years before. However, His message was about spiritual freedom first—this internal freedom, which came through the gospel. This is the essence of the message of this book, that God deals with injustice at its source.

Value: The message throughout the entire Bible is that all humans are created in God's image and have value—regardless of ethnicity, economic status, age, or gender. There is a consistent theme in Scripture that God is the defender of the least and the lowly. He warns against taking advantage of the poor and helpless (Matthew 25:45). The New Testament clearly states that there is no distinction in God's eyes between Jew or Greek, slave or free, male or female (Galatians 3:28).

Emancipation: The Ten Commandments begin by stating that God is the emancipator from slavery: "I am the LORD your God, who brought you out of Egypt, out of the land of slavery. You shall have no other gods before me" (Exodus 20:2–3). Where slavery has ended, it has been because of the force of the gospel. Sadly, slavery is still practiced in the twenty-first century practically unhindered in places where the proclamation of the gospel is outlawed.

Redemption: It is safe to say that you can't really understand the message of the Bible without understanding God's plan to redeem mankind from the spiritual slavery and bondage to sin and Satan. The concept of redemption is introduced in the Old Testament and finds its ultimate fulfillment in Christ. He is our Redeemer! "For you know that it was not with perishable things such as silver or gold that you were redeemed from the empty way of life handed down to you from your ancestors, but with the precious blood of Christ, a lamb without blemish or defect" (1 Peter 1:18–19).

Rear Admiral Barry Black (ret.), chaplain of the Senate and an African American, quoted that verse at the 2017 National Prayer Breakfast when explaining what Christ's sacrifice on the cross means to him: "The value of an object is based upon the price someone is willing to pay. When it dawned on me that God sent His only begotten Son to die for me, no one was ever able to make me feel inferior again."[18]

While skeptics mention slavery as evidence of the Bible's alleged injustice, it is actually a picture of just the opposite: God's love, justice, and freedom offered to us through Jesus Christ.

These points won't answer every objection that skeptics will raise. There are passages in the Old Testament that sound shocking to our modern ears. Take the example of polygamy. Even though God seemingly permitted people to have multiple wives, this was not what He originally intended. Because of the impact of sin, the culture digressed to a point where the primary issue was dealing with people who worshipped multiple gods, not who had multiple wives. Polygamy stopped eventually because of the understanding of God's original design for marriage between one man and one woman. As the apostle Paul stated, "In the past God overlooked such ignorance, but now he commands all people everywhere to repent" (Acts 17:30).

This was certainly true of slavery as well. God never intended humans to enslave one another. As society fell under the power of darkness and sin, slavery became part of the fabric of the ancient world. God's plan was to give regulations—restrictions as well as the understanding of the rights of those in slavery. In due season, the understanding of value and dignity of every human that the Scripture taught caused the evil institution of slavery to be dismantled.

Though there are other issues besides these two that skeptics raise, many of them come up when the claim that the Bible is God's inerrant message to man is broached. It is vital that we address what it really means to say that the Bible is the inspired, inerrant Word of God.

Understanding Inspiration and Inerrancy

From the very beginning of mankind, the central challenge of Satan to man could be summed up with the first accusation ever recorded: *Has God really said . . .?* Adam and Eve certainly didn't doubt God's existence; they doubted the authority of His words. This remains the Enemy's consistent tactic to deceive human-kind and subvert our trust in God and His Word. If God's Word is discredited, then humans can create their own standards and com-mands and be free from the responsibility that comes from clear and unequivocal demands of the Creator.

The rise in biblical criticism was the reason almost three hun-dred scholars gathered at the Hyatt Regency in Chicago in 1978 to draft a statement of the doctrine of biblical inerrancy. Convened by the International Council of Biblical Inerrancy, it included key figures such as Norman Geisler and R. C. Sproul. The result was a statement with five central points accompanied by nineteen articles consisting of affirmations and denials. The wisdom of this state-ment is so important that I feel I should give you a closer look at what it says. We must regain confidence in the truth and authority of Scripture, as well as the knowledge of how to present it to others. I must continue to stress that the Christian faith is not based on the belief in the inerrancy of Scripture. It is founded on the resurrection and is supported by belief that the Bible is minimally a historically reliable set of documents, as we have discussed. However, its inspi-ration is still central to Christian faith and doctrine.

Here are the statement's five key points:

1. God, who is Himself Truth and speaks truth only, has inspired Holy Scripture in order thereby to reveal Himself

to lost mankind through Jesus Christ as Creator and Lord, Redeemer and Judge. Holy Scripture is God's witness to Himself.

2. Holy Scripture, being God's own Word, written by men prepared and superintended by His Spirit, is of infallible divine authority in all matters upon which it touches: it is to be believed, as God's instruction, in all that it affirms; obeyed, as God's command, in all that it requires; embraced, as God's pledge, in all that it promises.

3. The Holy Spirit, Scripture's divine Author, both authenticates it to us by His inward witness and opens our minds to understand its meaning.

4. Being wholly and verbally God-given, Scripture is without error or fault in all its teaching, no less in what it states about God's acts in creation, about the events of world history, and about its own literary origins under God, than in its witness to God's saving grace in individual lives.

5. The authority of Scripture is inescapably impaired if this total divine inerrancy is in any way limited or disregarded, or made relative to a view of truth contrary to the Bible's own; and such lapses bring serious loss to both the individual and the Church.[19]

Having these statements stipulating the broad parameters of what is meant by inerrancy helps us grasp what this belief really means versus what some assume it should mean.

What This Means Practically

Looking over all the dimensions of this statement, it should be clear that a belief in the inerrancy of Scripture is backed by a multifaceted argument that saves the Scripture from an arbitrary dismissal at the sight of the first apparent problem or discrepancy. The nineteen affirmations and denials give greater clarity about the practicalities of what it means to claim the Bible is inerrant. Article XIII illustrates this point:

> WE DENY that it is proper to evaluate Scripture according to standards of truth and error that are alien to its usage or purpose. We further deny that inerrancy is negated by Biblical phenomena such as a lack of modern technical precision, irregularities of grammar or spelling, observational descriptions of nature, the reporting of falsehoods, the use of hyperbole and round numbers, the topical arrangement of material, variant selections of material in parallel accounts, or the use of free citations.

We cannot import twenty-first-century expectations of how Scripture should function into documents that are more than two thousand years old. God communicated His message in history using the minds and personalities of the writers. They were not passive bystanders, as if they were receiving a text message from heaven. We might assume that's the way God should have communicated the message, but in His wisdom and sovereignty, He didn't. However, the writing of Scripture was not solely initiated by man's will; it was initiated by the Spirit of God. The apostle Peter explained this process of how God spoke to and through humanity: "Above all, you must understand that no prophecy of Scripture came about by the prophet's own interpretation of things. For prophecy never had its origin in the human will, but prophets, though human, spoke from God as they were carried along by the Holy Spirit" (2 Peter 1:20–21).

Summary

It is important to keep this chapter in perspective in terms of how it relates to the overall theme of this book. The great question that we are seeking to answer could be framed simply: *Has God spoken to us?* In other words, is there evidence that God has communicated to us as His creation? The answer is yes. Not only has He given evidence of this through the order and intelligent information in the world He created, but He has spoken to us through Christ and the Scriptures. On the basis of His resurrection, we can trust Christ as an authoritative witness to this. We take much of what we believe in this world on the basis of authority. This is especially true when it comes to scientific knowledge.

Looking deeper at the Bible, we can clearly see that it is a historical record of the dealings of God with humanity, not a collection of mythological tales. The historical reliability of the Scripture adds an important pillar of support to the claim that the Bible is true and trustworthy. The field of archaeology offers abundant attestation to the fact that the various books of the Bible are set in a real historical context. A trip to the British Museum in London or the Israel Museum in Jerusalem will establish this as fact, not fiction. Furthermore, we can have confidence that what we have now is what the writers wrote then. The belief that we have an inerrant Bible doesn't refer to the text of a particular translation but to the inerrancy of the message. God has indeed spoken to us in Scripture. The objections that concern the instances of disturbing practices mentioned, such as violence or slavery, must be viewed in terms of the historical context and the complete teaching throughout the entire Bible.

The overall message of Scripture is that God has sent His Son to redeem humanity from the bondage of sin—an injustice. This is the message of the gospel that is detailed and explained in the pages of Scripture.

CHAPTER 7

JESUS VERSUS THE WORLD RELIGIONS

The Exclusivity of Christ

Salvation is found in no one else, for there is no other name under heaven given to mankind by which we must be saved.

—ACTS 4:12

I have traveled more than 3 million miles on airplanes over the last thirty-five years and have had countless discussions with people on these trips from a variety of religious and nonreligious backgrounds. Once someone finds out that I'm a Christian minister, the floodgates open, and most ask me questions that have troubled them, tell me their life stories, or seize the moment to complain about "organized" religion. I usually respond by saying that disorganized religion is really bad. These moments are so frequent that I call it "the church at thirty-five thousand feet." Some of these encounters have been really humorous (like the woman I met who told me she was God) while others have been very emotional, as in the case of someone traveling to a loved one's funeral.

In the last few years I have boarded airplanes with the express goal of *not* getting into a conversation unless I have a reason to believe I really need to talk to the stranger sitting next to me. The time on the plane usually provides me a needed break from the phone and a chance to read or work on a writing project. A few months ago I was actually working on this book while returning to the States from an international trip and had what could be called a reluctant conversation. We had been flying for a few hours, and I had managed to stay out of any discussion with the man sitting next to me (wearing headphones is the trick). Unfortunately I was seated by the window in a row of three people and had to ask to get out to visit the facilities. When I returned to my seat, a brief exchange with my fellow passengers led to a conversation that I soon realized was an important one.

The man said he was an executive with a company based in Japan and had the responsibility to travel the world representing the company. He then asked me the question that I'd hoped he wouldn't: "What do you do for a living?" When I revealed I was a Christian minister who spoke on university campuses and a writer, he was quick to tell me his beliefs. He told me he was a Muslim and was troubled by the lack of faith in God among university students. I showed him a copy of my book *Man, Myth, Messiah* and explained my motivation for showing the evidence of the historical Jesus and His resurrection, something that

Muslims reject. I then decided to engage the man truthfully and respectfully about why Christianity was true and Islam was not.

"My problem with Islam is that it simply is wrong about the statements made in the Quran saying that Jesus was not crucified," I told him calmly. "You are obviously an intelligent man, but it seems you are accepting a set of beliefs that are more cultural rather than ones you have objectively investigated." This led to a lengthy exchange during which I respectfully listened and asked him questions. I did not try to win an argument. I simply wanted to give him as much evidence as possible that Christianity is true.

When the plane landed, I said goodbye and proceeded to go through customs in the Atlanta airport. After I did that and rechecked my bags to Nashville, the man approached me and asked how long my layover was until my flight departed for Nashville. Though I had dreaded it, I was suddenly thankful for the more than two-and-a-half-hour wait for my final flight home. The man followed me to my gate and sat for more than an hour, asking me questions about my beliefs. Having such a respectful dialogue about truth with someone from another religion was refreshing. My final challenge to him was that he be willing to follow the evidence regardless of the implications with regard to his faith as a Muslim. I think he walked away reconsidering his lifelong assumptions about what is true about Jesus Christ.

This is an example of one of the most daunting issues facing you as a Christian—how to dialogue with people of other religions. We have to balance speaking the truth about Jesus' unique authority and role in our salvation with treating others' beliefs with respect. We also must realize that every belief people hold that does not correspond to reality will ultimately undermine individuals' lives and society as a whole.

Exclusivity and the Fear of Intolerance

Before we look at the specifics of three of the world's most followed religions, I want to talk about the exclusivity of Christ as
Savior and Lord and the fear that those who adhere to this belief
will necessarily be intolerant toward others. I have mentioned
this issue before, but feel I must revisit it now as we examine and
critique other belief systems. In a pluralistic society, where there
are multiple beliefs (as well as nonbelief), the pressure mounts
for everyone to hold their beliefs loosely. The twisted logic goes
something like this: the truly tolerant are those who possess no
dogmatic convictions and accept everyone's beliefs as equally
true. As I mentioned in chapter 4, truth by its very nature is exclusive. All of the religions we will examine make exclusive claims
and cannot all be right.

As Lesslie Newbigin stressed, we don't engage others by
abandoning our convictions but by standing firm and engaging
in respectful dialogue:

> The framework that I devise or discern is my ultimate commit-
> ment or else it cannot function in the way intended. As such
> a commitment, it must defend its claim to truth over against
> other claims to truth. I have no standpoint except that point
> where I stand. The claim that I have is simply the claim that
> mine is the standpoint from which it is possible to discern the
> truth that relativizes all truth. That claim is the expression
> of the ultimate commitment that is my real religion. If this
> argument is valid, it follows that the Christian will meet his
> or her friend and neighbor of another faith as one who is com-
> mitted to Jesus Christ as their ultimate authority, who openly

acknowledges this commitment, and seeks to understand and to enter into dialogue with a partner of another commitment on that basis.[1]

Respectful, meaningful dialogue with people from other religions happens best when you stand fully in the position that your belief represents ultimate truth. It doesn't happen when you surrender that position of truth in the name of tolerance. This seems counterintuitive, but it is dishonest to abandon your belief in what is true to accomplish an idealistic place of peace with others. Scientists certainly wouldn't think that way when it comes to truth. Why should we have a lesser commitment to our views of ultimate reality?

In this chapter I want to examine three of the major world religions in the light of the truth claims of Christianity: Islam, Hinduism, and Buddhism. I omitted Judaism because of the extensive writing done on the subject in *Man, Myth, Messiah*.

There is no way to give each of these topics the time it deserves within the scope of this book. I am hopeful that these brief descriptions of the central beliefs of each of these religions and some responses to these beliefs will serve as a primer for further study.

Islam

The religion of Islam has taken center stage in the news and in the minds of many in the world since the terrorist attacks in New York City on September 11, 2001. Since that time countless debates in the media have centered on whether Islam is inherently a religion of peace or one of violence. Islam actually means "submission," and the term *Muslim* means "one who submits." Technically, the vision of Islam is to achieve world peace—once everyone has either voluntarily or forcibly submitted to Allah.

It is important not to stop there in understanding the distinctions of Islam compared to Christianity and to be able to engage Muslims in a respectful dialogue concerning the gospel. The challenge to this effort is that the world's second-largest religion, with more than a billion adherents,[2] has many variations and sects that follow different traditions that have developed over the fourteen hundred years since Muhammad first recited his messages to his followers. For instance, a major division exists between Sunnis and Shias—the Sunnis believe Muhammad's successor should be chosen by the Muslim community, while the Shias hold the successor should come from Muhammad's family lineage.

The Quran, considered Islam's most holy book, can be difficult to understand because its chapters (suras) are from longest to shortest (thus not in chronological order) and the context of what is being stated is often missing. Muslims who take their faith seriously and attempt to share it with others supplement the Quran with the Hadith, which are collected sayings of Muhammad, and the Sira, the collection of biographies of his life. These sources are essential since the Quran teaches several times that Muslims should follow the example of Muhammad's life, and the additional material provides the historical background needed to understand the meaning of many of the verses. Reading all of these sources together provides a clear picture of Muhammad's life and teaching.[3]

Muhammad was born in Mecca in AD 570. His parents died when he was a child, and he was raised by his uncle, who was a merchant. Throughout his youth Muhammad interacted with Jews, Christians, and people of other faiths. He married a wealthy widow, which greatly improved his social status. He then made a regular habit of visiting a cave to pray. During one visit at the age of forty, he claimed to have fallen into a trance and encountered the angel Gabriel, who told him to "Proclaim!" (Sura 96:1–5). After this, he received his first revelation. Over the next several years, he received many more, which he recited to his followers. His recitations were eventually collected together into the Quran.

The core message includes the teaching of monotheism and a moral system similar to Judaism. The five pillars include professing Allah as the only true God, and Muhammad as his prophet (*Shahadah*); daily prayer five times a day while facing Mecca (*Salat*); giving alms for the poor (*zakat*); fasting from sunup to sundown during the month of Ramadan (*Sawm*); and pilgrimaging to Mecca (*hajj*) at least once in a lifetime.[4] The Quran also describes Muhammad as the last prophet, who would correct the corruption in the messages of previous prophets. In addition, Muslims must spread Islam until people submit to its authority through conversion or subjugation (Sura 9:29). Finally, the Quran speaks repeatedly of a day of judgment, with some going to paradise and some to hell, depending on whether their good deeds outweigh their bad ones (Sura 2:281).

Conquest by the Sword

Muhammad started his career in Mecca, where he preached against the local paganism, which consisted of numerous tribal deities. His message started as tolerant and peaceful, particularly toward Christians and Jews, whom he saw as recipients of God's revelation. He even stated, "There shall be no compulsion in the religion" (Sura 2:256). Yet in the same sura you find the command, "Fight them until there is no [more] fitnah (divergent opinions about faith) and [until] worship is [acknowledged to be] for Allah. But if they cease, then there is to be no aggression except against the oppressors" (2:193).

Within a few years, Muhammad's tone morphed from that of a "prophet" to that of a military leader with a mandate from Allah to fight the infidels. His revelations shifted to commanding his followers to fight against unbelievers (the *kafereen*) until they submit:

> Make war on those who have received the Scriptures [Jews and Christians] but do not believe in Allah or in the Last Day. They do not forbid what Allah and His Messenger have forbidden. Christians and Jews do not follow the religion of truth until they submit and pay the poll tax [*jizya*], and they are humiliated. (Sura 9:29)

From his base in Medina, Muhammad organized a military force and sent them to raid caravans and loot their possessions. He eventually fought brutal campaigns against Meccan military bands and conquered the city. After feeling threatened by a Jewish tribe, he conquered them and had the men of the city beheaded as he watched with his nine-year-old bride, Aisha. He then had the women and children sold into slavery. His every action seemed to correspond to a new revelation that authenticated his increasing brutality. His most strategic and motivating innovation was promising paradise to anyone who died in the cause of Islam. This enticement turned his army into a relentless fighting force, which could challenge armies far greater than its own size. By the end of his life, Muhammad was the most powerful leader in the Arabian Peninsula.

Muhammad passed his expansionist vision on to the future caliph (leader of Islam) who succeeded him. After Muhammad's death in 632, several tribes attempted to break away from the control of the new Islamic state, but the first caliph, Abu Bakr, ensured militarily that they remained under his control. He eventually unified the entire region. His successors turned the Islamic state into an empire and conquered enormous regions of the Middle East and Africa. Future leaders expanded farther into Asia, including modern-day India, Pakistan, and central Europe.

Many Christian lands (Syria, Turkey, and North Africa) were conquered, and Christians and Jews were forced to live as second-class citizens and pay a tax (*jizya*). If they converted a Muslim, both the Christian and the new convert could be exiled, imprisoned, tortured, or executed. Adherents to other religions faced fewer choices. They were forced to convert to Islam, flee, or face execution. During the Middle Ages, Europe had to defend itself against several attempted Islamic invasions. In fact, the Crusades were initiated in response to the pleas of Byzantine emperor Alexios I Komnenos for help against Islamic invaders who had committed great atrocities against Christian cities. The threat only subsided after European military technology advanced beyond that of the Islamic world. Today the challenges of ISIS and Islamic terrorism are partly a continuation of Islamic expansionism, which temporarily fell into remission.

Engaging Our Muslim Neighbors

Our call as followers of Christ is to love our neighbors and pray for our enemies. For many, these commands are far more challenging than any of us in America could imagine. If you are reading this book in the Middle East, you have a far more complicated challenge than if you live in Middle Tennessee. Like many who call themselves Christians but have little understanding of the Bible or Christian theology, many Muslims have little understanding of their faith, and they have accepted revisionist versions of history, which soften Islam's violent past. Many believe Muhammad was a man who promoted peace, and they have mainly focused on the earlier Quranic verses, which promote tolerance. They give away the ultimate distinction between these two competing belief systems—the idealized vision of Muhammad they desire can only be found in the person of Jesus Christ, and the religion of peace and justice they wish to follow comes from Jesus' teaching, not the Quran.

Understanding that the nature of the God of the Bible is not the same as the nature of Allah in the Quran is critical. Though Islam believes there is only one God, like Judaism and Christianity, there is little resemblance to the God of Scripture. In Islam, God is not a God of love. There is no comprehension of what is described in John 3:16, in which God so loved the world that He came to earth to die for our sins. Furthermore, there is no clear concept of sin and separation from God in Islam. The truth that God wants a relationship with us as sons and daughters is also nonexistent. In Islam, because humankind was never separated from God because of sin, there is no understanding of our need for Christ to die for our sin to reconcile us back to God.

The earliest Quranic verse is found inscribed on the Dome of the Rock, a landmark in Jerusalem that was built in 691. It reads, "God had no Son." Yet the Quran mentions Jesus in many places and acknowledges that He was born of a virgin, performed miracles, and was a prophet. Muslims don't believe God would have allowed a true prophet to suffer and be crucified, so they allege that Allah tricked everyone and replaced Jesus with Judas on the cross.

In terms of its historical reliability, the Quran has serious issues. Many versions of it existed during the time of the third caliph, Uthman (AD 644–656). To perpetuate the perception that there was only one version, he had all but one version burned and sent copies of it to the cities of Medina, Kufa, Basra, Damascus, and possibly to Mecca.[5] The destruction of those then existing Qurans places great doubt on the actual content of the original. This is in stark contrast with the New Testament; thousands of extant manuscripts exist today, some from the early second century. Scholars can reconstruct the originals with up to 99 percent accuracy (see chapter 6). In addition, many of the stories in the Quran appear to have been copied from earlier writings, such as fictitious writings about Jesus that postdate the Gospels. Muhammad had ample opportunity to hear these stories, and he apparently incorporated them into his recitations. Since these stories are known to be fictitious, little doubt can remain that these suras are historically unreliable. Furthermore, the Quran's stories about the past cannot be authenticated by any archaeological discoveries, and one of its central claims—that Jesus was not crucified—contradicts enormous historical evidence. As such, the evidence behind the reliability of the Gospels dwarfs that of the Quran.

The Quran itself also confirms that the Gospels (*injeel*) are inspired by God, and it affirms that Christians could consult them at the time of Muhammad:

We sent Jesus, the son of Mary, confirming the Law that had come before him. We sent him the Gospel. . . . Let the people of the Gospel judge by what Allah hath revealed therein, if any do fail to judge by the light of what Allah hath revealed, they are (no better than) those who rebel. (Sura 5:46–47)

Perhaps the most challenging issue is the deity of Jesus. In Islam, Jesus is considered a prophet. The Scriptures teach that Jesus Christ is the incarnation of God, not a son in a biological sense, but the perfect representation of the Father in human form (Hebrews 1:3). I wrote in greater detail about the deity of Christ in *Man, Myth, Messiah*. The very essence of the gospel is that God became man in Jesus Christ. Every prophet who spoke in Scripture would preface his remarks by saying, "Thus says the Lord." When Jesus spoke, He said, "Truly I say to you." This was because the Lord was speaking! Jesus said, "Heaven and earth will pass away, but my words will not pass away" (Matthew 24:35 ESV). The confession that Jesus is Lord means that Jesus is indeed God. This is a vital aspect of the plan for our salvation (Romans 10:9–10).

They Deserve to Know the Truth

Much more could be said about the differences between Islam and Christianity, from Islam's view of women and their deliberate subjugation, to the Quran's teaching that assurance into paradise can be obtained by dying as a martyr in jihad (holy war). The motivation behind suicide bombings and terror attacks is not just in obedience to the command to fight the infidel but also in the hope of gaining paradise by being a martyr (*Shaheed*).

Radicalization isn't the fate of just the ignorant and illiterate masses in an impoverished or war-torn part of the world; it is seen as the logical conclusion of those who read the Quran and seek to be faithful to the words of Muhammad.

The answer is to engage Muslims with the truth and power of the gospel. It offers them the freedom from sin and its penalty of eternal separation from God. The idea that God is a Father who desires a relationship with us is good news and needs to be told to every Muslim. The Quran itself acknowledges that Jesus was born of a virgin, performed miracles, was sinless, and was a prophet. To understand that He was all this and more and that He died and rose again to secure our salvation is news that they deserve to know. God is at work in the Muslim world, and literally millions are coming to faith in Christ. As David Garrison documents in his book *A Wind in the House of Islam*, thousands of movements of Muslims toward Christianity have occurred in the last two decades alone.[6] God has prepared them to hear. We must be willing to reach out to them with love and the offer of friendship and be prepared to share with them the life-giving message they desperately need.

Hinduism

Hinduism is the world's third-largest religion, with more than a billion adherents. Its worldview and teachings are being popularized in the West with the spread of the practice of yoga. A generation ago celebrity participation, such as the Beatles in the 1960s, and the introduction of TM (transcendental meditation) and Hare Krishna gave the practice a big boost. The term *Hinduism* actually encompasses a wide range of belief systems that originated out of the region of modern-day India and Pakistan. While the term itself is recent, some of the ideas originated from as early as 2000 BC. Despite the diversity of beliefs and the recognition of more than three hundred million various gods, most Hindu sects share some themes in common; therefore, the term *Hinduism* can be applied to all of them.

For example, many Hindus believe that everything emanates out of one ultimate reality, or absolute, commonly called Brahman.[7] The different deities, such as Vishnu, the dreamer, or Shiva, the destroyer, are emanations from that same source. This absolute also manifests as people, animals, and the entire world. That is why a Hindu can worship a stone or a star, a serpent or a cow, an ancestor or a living guru; everything is god. Osho Rajneesh, one of the most popular gurus of the seventies and eighties, taught that "the world and God are not two things. The creation is the Creator."[8]

Normal perception that every individual is a distinct person, that a bird is separate from the branch on which it sits, is illusion. It is called *māyā*. This false perception, *māyā*, is the fundamental evil in the world. It constitutes our ignorance (*avidya*) of our own oneness with everything, including Brahman.

Since ignorance of our intrinsic divinity is our fundamental problem, salvation is to obtain the true, mystical knowledge (*jñāna*) that our individuality is illusion, our self is the divine Self. It is one with everything. You are god—the absolute, Brahman.

The idea that everything is one—divine—means that everything is spirit and spirit is god. There is no final distinction between good and evil, deities and demons, god and the devil. Rajneesh repeatedly taught that we, the ignorant ones, "have divided the world into the good and the evil. The world is not so divided. . . . There is no good, there is no bad."[9] This worldview makes it possible for a Hindu to go to a temple and worship a demon before worshipping the deity in the same temple.[10] This worldview makes it very difficult for India's well-intentioned politicians to fight corruption, so rampant in its public life.[11]

Because the *atman* (self or soul) is the eternal, infinite, absolute, it survives death. As long as an individual remains ignorant of his oneness with god, his soul keeps reincarnating in a continuing cycle of rebirths. This is known as *samsara*. Each rebirth is subject to "moral" consequences depending on one's actions. This belief, known as *karma*, explains people's suffering as payment for "evil" in their past lives.

It is important to remember that terms such as *good karma* and *evil karma* do not imply abiding by or breaking of an absolute moral code. In Hinduism goodness or badness of a karma (deed) is related to one's *dharma*—socially assigned duty. A woman's *dharma* or duty is different from a man's. A sweeper's *dharma* is to sweep; if he becomes a physician instead, he is guilty of bad karma. The end goal for a religious Hindu is to break free of the karma-reincarnation cycle and reach liberation (*moksha*). In liberation from life, he merges with Brahman and ceases to reincarnate. Salvation, in other words, is eternal death—ceasing to exist as an individual soul.

Practically every Hindu believes that there are many ways to salvation. This is because they assume that salvation is a matter of perception, called *self-realization*. Since perception depends on the nervous system, there are indeed many ways to alter your consciousness or perception. That is why a typical guru can mix meditation with physical exercises (*asanas*), chanting, drugs, and sex. The path to altering perception (salvation) is flexible. One devotee may detach from the world and focus on meditation to connect to his soul, or *atman*. This is called *jñana-marga*—the path of (mystical) knowledge. Another may focus on performing duties. These could be ritual, family, and social duties. This is called *karma-marga*—the path of duty. Still others choose the path of self-surrender to one of Hinduism's millions of deities. One of the most popular deities is Krishna. This path requires devoting time to chanting and singing. It is called the path of devotion, or *bhakti-marga*.

Hinduism gives you the freedom to create your own god or to choose one invented by sages and honored by tradition. It also gives you the freedom to choose your path of salvation. It can be the path of intense discipline (yoga) or of complete indulgence (tantra). What gives unity to this unfettered diversity is veneration of the priestly class (the Brahmins) and participation in rituals, festivals, and pilgrimages to holy sites. For example, every year millions come to bathe in the river Ganges to attempt to expunge themselves of bad karma: "Hindus believe that sins accumulated in past and current lives require them to continue the cycle of death and rebirth until they are cleansed. If they bathe at Ganges on the most auspicious day of the festival, believers say they can rid themselves of their sins."[12]

Yet tragically the government of India concedes that the Ganges is one of the world's dirtiest rivers. It has appointed a federal minister to clean up the millions of liters of sewage and contaminants that are released into its waters every day. Far from cleansing people of sin or disease, it is deemed responsible for the thousands, if not millions, of deaths each year due to water-borne diseases. Educated Hindus think that, despite all evidence, myths about Ganges purity persist because these myths undergird priests' livelihoods. Accepting truth may liberate people, but myths sustain the religious "shops" that dot the river's banks.

Clash of Values with the West

Dramatic social implications of Hindu beliefs are apparent to any visitor to India. To see suffering as punishment for wrongs in a previous life is to condemn the impoverished and the oppressed. It is to view them as cosmic criminals, paying back their debt to society. This worldview does not motivate people to serve their unfortunate neighbors. The victims need to endure their suffering as payment for their bad karma. This perspective sustains the traditional Indian caste system, where different people are designated at birth to a particular role in society. Those of the lower caste are tasked to perform menial and even dangerous jobs. Today the concepts of human rights, charity, and social justice are challenging traditional Hinduism.

Not too long ago the Bible's notion that all people are created equal was alien to Hinduism. That is why the positive changes to the traditional mind-set did not come to India from Hinduism but from the impact of Christian missionaries who came to India in the 1800s. As we learned in chapter 6, the influence of the Bible and its view of a rational Creator, who intelligently designed the universe and then created humans in His image, produced modern education, science, and the view of humans that all were created equal. As Indian intellectual Vishal Mangalwadi stated, "I first discovered the Bible as a student in India. It transformed me as an individual and I soon learned that, contrary to what my university taught, the Bible was the force that had created modern India."[13]

Studying science requires belief in a God who transcends the physical world so He could create it according to laws that can be studied. In addition, people need to believe that the world is real and important or else no motivation would exist for scientific inquiry or alleviating physical need. Western thought (based on the biblical worldview) had to influence India before its citizens could enjoy the fruits of the scientific revolution.

Equally problematic is the rejection of reason and logic in favor of the pursuit of a nonrational (mystical) bliss that comes when the human mind rejects truth and logic. Orthodox Hindus don't translate their most sacred scriptures, the Vedas, from Sanskrit into Hindi or other Indian languages. They view the Vedas to be magical mantras. They are for the priests, to be chanted as the priests' secret source of power—a magical power released through correctly performed rituals. Later scriptures, such as the Mundka Upanishad, explain why study of the Vedas cannot lead to truth.[14] In Hinduism the Creeds (words with content) aren't important. One has to meditate on inner silence to escape thought. That is the way to experience ("realize") mystical, no-content silence or bliss.

Engaging Hindus

Hinduism and Christianity have many points of contact where a conversation can begin. The concept of karma can be used to help Hindus understand the doctrine of sin—breaking God's law, not the duties (*dharma*) assigned to caste. The crucial difference—the good news—is that Jesus paid the penalty for our sins on the cross. He removes sin, its guilt, and its punishment from our lives.

Hinduism sees Jesus merely as one of many emanations (avatars) from God, not His perfect representation. In fact, all religions are seen as different interpretations of the absolute, much like the different-colored rays of light from a prism. Hindus need to recognize that Jesus claimed to be the unique incarnation of God. He was with God at creation, and everything was created through him (John 1). The Lord Jesus did not teach meditation techniques to help us obliterate our individuality. He died to give us eternal life. To receive Him as our Savior is to crucify the sinful core of our being and to receive His resurrected life.

Willful disobedience to God (sin), not ignorance, is humanity's root problem. No one, except Jesus Christ, has taken our sin upon himself. He took the punishment of our sin—death. Through His resurrection He conquered sin and death. Therefore, He alone is the Savior. Christ's character and teachings are distinct and often in contradiction with core Hindu teachings. That is why they could not both be correct. Because of Jesus' death and resurrection, we aren't doomed to pay off our own karmic debts in the continuous cycle of *samsara*. This is the message of freedom and deliverance that Hindus so desperately need to hear.

Though the world is a place filled with corruption and evil, our role is not to detach ourselves in search of some meditative state of bliss but to engage the world through the power of the Holy Spirit and the liberating truth of the gospel. The poverty that is the result of the Hindu worldview is self-evident and demonstrates that beliefs have consequences.

Buddhism

Thanks to Tibet's exiled theocratic ruler, the Dalai Lama, the West has a highly positive picture of Buddhism. In the 1960s, Hollywood celebrities began courting him as their spiritual mentor. This created Buddhism's current image as a benign religion that gives one inner peace through meditation, in contrast to more aggressive religions that seek to evangelize others or demand that society embrace their moral code. This Western conception of Buddhism is quite different from the way it's practiced in Buddhist lands, such as Thailand and Japan (where I wrote this portion of the book).

Buddhism, the world's fourth-largest religion, with more than 300 million adherents, was begun in northern India around 500 BC by Siddhartha Gautama. By 250 BC it had become India's dominant intellectual-political force, expanding into Tibet, China, Korea, Japan, and the Far East. By the fourteenth century, however, Buddhism was practically extinct in India, the land of its origin. Its revival began only in 1956.[15]

Siddhartha, the future Buddha, was born into a wealthy ruling family. His father attempted to shelter him from the misery of the world, but Siddhartha ventured into the city and observed sickness, poverty, old age, and death. This exposure greatly disturbed him, and he contemplated the meaning of and remedy for suffering. Many years later he experienced what he believed to be enlightenment, where he recognized the Four Noble Truths, which are Buddhism's cornerstone:

1. *Dukkham* (Suffering): Life involves suffering at every step.
2. *Samudaya* (Source): The source of suffering is desire or craving for what is impermanent (*annica*) and always changing.
3. *Nirodha* (Cessation): Suffering ceases by eliminating all desire for what is impermanent.
4. *Magga* (Path): Following the Eightfold Path eliminates desire for impermanent things and ends suffering. [16]

The Eightfold Path can be broken into three categories. The first category, *wisdom*, includes right understanding and right thought. Followers must understand that the world is impermanent, and our self, unlike in Hinduism, does not exist (the doctrine of *annata*). The second category, *ethical conduct*, includes right speech, right action, and right livelihood. These three directives involve following a moral code similar to the Ten Commandments. It also includes never speaking negatively about others and choosing a vocation that does not violate Buddhist principles. Following these directives is enabled by following those in the first category. For instance, recognizing that one has no self enables a person to act selflessly. The final category, *mental discipline*, includes right effort, right awareness, and right meditation. They involve preventing evil thoughts from entering one's mind and meditating to obtain the bliss of enlightenment.

Buddhism attracted the masses because it was a reaction to Hinduism. It taught that the priestly class (Brahmins) had invented capricious gods and their myths to terrorize and exploit people through spiritism, astrology, fortune-telling, and elaborate magical, even sexual, rituals. Their gods extracted appeasements.

The difficulty was that having rejected God, the Buddha doubted the reality of human soul.[17] Nor could he offer a credible explanation for creation. Since there was no god in the beginning, there could be no word *(logos)*, sense, reason, or logic at the source of creation. Buddha's cosmos had to begin with Silence or Nothingness or *Shoonya,* which is primeval Ignorance, called *Avidhya.* Everything, including the intellect, came out of that Ignorance. Therefore, the intellect could not be a means of discerning truth. Thought and word had to be eliminated through psycho-technologies or meditation. This anti-intellectualism had tragic consequences.

In ancient South Asia, for example, Buddhism received so much popular support and political patronage that it built vast *viharas* (monasteries),[18] great statues, sculptures, and monuments. Some of these viharas, such as in Taxila (Pakistan) and Nalanda (India), attracted students from all over Asia. They were centers of learning. They produced philosophical and religious writings, but they were very different from European monasteries, such as Oxford and Cambridge, which grew into universities. Buddhist viharas were pioneered by brilliant philosophers, but they were dedicated to teaching how to empty one's mind of thoughts and words. Therefore, these institutions produced no useful knowledge and lost popular support.

The Buddha's teaching that the ultimate reality was not God's Wisdom (*logos*/word) but *Avidhya* (Ignorance/Silence) gave birth to the Indian word for an idiot—*buddhu*: an individual who knows nothing.[19] Students came to these viharas to become "Nothingness," and far too many of them succeeded.

Buddhism's decline and disappearance in the land of its birth can hide its perennial appeal. The Buddha appealed because back then, everyone did experience life as suffering. As English philosopher Thomas Hobbes put it, life was "solitary, poor, nasty, brutish, and short."[20] However, making suffering the First Noble Truth created major problems.

To begin with, the Buddha's dictum, *Servam dukkham*, or everything in life is suffering, bred fatalism. Buddhists began to think that life without suffering is impossible. There never was the garden of Eden, and there will never be a paradise. Therefore, one should not seek eternal life. The only way to escape suffering is to escape life itself. That is the Buddhist idea of salvation. It is called *Nirvana*: cessation of existence—i.e., eternal death.

Assuming suffering to be the primary problem precluded seeing sin as the ultimate cause of suffering and pain. Rejecting God made it difficult to grasp that He may love us enough to come to this world to save us from our sin.

The immediate goal of the Eightfold Path is to eliminate suffering. Its ultimate goal is to break free of the cycle of reincarnation. That requires eliminating belief in having an immortal soul or self. Once the soul is extinguished, karma has nothing to hold on to. A person is liberated, at least in theory, into the void, *Shoonya*, or Nothingness. That alone, the Buddha thought, is permanent and unchanging. After Buddhism came in contact with Christianity in South India and Sri Lanka, a new school of Buddhism developed that believed that some who have achieved enlightenment (*bodhisattva*) can remain in the world to help others obtain enlightenment.[21]

Christian Response

Many teachings of Buddhism directly conflict with Christianity. First, it views absolute reality as an impersonal void. Reconnecting with that reality involves denying your own existence, which is completely absurd. Once it is assumed that "desire" is the source of all the problems in the world, the path to salvation requires you to deny your own humanity. It demands that you suppress all desires and break free completely from the world. The Buddha renounced his wife and son in order to attain enlightenment. In the Bible, family and community relationships reflect God's own being as Trinity, bound together in perfect love.

Christianity teaches that ultimate reality is a loving God who created the world as good. He made our minds in His likeness so that we may understand the world and take care of it as the

Creator's vice-regents. The evil and suffering in the world do not come from our desire to love one another and care for the creation. Our problems are a result of our rebellion against God and breaking away from His loving presence and provision. As such, the problem is not desire in itself but wrongly ordered desires. Once our deepest longings are met in God, then we can enjoy the pleasures and beauty in the world that He gives to His children. Finally, salvation aims for reconnection, not to an impersonal void, where we are extinguished, but back to God, where we find our true selves.

A second contrast is in the person of Jesus. Buddhists believe He is one of many *bodhisattvas* who come to show the path to enlightenment. In contrast, Christ revealed Himself to be the path. And He took our "karma" on Himself to eliminate it since no actions we could take alone could reconnect us to truth and transform us. His rising from the dead demonstrated that His words are true and carry ultimate authority.

A third contrast is the different perspectives on social justice. Moses learned that life need not be slavery. Therefore, he renounced fatalism and became God's instrument for liberating slaves. Moses taught them how faith and obedience enable God to give them shalom in the promised land flowing with milk and honey.

Initially, Buddhism attracted Indians because it began as a protest against a religious system that exploited the common man. Indians lost interest in Buddhism when they saw that the Buddhists were eliminating the very desire to improve this world. The quintessential image of a faithful Buddhist is a monk on a mountain, closing his eyes to the suffering of the world while meditating in search of inner bliss. In contrast, the highest ideal for a Christian always includes feeding the poor, visiting the orphan, and taking care of the widow (James 1:27).

The Dalai Lama continues to be a media celebrity. However, not many realize that he is the fourteenth Dalai Lama. Before him thirteen others had "reincarnated" to govern Tibet as religio-political rulers with totalitarian powers. Their rule brought only suffering and superstitions. It did not bring the kingdom of peace and freedom. Hardly anyone is now interested in reestablishing Buddhist theocracy in Tibet. Therefore, the current Dalai Lama has announced that he will not reincarnate.[22] Tibetan Buddhists must choose their religious leader democratically. One could add that they should also seek God's kingdom and His righteousness.

Engaging Buddhists

Today, on a university campus, a Christian is likely to meet a fellow student who is excited about going to a ten-day retreat to practice Vipassana.[23] This meditation technique was developed in ancient India and dumped in medieval times. In the 1970s many young people discovered it in Burma (now Myanmar) and brought it to the United States.

Vipassana is the opposite of yoga. In yoga you control breathing to reduce oxygen intake. That affects your nervous system and may give you hallucinogenic ecstasy. In Vipassana you don't control but "observe" breathing. You meditate quietly on inhaling and exhaling. That rhythm becomes a mantra, which eventually helps you stop thinking and experience emptiness—Nothingness or *Shoonya*.

Practicing Silence for ten days can be a mind-blowing experience for students who are addicted to music, movies, and mobile devices, besides being in engaged in lectures, discussions, and studies. Typically there are several hundred people in a retreat, but no one is allowed to talk to anyone. You may hear a video lecture and meet with a mentor, but participants are encouraged not to ask any philosophical questions. The goal is to empty the mind of thoughts and questions. The one-on-one conversation with a mentor is limited to finding out "how to experience complete inner silence." Buddhist mentors in these retreats attract students because they are unapologetic about their faith that since there is no God, the human mind is a product of primeval Ignorance (*Avidhya*). It can neither know the truth nor communicate it in rational words.

This context provides an excellent opportunity for Christians to explain to Buddhist students that we can know truth because God is here, and He is not silent. Parents teach their children language so that parents, teachers, and experts may teach children things they know. Likewise, our heavenly Father made our minds in His likeness and gave us the gift of language so that He may communicate truth to us. He gave us intellect so that we may explore and find truth.

Christians often encounter a number of common challenges in sharing their faith with Buddhists. First, the view that God has emotions will prove challenging to convey since the goal of their faith is often to remove emotions, which are believed to anchor them to a false self. Even the Christian promise of eternal life is challenging to convey, when the Buddhists' goal is to extinguish self. They will also have difficulty with Jesus being the unique path to God because they feel many paths are equally valid. However, several points of contact can be used to guide conversations. In particular, both faiths recognize that people live in deception, and many aspects of their sense of self need to change. They also both recognize that desire for the impermanent (e.g., career advancement) can lead to suffering and even self-destructive actions. And peace comes through connecting with that which is permanent and in turning toward such beneficial patterns as compassion.

After discussing points in common, the conversation could turn to the nature of God as the permanent foundation for reality and as personal and loving. Since God is a person, the fall is not simply a result of desire but of a broken relationship, and salvation comes through reconciling with God to restore that relationship. And the reconciliation was initiated by God through Jesus. These truths naturally lead to the belief that desires are not bad; we are to seek God's kingdom and His righteousness. Our desires must be rooted in our connection with God because He is the source of our hope, joy, and purpose.

Summary

As we present the gospel in the public arena, we must contend for its truth in the face of the challenges presented by other religions and worldviews. While we are to treat others with respect and dignity, we are to boldly, lovingly proclaim the message of Christ. Every religion makes claims about the nature of reality that should be evaluated in terms of whether the statements should be considered true or false. This is also true when it comes to historical claims.

Looking closer at the three largest religions, we see how vast the differences are compared to Christianity. Anyone who says "all religions are the same" has not studied them closely. There may be a few similarities, but they differ greatly in terms of describing the nature and character of God, humanity's need for salvation, and how that salvation and deliverance are accomplished. Understanding these distinctions gives you confidence in any dialogue with someone with a different belief system.

Before we leave the discussion about engaging world religions, we must discuss one of the greatest tragedies of our times—that is, the persecution of Christian believers around the world. In many parts of the world, especially the Middle East, believers are being martyred more today than in any other time in history. The onslaught has reached such proportions that the media has been forced to call attention to this injustice and pressure governments in the nations where this is taking place to uphold the basic human right of individuals to have the freedom of religion.

Christians throughout the centuries have been willing to lay down their lives for the truth of their beliefs. This is far from the insanity of suicide bombers who die while killing others in the name of their religion. Christians are called to love our enemies and pray for those who persecute us. The witness of these suffering believers should motivate us to take our stand for the message of the gospel regardless of the opposition.

CHAPTER 8

OPEN THEIR EYES

The Necessity of Words

*I am sending you to them to open their eyes and
turn them from darkness to light, and from the
power of Satan to God.*
—ACTS 26:17–18

D r. Ming Wang is one of the most respected eye surgeons in
the world. He is a Harvard-trained MD and holds a PhD in
laser physics. He has performed more than fifty-five thousand eye
procedures (four thousand of them on other doctors). His Wang
Vision Institute helps restore sight to people from around the
world who fly to Nashville to seek his help. Ming's story of coming to America from China and turning to Christ from atheism
was featured in the book *God's Not Dead* and inspired a character in the eponymous movie. The testimonies of people he's

helped—people who were blind but after surgery regained their sight either partially or fully—tell of true medical miracles.[1]

One of the most emotionally powerful examples is a young girl named Maria from Moldova. A genetic disorder and severe malnutrition from an early age rendered her completely blind. A Christian couple from Nashville met her while on a mission trip and brought her back to the United States to seek Dr. Wang's help. Her medical condition made it very difficult to repair her damaged eyes.

Dr. Wang explained to me that there are two distinct ways for eyesight to be restored. The first involves the structure of the eye. The question here is whether the physical apparatus of the various parts can be repaired. The second approach concerns function. This always involves helping the newly sighted understand what they are seeing. This requires communication from someone else. He said, "I can repair the physical parts of a damaged eye, and people will still not be able to see properly. We have to work with them through cognitive therapy to help them understand what they are seeing."[2] Through this process of repairing structure and building function, people can learn how to see. In other words, if they have never seen the color red, they don't really know what they are seeing.

In Maria's case she was able to regain almost 30 percent of her sight as a result of Dr. Wang's surgery on her eyes' physical structure. Three years later the communication process that helps her understand what she is seeing is still ongoing.

The all-important communication dimension of restoring a person's physical sight struck me as a vivid illustration of the importance of words in helping others gain *spiritual* sight. In fact, our role in helping others understand the gospel is indispensable. We have been called to help open people's eyes to grasp the reality of God's existence and the truth of the Christian faith. We do this by speaking words to others, backed up by a lifestyle consistent with this confession. The apostle Paul experienced a dramatic transformation when he encountered a vision of the risen Jesus. He recounted what he was told by the Lord and the calling he was being given: "I am sending you to them to *open their eyes* and turn them from darkness to light, and from the power of Satan to God, so that they may receive forgiveness of sins and a place among those who are sanctified by faith in me" (Acts 26:17–18).

Paul said that he was being sent to "open their eyes." I don't know why I missed the significance of this phrase for years as I read this passage. In my mind, I assumed that only God can open people's eyes, so I didn't grasp what the text was saying. Paul was told he was being sent to open people's eyes so that they could turn from darkness to light. This is what happens when we tell others about the gospel and help answer any questions and objections that block them from seeing the truth of the message.

Dr. Wang related another example of a person who was completely blind from birth and had no repairable eye structure at all. It would be impossible, barring a miracle from God, to do anything about the missing structure. However, he said that the woman still possessed what he called "a sense of sight," because she'd had constant communication from others helping her relate what she could touch and smell with a mental image of what these things looked like. In both cases—this woman and Maria—communication with words was essential.

Our Words Can Help Open People's Eyes

Unfortunately this principle happens in a negative sense as well. I remember walking home from school in the third grade and a classmate running to tell me something perverse he had heard. As he spoke that day, my eyes were opened and my innocence pretty much ended abruptly. The way he related his twisted vision of sexuality made me feel dirty. He indeed opened my eyes to evil that day.

The Knowledge of Good and Evil

Adam and Eve were warned to avoid the tree of the knowledge of good and evil. Skeptics mock the notion of this being a true story. In *Man, Myth, Messiah*, I explained the case for the historical Adam and Eve. Here I want to focus on the idea of ingesting knowledge by eating the fruit of a tree like the one mentioned in the book of Genesis. While it's not necessary to try to force some kind of wooden literalism on the text, it is important to understand the plausibility of the stories.

I listened recently to a TED talk by a man named Nicholas Negroponte.[3] He has spoken more than fourteen times at TED and is considered one of the world's leading futurists. In 1984, he gave his predictions of what would happen within thirty years. Many of those things he spoke about came true. Thirty years later, in 2014, he was asked to give another prediction. What he said sounded as though it came right out of the movie *The Matrix*, in which people learn languages or jujitsu simply by taking a pill. Negroponte said that within the next thirty years, it will be possible to ingest knowledge in pill form. This isn't just reminiscent of a science fiction movie; it sounds similar to what happened in the record of humanity's beginnings in Genesis:

> When the woman saw that the fruit of the tree was good for food and pleasing to the eye, and also desirable for gaining wisdom, she took some and ate it. She also gave some to her husband, who was with her, and he ate it. Then *the eyes of both of them were opened*, and they realized they were naked; so they sewed fig leaves together and made coverings for themselves. (Genesis 3:6–7)

The result of eating this forbidden fruit was that "their eyes were opened," and they knew good and evil. The point is simply this: we can open people's eyes to good or evil depending on the *knowledge* we speak to them. This may seem elementary, but in times like these, when people question everything, we need to explain the basic fact that people must first hear the message of the gospel before they can possibly believe.

Words Are Necessary

One of the most oft-quoted statements when it comes to evangelism is "Preach the gospel, and, if necessary, use words." This quote is attributed to St. Francis of Assisi, a thirteenth-century monk. The quote suggests that we should let our lives represent the gospel while keeping our words at a minimum. This kind of thinking might be understandable for monks, who were likely to take vows of silence and live an ascetic lifestyle, detached from the world. But the fact is, Francis didn't say it. There is no record of it. No biographer records it, nor is anything like it found in the records of Francis's life and words. More important, he was an itinerant preacher who was very much engaged in taking the gospel to the crowds:

> He usually preached on Sundays, spending Saturday evenings devoted to prayer and meditation reflecting on what he would say to the people the next day.
>
> He soon took up itinerant ministry, sometimes preaching in up to five villages a day, often outdoors. In the country, Francis often spoke from a bale of straw or a granary doorway. In town, he would climb on a box or up steps in a public building. He preached to serfs and their families as well as to the landholders, to merchants, women, clerks, and priests—any who gathered to hear the strange but fiery little preacher from Assisi.[4]

His very actions demonstrated the importance of preaching the gospel—definitely using words. The notion that people should somehow stop speaking is deeply problematic in a variety of ways. To begin with, the gospel is good news. The very fact that it is called *news* indicates that it is a message that is announced. How absurd would it be to say, "Publish newspapers, and if necessary, print words"? The gospel is a message that must be shared with others, as missiologist Ed Stetzer affirmed:

> The gospel is the declaration of something that actually happened. And since the gospel is the saving work of Jesus, it isn't something we can do, but it is something we must announce. We do live out its implications, but if we are to make the gospel known, we will do so through words.[5]

It could be no less than a scheme from Satan himself to convince people that words were not at the heart of the communication. The apostle Paul told the believers in Thessalonica that the religious authorities that were opposing him were being motivated by the evil one.

> They displease God and are hostile to everyone in their effort to keep us from speaking to the Gentiles so that they may be saved. In this way they always heap up their sins to the limit. The wrath of God has come upon them at last.
>
> But, brothers and sisters, when we were orphaned by being separated from you for a short time (in person, not in thought), out of our intense longing we made every effort to see you. For we wanted to come to you—certainly I, Paul, did, again and again—but Satan blocked our way. (1 Thessalonians 2:15–18)[6]

The greatest level of what is called *spiritual warfare* takes place around the preaching of the Word of God. When the gospel is preached, people believe. If people never hear the gospel, they will never know the gift of eternal life that has been provided for them. It was because the early apostles and Christians preached the gospel openly that they were persecuted. If the apostles would have simply engaged in deeds of benevolence and not spoken the truth of the gospel, they would have undoubtedly lived longer lives. When they were threatened by the authorities to cease and desist all of their evangelistic activities, "Peter and John replied, 'Which is right in God's eyes: to listen to you, or to him? You be the judges! As for us, we cannot help speaking about what we have seen and heard'" (Acts 4:19–20).

God has chosen the message of salvation to be communicated with words. Jesus Himself was called the Word. Paul understood this from the very beginning, when he was dramatically called by God on the road to Damascus (Acts 9). Even though he saw a vision of the resurrected Christ, he needed to hear the gospel from someone. Ananias was sent to speak to him and baptize him.

Faith Comes by Hearing

The importance of using words to communicate the gospel was so urgent that Paul would write to the Romans:

> For there is no difference between Jew and Gentile—the same Lord is Lord of all and richly blesses all who call on him, for, "Everyone who calls on the name of the Lord will be saved."
>
> How, then, can they call on the one they have not believed in? And how can they believe in the one of whom they have not heard? And how can they hear without someone preaching to them? And how can anyone preach unless they are sent? As it is written: "How beautiful are the feet of those who bring good news!"
>
> But not all the Israelites accepted the good news. For Isaiah says, "Lord, who has believed our message?" Consequently, faith comes from hearing the message, and the message is heard through the word about Christ. (Romans 10:12–17)

Please go back and read this passage slowly. Paul asked a series of rhetorical questions. The key question is, *how can they believe in the one of whom they haven't heard?* Most people have made up their minds about the existence of God and the truth of the faith without all the facts. This is why we must stress that the gospel isn't only public truth, but hearing it should be viewed as a fundamental human right. Time and time again, I tell skeptics that they are free to believe or disbelieve the message, but they should at least hear it first before they decide. It's foolish to reject a caricature of the gospel instead of the real thing.

As we saw in chapter 2, the gospel is public, not private, truth. When we fail to speak clearly and boldly, we are in danger of denying the very thing Christ called us to do, as Stetzer pointed out:

> The apostle Paul summarized the gospel as the life, death, and resurrection of Jesus Christ, through whom sin is atoned for, sinners are reconciled to God, and the hope of the resurrection awaits all who believe.
>
> The gospel is not habit, but history. The gospel is the declaration of something that actually happened.[7]

This doesn't mean that our actions are unimportant. With this understanding of the necessity of words firmly grasped, we can now discuss the importance of our actions in terms of living the life of a true disciple of Christ and serving others as a demonstration of His love and mercy.

Our Actions Impact the Message

Of all the objections to Christianity, the two most common and evocative ones are the problem of suffering and the hypocrisy of self-described Christians.

The latter was certainly a stumbling block for me. Most of the people I knew who called themselves Christians had no visible difference in their lives compared to mine, or anyone else's, for that matter. The consequences of misdeeds committed by those who profess to be Christian but fail to behave accordingly live on for hundreds of years. For some, the eleventh-century Crusades are still valid reasons to reject the message of the gospel.

Yet, while there is no excuse for any violence committed in Christ's name, we must be consistent logically as well as historically fair. Jesus was the chief critic of religious hypocrisy and duplicity and gave the strongest warnings about the judgments awaiting such actions. One of the first passages I read in Scripture about this condemns those who do mighty works in the name of the Lord yet do not know Him:

> Not everyone who says to me, "Lord, Lord," will enter the kingdom of heaven, but only the one who does the will of my Father who is in heaven. Many will say to me on that day, "Lord, Lord, did we not prophesy in your name and in your name drive out demons and in your name perform many miracles?" Then I will tell them plainly, "I never knew you. Away from me, you evildoers!" (Matthew 7:21–23)

Paul strongly rebuked the outwardly religious but internally corrupt, indicting any witness of the gospel whose credibility is marginalized by un-Christian actions. His words should make anyone shudder at the thought of being the cause of someone's lack of faith:

> If you are convinced that you are a guide for the blind, a light for those who are in the dark, an instructor of the foolish, a teacher

of little children, because you have in the law the embodiment of knowledge and truth—you, then, who teach others, do you not teach yourself? You who preach against stealing, do you steal? You who say that people should not commit adultery, do you commit adultery? You who abhor idols, do you rob temples? You who boast in the law, do you dishonor God by breaking the law? As it is written: "God's name is blasphemed among the Gentiles because of you." (Romans 2:19–24)

This passage should leave no doubt that evil deeds can discredit the words you communicate to others. The encouraging thought in considering this grave reality of hypocrisy is the powerful effect just one genuine follower of Christ can have on others. For me, that one true believer was a college classmate whose godly lifestyle stood out as a light in the darkness and proved that it was still possible for a twentieth-century Christian to live the way Christians did in the first century. Because of his example, I determined I needed to give my life fully to Christ if I was going to be an encouragement to others instead of a stumbling block. It's no cliché to say that "by the grace of God" it's possible. In chapter 10 I discuss the mystery of godliness, looking more closely at how we can live in a way that is honorable in the midst of a "crooked and perverse generation" (Philippians 2:15 NKJV).

Signs and Wonders

The gospel was confirmed in the New Testament by signs and wonders. There were miraculous healings and answers to prayer. Because God exists, He can step into history and act on behalf of humanity in response to prayer. These types of confirming signs are happening all over the world. Whether it be near-death experiences (as we discussed in chapter 4) or visions of Jesus being seen across the Muslim world, there is overwhelming evidence that God is at work on the earth just as much if not more than He was during the times the Scriptures were written. In fact, the Bible confirms that the promises for healing are still valid today. Jesus is said to be "the same yesterday and today and forever" (Hebrews 13:8).

Over the years the stories of supernatural answers to prayer are too many to dismiss. In *Man, Myth, Messiah*, I devoted an entire chapter to miracles. I highlighted Dr. Craig Keener's work chronicling the evidence for miracles in modern times. Keener, a professor at Asbury Seminary, is considered one of the foremost New Testament scholars in the world and confirms that the scriptural promise for healing and supernatural answers to prayer are available for us today. Indeed, our trust is not in an answer to our prayers or whether someone is healed or not. Our confidence is in the death, burial, and resurrection of Christ. That event helped provide the greatest miracle a person can receive—the gift of eternal life.

Servant Evangelism

One of the most effective confirmations of the truth of the gospel is the service and love we show as believers to one another and to the world around us. As I mentioned in chapter 3, the church has been the source of so many good things that have blessed humanity—from hospitals, orphanages, universities, and education in general to relief efforts in crisis situations and so much more. On a very individual and practical level, everyone can make a huge difference by simply showing kindness and consideration through acts of kindness.

Sometimes the deeds that make an impact are so small and

seemingly insignificant that they can be dismissed in our minds as having a negligible impact on others. Nothing could be further from the truth. One of the men who has made a huge impact on the world by stressing this important truth is Steve Sjogren (pronounced "show grin"). His book *Conspiracy of Kindness* helped launch what came to be known as servant evangelism. Thousands of churches and millions of believers have helped demonstrate the love of God and the truth of the gospel by simply serving others in a multitude of helpful ways. I have been with Steve when he would go into bars and ask the manager if he, Steve, could clean the toilet. The look on the manager's face when Steve explained his intentions was priceless. He would say, "We just want to show you God's love in a practical way."

In other cases he would lead Christians into their communities to do a variety of community service projects. The number of hours given freely each year by Christians in community service to cities and neighborhoods around the world is conservatively estimated to be in the millions. The majority of them do this simply to follow the example of Christ in serving others. God uses the collective efforts of millions of believers to daily demonstrate the power and priority the gospel deserves. In view of that, it is shocking to see the resistance to such a message of hope and the accompanying benefits to humanity. It is due, however, to the spiritual conflict that centers on the advancement of the gospel.

The Very Real Spiritual Conflict

When it comes to opening people's eyes, there are many questions that unbelievers have about God and spiritual things, as well as many important truths that need to be explained. In virtually every conversation with an unbeliever, I spend time asking questions and intently listening to the person's answers in order to be able to grasp the areas where there is confusion, doubt, or simply a lack of knowledge.

After having these conversations for years, I've come to realize how common the intellectual objections are. With a little effort we can help unbelievers deal with the speculations and deceptions that are so prevalent in their arguments.

Beyond addressing unbelievers' intellectual and emotional arguments, there is another consideration to take seriously. Scripture explains the importance of dealing with the spiritual conflict evident in many arguments: "And even if our gospel is veiled, it is veiled to those who are perishing. The god of this age has blinded the minds of unbelievers, so that they cannot see the light of the gospel that displays the glory of Christ, who is the image of God" (2 Corinthians 4:3–4).

When someone has been blinded by spiritual deception, we need to pray for wisdom as well as for God to remove the obstructions from an unbeliever's mind. If we are willing, God will use us to help open the eyes of others to His existence and the credibility of the gospel. The truth of God is like a sharp scalpel that helps us help others. *We must always be aware that we are not in a war with people.* We are in a spiritual war against the gospel, on behalf of those who need to hear it. Having this mind-set keeps us from getting angry with those who do not believe or who are resistant or antagonistic of any evangelistic efforts. This should draw us ever closer to God in prayer as we embark on any endeavor to help others come to Christ.

For though we live in the world, we do not wage war as the world does. The weapons we fight with are not the weapons of the world. On the contrary, they have divine power to demolish strongholds. We demolish arguments and every pretension that sets itself up against the knowledge of God, and we take captive every thought to make it obedient to Christ. (2 Corinthians 10:3–5)

Speculations and doubts can enter our minds subtly and oftentimes undetected. In other instances there can be dramatic trauma or pain that can cause someone's spiritual eyesight to be lost or impaired. Regardless of how it happens, the end result is a blindness to the truth of the gospel.

As I discuss in more detail in the next chapter, a vital partnership exists between us and the Holy Spirit in communicating the truth to unbelievers. Ultimately God is the one who opens people's eyes. He could certainly do this without us but has chosen to involve us in this great mission. In a way, we need our eyes opened to the power of God and His Word so we can enter any situation with the confidence that truth is greater than any lie.

We Must Open Our Eyes

All the things included in this book are obviously important truths that people need to understand. I have tried to cover the key areas that most people have not considered when presenting the gospel. These are the truths I spend much time explaining in detail when sharing the message of Christ with others. While I am deeply concerned about engaging unbelievers, I've realized that many believers need their eyes opened as well. The spiritual warfare I mentioned is not just around skeptical unbelievers but also "unbelieving believers." This can be shocking and disheartening to anyone attempting to train and mobilize others to be involved in what has been called the Great Commission given by Jesus:

> Then the eleven disciples went to Galilee, to the mountain where Jesus had told them to go. When they saw him, they worshiped him; but some doubted. Then Jesus came to them and said, "All authority in heaven and on earth has been given to me. Therefore go and make disciples of all nations, baptizing them in the name of the Father and of the Son and of the Holy Spirit, and teaching them to obey everything I have commanded you. And surely I am with you always, to the very end of the age." (Matthew 28:16–20)

When you consider that the God who created the universe became a man in Jesus Christ and suffered and died for the sins of the world, there could be no greater mission or cause than telling others about these momentous events. If the gospel is true, then it should impel and captivate everyone in terms of finding ways to tell others. If it is not true, then it is a cruel distraction from the real needs and struggles of our lives or the rest of humanity's concern.

This is why I am speaking of the gospel as the ultimate human right. When I frame it in this language, I can almost see people's eyes being opened to the urgency and priority the message deserves. Then when they begin to learn about truth, the reality of the soul, the gospel as public truth, and the other vital topics, they realize that the claims of the gospel are true and defensible in the public arena. There is also the realization that they must get prepared.

Over the past few years a resurgence has taken place in what is called Christian apologetics. The term *apologetics* comes from the Greek word *apologia* and means "to give a defense." This charge is given to us by the apostle Peter, who has the dubious distinction of denying Christ three times on the night before His crucifixion. Peter recovered and became one of the great defenders of the faith, so much so that we look to his words today to guide us in this important matter of confidently sharing the gospel:

> Who is going to harm you if you are eager to do good? But even if you should suffer for what is right, you are blessed. "Do not fear their threats; do not be frightened." But in your hearts revere Christ as Lord. Always be prepared to give an answer to everyone who asks you to give the reason for the hope that you have. But do this with gentleness and respect, keeping a clear conscience, so that those who speak maliciously against your good behavior in Christ may be ashamed of their slander. (1 Peter 3:13–16)

There is so much in this passage we are to be aware of. First, we are not to be frightened by any external threats. As we saw in chapter 7, a real danger exists when sharing Christ, especially in certain parts of the world. Even in the West, where there may not be physical danger, we can lose our jobs or reputations whenever we dare to stand for truth. I was in a meeting with Christian educators when a leading professor in a mainline denomination told us he almost lost his job for explaining, in answer to a question, that marriage is between a man and a woman.

Truth has, indeed, stumbled in the streets. That's why the Bible tells us, second, to be prepared to give an answer (apologia) to everyone who wants to know the reasons for our hope. This underscores the fact that we are to have a faith that is backed by reason and evidence.

Third, Peter tells us that we are to speak truth with gentleness and respect. If you think about the metaphor of opening people's eyes, it is good to remember how gracious we must be in dealing with such sensitive areas. If you have ever been to an eye doctor for an exam, you know how slowly and cautiously he approaches your eyes. He avoids making any rash or careless motions in the vicinity of your eyes. I try to remember this when talking to others and attempting to open their eyes. There is no substitute for this kind of demeanor when dealing with others.

Finally, Peter links our behavior to the verbal defense of our faith. He tells us to keep a clear conscience and to model good behavior that will silence the accusations of those who oppose the message.

Closing Our Eyes Intentionally

One of the very first lessons I learned in the Gospels is the parable of the sower and the seed. It is referenced by three of the four gospel writers (Matthew, Mark, and Luke). In the parable, Jesus told how a farmer goes out to sow his seed and birds of the air come immediately to eat the seed. He later explained this as a picture of Satan coming to steal the Word of God sown in people's hearts. He also said some people were simply unwilling to open their eyes—regardless of the evidence:

> His disciples asked him what this parable meant. He said, "The knowledge of the secrets of the kingdom of God has been given to you, but to others I speak in parables, so that,
>
>> 'though seeing, they may not see;
>> though hearing, they may not understand.'
>
> "This is the meaning of the parable: The seed is the word of God. Those along the path are the ones who hear, and then the devil comes and takes away the word from their hearts, so that they may not believe and be saved." (Luke 8:9–12)

Jesus spoke of this spiritual battle and confirmed the focus of the Enemy's efforts. The very epicenter of the battle is the Word of God and a person's ability to understand and believe it. That is why I have labored to help you grasp why the Bible is true and trustworthy. If the Word is stolen from a person's heart and mind, then the basis for faith is lost.

Within this parable Jesus referenced the prophet Isaiah from more than six hundred years earlier. Isaiah was commissioned in a time of political and spiritual upheaval; then he was charged with the difficult task of speaking to people who did not have eyes to see or ears to hear his message:

> Then I heard the voice of the Lord saying, "Whom shall I send? And who will go for us?"
>
> And I said, "Here am I. Send me!"

He said, "Go and tell this people:

'Be ever hearing, but never understanding;
be ever seeing, but never perceiving.'
Make the heart of this people calloused;
make their ears dull
and close their eyes.
Otherwise they might see with their eyes,
hear with their ears,
understand with their hearts,
and turn and be healed." (Isaiah 6:8–10)

The warning given to Isaiah applies to us today. Many people simply don't want to see. Jesus made this very point in His explanation of the parable, as did the apostle Paul at the very end of the book of Acts:

They arranged to meet Paul on a certain day, and came in even larger numbers to the place where he was staying. He witnessed to them from morning till evening, explaining about the kingdom of God, and from the Law of Moses and from the Prophets he tried to persuade them about Jesus. Some were convinced by what he said, but others would not believe. They disagreed among themselves and began to leave after Paul had made this final statement: "The Holy Spirit spoke the truth to your ancestors when he said through Isaiah the prophet:

'Go to this people and say,
"You will be ever hearing but never understanding;
you will be ever seeing but never perceiving."'"
(28:23–26)

After speaking with these people all day, Paul realized that they simply refused to see anything that challenged their beliefs. He then quoted the very same words of Isaiah that Jesus referenced. Afterward Paul rented a house and began to minister to anyone who was willing to come and listen. To this day he models the fact that even if some are not willing to listen, plenty of others will. This is why we must be willing to persevere through all the complexities that can arise when trying to help others grasp the gospel and be transformed by its message.

We must even be willing to suffer rejection in our efforts to help others. Rejection is a horrible curse that makes us run away from the things we must do. For every encouraging story I could tell, there are two others that didn't turn out so well. What I have learned is to persevere. Each encounter with an individual is a chance to start fresh and to take what I've learned from past encounters and hopefully not make the same mistakes.

Don't Always Trust What You See

I'm not trying to speak as a mystic (like a Jedi knight in *Star Wars*), but our eyes can fool us by misjudging the impact of our words on others. I've spoken to people who seemed to be visibly moved by the gospel and found out that it really didn't last. All the signs pointed to their eyes being opened, but in the end it proved to be a temporary emotional response.

On the other hand, there are those who give no indication that what you are saying is affecting them, but the truth is actually sinking deeply into their hearts and minds. I truly couldn't count the number of people who've told me that what I said to them was forcing them to retreat and ponder the implications for their lives. Many times those are the types of decisions for Christ that are genuine and lasting. Again, the prophet Isaiah spoke of this:

> A shoot will come up from the stump of Jesse;
>> from his roots a Branch will bear fruit.
> The Spirit of the LORD will rest on him—
>> the Spirit of wisdom and of understanding,
>> the Spirit of counsel and of might,
>> the Spirit of the knowledge and fear of the LORD—
> and he will delight in the fear of the LORD.
> He will not judge by what he sees with his eyes,
>> or decide by what he hears with his ears. (Isaiah 11:1–3)

This means that we should simply focus on ministering the gospel and leave the ultimate results up to God. Our calling to tell others about the good news doesn't depend on whether they respond.

Bringing Joy and Evangelism Together

The charge to open people's eyes sounds daunting, but it can be quickly turned into the joy and delight of your life. There is more joy in heaven over one sinner who repents than over ninety-nine that need no repentance (Luke 15:7). When Jesus sent out the seventy-two disciples, they "returned with joy" at what had happened (Luke 10:17). When Jesus heard their stories, Scripture says He was filled with joy. His response is worth reading in full:

At that time Jesus, full of joy through the Holy Spirit, said, "I praise you, Father, Lord of heaven and earth, because you have hidden these things from the wise and learned, and revealed them to little children. Yes, Father, for this is what you were pleased to do.

"All things have been committed to me by my Father. No one knows who the Son is except the Father, and no one knows who the Father is except the Son and those to whom the Son chooses to reveal him."

Then he turned to his disciples and said privately, "Blessed are the eyes that see what you see. For I tell you that many prophets and kings wanted to see what you see but did not see it, and to hear what you hear but did not hear it." (Luke 10:21–24)

The call to tell others about the ultimate human right provided in the message of the death, burial, and resurrection of Jesus Christ along with all the incredible implications—such as receiving forgiveness of sins and eternal life—will be the source of inexhaustive joy to all involved. We are able to see things happen today that the prophets of old, such as Isaiah, longed to see. It is my job as an evangelist and apologist (along with any others with these gifts) to help equip believers in this awesome task.

Several tools have been developed that can significantly assist you in starting conversations with people and helping them to open their eyes to the glorious gospel of Christ. One of these tools is the God Test (for a free download, go to http://www.thegodtest .org/get-the-app/) The survey has been utilized in more than 170 countries, and people's answers are anonymously recorded and evaluated. The impact of this evangelism tool has been truly amazing. Thousands of Christians who have never shared their faith with others have used the God Test and experienced the joy of helping others with matters concerning faith, skepticism, and the meaning of life.

In keeping with the theme of this book, we also have developed the Human Right Survey. This tool is included in the God Test app, or you can order a hard copy from EngageResources.org. Both surveys comprise questions that facilitate a discussion. They both require some preparation to make certain you can respond credibly to any questions you might receive. One of the built-in aspects of both surveys is there is no obligation for you to respond with answers. If nothing else, just asking the questions and then listening can sow seeds in the hearts and minds of unbelievers.

By the way, one of my favorite endorsements of the God Test is from a campus pastor in Poland named Przmek Sielatycki (first name pronounced "shimek"). He said, "The God Test brought joy and evangelism back together."

Summary

We have been given the opportunity to help open people's eyes to the reality of the existence of God and the veracity of the gospel—and we dare not ignore it. Believing that knowing Jesus Christ is a fundamental human right motivates us to tell as many people about Him as we can.

It begins with our announcing and proclaiming the gospel message. Merely performing acts of kindness is not the same as sharing the gospel. We must confidently and respectfully engage others with truth. This seems so obvious, yet there has been a disturbing trend of distortion that suggests that communicating the message is not as important as serving others and living a life in front of them that models Christian character and values. Of course the latter must be done, but not to the exclusion of sharing the good news *as news*.

We believers also need to have our own eyes opened to the harvest fields of opportunity. Jesus said, "The harvest is plentiful but the workers are few" (Matthew 9:37). He then told His disciples to lift up their eyes and see that the fields were ripe for harvest (John 4:35). This metaphor doesn't mean much to those of us who do not live in an agrarian society. We wouldn't understand the opportunity or urgency of such a situation. When we realize what's at stake when we refuse to tell others, we are in a sense closing our eyes and ears intentionally to the calling of Christ. When the Human Right project was first launched in Cincinnati in front of fifteen thousand young people, Heath Adamson, who was the national youth leader for the Assemblies of God at the time, said, "Silence is the enemy of truth." This is simply because truth is a human right and contains the power to set humanity free.

CHAPTER 9

THE MINISTRY OF RECONCILIATION

Healing a Broken World

All this is from God, who reconciled us to himself through Christ and gave us the ministry of reconciliation.

—2 CORINTHIANS 5:18

In June 1967, Israel went to war against three neighboring countries—Egypt, Syria, and Jordan. Egypt's President Nassar had vowed to wipe Israel from the face of the earth and proceeded to set in motion a chain of events that would lead to war. Because the combined forces of these Arab nations overshadowed Israel's forces in number and strength, it seemed the Israelis had little chance to survive. Yet in one of the most remarkable battles in history, Israel prevailed in just six days. Israel was able to push the Syrians out of the Golan Heights in the north and the Jordanians out of the West Bank and the Old City of Jerusalem. For the first time since the time of Christ, Jerusalem—and, importantly, the Western Wall—was now back under the control of the nation of Israel. *New Yorker* magazine summed up the significance of this event:

> For the Israelis, the 1967 war was a triumph of such miraculous speed and fantastic territorial consequences that its leading military commander, Moshe Dayan, quickly helped brand it "the Six-Day War"—a deliberate echo of the six days of creation in Genesis. (In the Arab world, the defeat was such a humiliation that when it was spoken of at all it was commonly referred to as *an-naksah*, the "setback," an echo of *al-nakba*, the "catastrophe," of 1948.)[1]

Fifty years later the outcome of the war is still a focal point for Israel's enemies, who claim the territory lost in the war is actually occupied. Israel claims the land was secured not only as the result of winning a war, but by divine right. As Golda Meir, the first female prime minister of Israel, said, "This country exists as the fulfillment of a promise made by God Himself. It would be ridiculous to ask it to account for its legitimacy."[2] On and on the debate rages, decade after decade with no sign of resolution or hope for lasting peace.

On a personal note, I believe Israel has tried to honor the various peace treaties it has signed with its neighbors, but the long history of mistrust between them and the Arab states has swamped any hope for lasting reconciliation. On top of that is the unyielding refusal of the Palestinian leadership even to acknowledge

Israel's right to exist, as well as their expressed desire to destroy the Jewish state.

You could label this one of the most notable cases of irreconcilable differences that exists in our world. Scores of presidents, prime ministers, and other world leaders have tried to help solve this conflict but to no avail. The answer seems beyond our reach as humans. As a result, the possibility of world peace continues to evaporate like a mirage.

Who Can We Trust?

The question that seems to continually go unanswered is, *who can we trust to fix our problems?* To untie this Gordian knot, we would first need a mediator both sides could trust, someone each party believed had their best interests at heart, who understood their point of view. Beyond that, all parties would have to have a fundamental change of heart. Hate would have to be turned into love and trust. Forgiveness and grace would have to replace the endless cycle of attack and reprisal. In short, it would take a miracle. This is the kind of miraculous reconciliation and peace that Christ offers all who come to Him. He is *the* mediator that all nations and peoples should trust in light of His death on the cross for everyone:

> This is good, and pleases God our Savior, who wants all people to be saved and to come to a knowledge of the truth. For there is one God and one mediator between God and mankind, the man Christ Jesus, who gave himself as a ransom for all people. (1 Timothy 2:3–6)

Christ offers to be the mediator not only between God and man but also between nations and individuals. He is the one person who resolves and heals any irreconcilable differences when both parties submit fully to Him. He does this by offering everyone a new heart that results in a fundamental change in the way each side views the other. Those who were once enemies can now be friends. *The definition of reconciliation is to restore to a friendly relationship.* Ethnic groups with long histories of hate toward other ethnicities make peace and are able to sit down together at the table of brotherhood. The dream of Dr. Martin Luther King Jr. can actually become a reality because of the promise of Jesus Christ.

It was Jesus who gathered the most unlikely group of followers, many of whom would have been natural enemies— fishermen and tax collectors, Zealots and Roman sympathizers. His ministry brought them together, and His message of "love one another" was the cohesive force that bound them together and kept them from the destructive forces that rip most people apart.

After His death and resurrection, Jesus sent them out to tell the world He had risen and that He offered peace and reconciliation to everyone. The key would be for all to come to Him and surrender their unforgiveness in exchange for His forgiveness of their sins. He would teach us to pray, "Forgive us our sins, as we have forgiven those who sin against us" (Matthew 6:12 NLT).

This simple exchange could produce the miracle of reconciliation that still eludes the masses. Whether it be marriages or family conflicts, business disputes or international standoffs, such as the one in the Middle East, all things are possible with Christ in terms of unraveling the tangled knots of human conflict. In short, this is the wonderful hope the gospel offers. As we have seen the evidence of its truth, we can also experience its awesome power. Humankind can be brought into a restored relationship with God and one another. In short, the gospel could be summed up in one word: *reconciliation*.

The apostle Paul stated this truth directly in his second letter to the Corinthians:

> Therefore, if anyone is in Christ, the new creation has come: The old has gone, the new is here! All this is from God, who reconciled us to himself through Christ and gave us the ministry of reconciliation: that God was reconciling the world to himself in Christ, not counting people's sins against them. And he has committed to us the message of reconciliation. We are therefore Christ's ambassadors, as though God were making his appeal through us. We implore you on Christ's behalf: Be reconciled to God. God made him who had no sin to be sin for us, so that in him we might become the righteousness of God. (2 Corinthians 5:17–21)

Paul mentioned twice in these few verses that God has both entrusted as well as committed to us the ministry and message of reconciliation. Who are those who have this commission and stewardship? Those who have been reconciled themselves. In the same way that God did not count our sins against us in order to reconcile us, so we must be willing not to count others' sins against them.

It seems to be an impossible proposition. How can anyone do something so monumental? The answer is: become a new creation in Christ. God doesn't just offer us a new set of rules to live by; He offers us a new heart that will overrule the natural tendencies and proclivities of human nature. We could never hope to achieve such lofty ideals as loving our enemies or forgiving someone seven times seventy in a day when he or she sins against us. This requires that we receive a new nature inside our own souls.

In this miraculous transformation lies the answer to humanity's greatest needs. We have been reconciled to God so that we can help others reconcile with Him and then with still others. Walls and conflicts that stand between us and our enemies will be torn down.

As we take this message of reconciliation to a broken and divided world, it will take all of our heart, soul, and effort as we seek to open people's eyes to the promises of God. We will have to give ourselves fully to defending the truth of the faith and answering the objections the skeptics raise. We will have to lovingly challenge opposing belief systems and present the truth of the gospel against every other competing voice. But all of this must be done with one clear goal in mind: helping others to reconcile with God and one another.

Looking back over the last thirty-five years of my Christian ministry, I can see the glorious results of those who heeded this call and chose to forgive and follow the narrow road of reconciliation. I have also witnessed countless tragedies in which people rejected this path and chose to give in to hate and unforgiveness— too many sad endings even to mention. In each case the truth of the gospel was vindicated. When Christ's commands are obeyed, you see life and peace; when they are disobeyed, you see the death and chaos He warned us about. Because of this, we should resolve to be available at all times and to be peacemakers and healers instead of troublemakers and sources of division. There is a blessing for those who choose to embrace this high calling of the ministry of reconciliation.

Let's now look deeper into this awesome responsibility to be the voice of God to others in need of reconciliation. May we be able to help open their eyes to their needs and to the promise of forgiveness and the new heart Christ promises.

Why We Need Reconciliation

One of the first theological truths I learned was that humankind was separated from God because of sin. This was a little confusing to me because of the other truth I knew—that God loved us all. How could God love us and yet allow us to separate from Him? This apparent dilemma is actually the framework for understanding why we need a Savior and God's use of Christ to reach out to us who are alienated from Him. The prophet Isaiah spoke of this separation between God and man:

> Surely the arm of the Lord is not too short to save,
>   nor his ear too dull to hear.
> But your iniquities have separated
>   you from your God;
> your sins have hidden his face from you,
>   so that he will not hear. (Isaiah 59:1–2)

The estrangement began at a real place in time and history, as we saw in chapter 6. This gives us a key insight into the purpose of life, as well as the primary reason we need reconciliation—the breach in relationship with Him.

We were created for relationship with God and one another. That's what we are searching for, and that's what the gospel is really about—restoring relationships. The virus of evil has spread because we constantly imitate Adam and Eve's original sin, not because we inherited it. By our own choices we have turned away from the truth and sought to be our own gods:

> So I tell you this, and insist on it in the Lord, that you must no longer live as the Gentiles do, in the futility of their thinking. They are darkened in their understanding and separated from the life of God because of the ignorance that is in them due to the hardening of their hearts. (Ephesians 4:17–18)

As the passage points out, we are separated not just from the physical presence of God but from the incomparable life of God.

Why Can't God Just Forgive Us?

The question is continually raised: *Why can't God just forgive us?* If He is all-powerful, isn't He able to simply pardon us without having to go through this excruciating process of coming to Earth as a man and dying on a Roman cross?

We can see a glimpse of the reason for this in our own systems of justice. If there is no punishment for crimes committed but blanket forgiveness—or, even more problematic, selective forgiveness—the idea of justice is completely lost. The very nature of God revealed in Scripture is that He is *just* as well as loving. The fact that sin is costly was demonstrated in the Old Testament in the fracturing of relationship and loss of innocent life as God required the death of animals to atone for iniquity and sins.

On the day I wrote these words, a shooter opened fire in the Fort Lauderdale airport, killing five innocent people. The police were able to capture him and place him in custody to stand trial for this unthinkable crime. What would be the public's reaction if he were released from jail because he had confessed his crime and asked for forgiveness? It is not to say that such an act would not be a good thing—that is, to confess and admit one's guilt. In fact, another shooter who opened fire on a church in Charleston, South Carolina, in 2015 said he was not sorry and had no regret. Regardless of the contrition or lack thereof on the part of those committing the crimes, what is required in both cases is just punishment.

Why Did Christ Have to Die?

Christ's death is the centerpiece of God's plan to reconcile humankind to Himself and to one another. The depth of the spiritual and theological significance of this heroic act is so vast that attempting to explain it in a few pages of a book seems to trivialize it.

The requirement of satisfying the justice of God is that punishment should be required for the crimes or sins committed. God could not forgive sins without requiring punishment any more than an earthly judge could let off his own child if he had been the perpetrator of one of the atrocities just mentioned.

The gospel tells us that God became a man in Christ and lived the life humanity should have lived—completely just and moral. He then died the death we should have died . . . in our place. Please take the time to slowly read this important passage of Scripture that connects Christ's death to the gracious gift of reconciliation:

You see, at just the right time, when we were still powerless, Christ died for the ungodly. Very rarely will anyone die for a righteous person, though for a good person someone might possibly dare to die. But God demonstrates his own love for us in this: While we were still sinners, Christ died for us.

Since we have now been justified by his blood, how much more shall we be saved from God's wrath through him! For if, while we were God's enemies, we were reconciled to him through the death of his Son, how much more, having been reconciled, shall we be saved through his life! Not only is this so, but we also boast in God through our Lord Jesus Christ, through whom we have now received reconciliation. (Romans 5:6–11)

The shedding of the innocent blood of Christ was greater than any of the blood of the animal sacrifices required in the Old Testament. Christ's death paved the way to forgive our sins and restore us into genuine friendship with God.

How Could Someone Else Die for My Sins?

The objection is raised from skeptics as well as members of other religions, such as Islam, as to the ability of someone to die for the sins of another. Both groups seem adamant that every person should be accountable for his or her own actions and pay the penalty for his or her own crimes.

On a human level this is certainly true. If you steal something from someone, you should be punished and made to return the stolen property. If a murder is committed, the guilty should bear the punishment. But what about sins against God? Who can pay the penalty for the crimes against the Creator? We are so focused on the human side of things that we miss the fact that there is an eternal repercussion for our actions. Because God is infinitely just, the payment for the crimes against Him have an infinite consequence. Christ, being God in the flesh, represented an infinite sacrifice for the sins of humanity.

Some have seen this as a form of child abuse or human sacrifice when objecting to the necessity of God requiring such an act in order to forgive us. This would be true if Jesus Christ were just a human:

> There is no difference between Jew and Gentile, for all have sinned and fall short of the glory of God, and all are justified freely by his grace through the redemption that came by Christ Jesus. God presented Christ as a sacrifice of atonement, through the shedding of his blood—to be received by faith. He did this to demonstrate his righteousness, because in his forbearance he had left the sins committed beforehand unpunished—he did it to demonstrate his righteousness at the present time, so as to be just and the one who justifies those who have faith in Jesus. (Romans 3:22–26)

Far from some kind of primitive, cruel act required to assuage a bloodthirsty deity, God Himself became a man and took on our punishment. This was not an act of barbarous evil but a demonstration of the love of God and the justice of God. This being a monumental act of love and grace is even more evident when you understand what really happened at the cross in terms of the blessings that God has provided for humanity.

What Happened at the Cross

In *Man, Myth, Messiah* I wrote extensively about how the cross of Christ disarms principalities and powers (Colossians 2:15), delivering us from the fear of death (Hebrews 2:14) and tearing down a wall of division between Jews and Gentiles, the ultimate divide that separated people in Christ's day. Many other vital truths were mentioned as well. In the end, everything Christ did had an impact on reconciling us to God and one another.

The verses we are focusing on here, 2 Corinthians 5:17–20, say that *God was in Christ reconciling the world to Himself.* Looking at the entire life of Christ as well as His death, we can see He was focused on reconciliation. As you see Jesus through the eyes of the writers of the Gospels, they tell of Him reaching out to men and women from a variety of ethnicities, beliefs, and moral behavior. Regarding those who seemed unreachable or hopelessly wicked, Jesus went out of His way to engage and forgive.

We see God in Christ offering reconciliation to the Roman centurion, a devoted enemy of the Jewish state, asking Jesus to heal his servant; the Samaritan woman, with whom Jews wished to have no dealings, who had been married five times and was living out of wedlock with yet another man; and the demon-possessed man living naked among the tombs in an area called Gadara, which was off-limits to observant Jews—one of the most moving encounters in Scripture.

At the cross, too, God, in Christ, offered reconciliation, suffering beyond description to pay the price for the sins that separated a holy God from an unholy humanity. On the surface it looked as though the Romans were merely dealing out their brutal justice to yet another rebel. But in reality it was the execution not of a man but of a plan. The divine plan was to make a way for human-kind to return back to God.

Not Counting Our Sins Against Us

To grasp the promise of reconciliation, it is very important to understand this part of the text. To reconcile us to Himself, God did not count our sins against us. What else could He do to accomplish His purpose? Without exception, every irreconcilable situation comes down to a list of wrongdoings, slights, offenses, and crimes that have taken place between people (or peoples). For God to reconcile us to Himself, He willingly sent Christ to assume the entire everlasting burden of our sins against Him. This is a staggering act of love. Even as Jesus was going to the cross to die for the sins of the world, the very people He was going to help gave Him every reason to abandon the plan of redemption and forgiveness and unleash the deserved judgment and retribution against them. But, no, He refused to count our sins against us.

I can't help but think of Peter, who came to Jesus and asked, "Lord, how many times shall I forgive my brother or sister who sins against me? Up to seven times?" (Matthew 18:21). If you read between the lines, Peter was a "counter" and didn't want to allow someone to take advantage of him as a follower of this radical idea of love and forgiveness that Christ was command-ing. Jesus' reply let Peter know the futility of trying to keep score that way. Jesus answered, "I tell you, not seven times, but seventy-seven times" (v. 22).

As King David observed more than three thousand years ago, "If you, Lord, kept a record of sins, Lord, who could stand?" (Psalm 130:3). Peter would learn after his tragic denial of Christ that he, of all people, didn't need to keep a record of offenses against others. Peter became a reluctant leader in being a reconciler and would be the first of the apostles to reach out to the Gentiles and actually enter the forbidden zone of a Roman centurion's house to preach the gospel. It took Peter receiving great mercy to be able to be a vessel of great mercy to others.

The Great Exchange

On the cross Christ became sin for us that we might receive the gift of His righteousness. In the classic book *A Tale of Two Cities* by Dickens, Charles Darnay is condemned to die by guillotine during the time of the French Revolution. At the last minute, he unwittingly exchanges clothes with a look-alike named Sydney Carton, not realizing Carton wishes to save Darnay's life and Lucie's, the woman both men love. It is a gripping story that illustrates the nature of true love described by Jesus when He said, "My command is this: Love each other as I have loved you. Greater love has no one than this: to lay down one's life for one's friends" (John 15:12–13).

This is the great exchange that took place at the cross of Christ. We were those who were condemned to die for our crimes. But unexpectedly, Christ exchanged clothes with us. He took on the filthy rags of our moral failings and gave us His righteousness. We escape the deserved sentence of death because of this great exchange. Understanding this incredible sacrifice gives us an overwhelming sense of the love of God for us. It is this love that should motivate us to tell others of God's amazing offer of forgiveness and reconciliation.

As Sydney Carton approached his death, he reflected on his decision to die so that others could live. He said, "It is a far, far better thing that I do, than I have ever done." The sacrifice of Christ at the cross is by far the best gift ever given to the human race.

Accusations Against Us Silenced

The torment experienced when being accused of some wrong-doing is almost too much to bear. The guilt and accusation unleashed against us keeps us from the peace of mind and the sense of confidence God offers us, His children. In Scripture Satan is called "the Accuser" (Job 1:6 NLT; 2:1 NLT). He is like a prosecuting attorney who is determined to have us pay for our sins in full. Christ took away the basis for this accusation by His sacrifice on the cross.

> For God was pleased to have all his fullness dwell in him, and through him to reconcile to himself all things, whether things on earth or things in heaven, by making peace through his blood, shed on the cross.
>
> Once you were alienated from God and were enemies in your minds because of your evil behavior. But now he has reconciled you by Christ's physical body through death to present you holy in his sight, without blemish and free from accusation—if you continue in your faith, established and firm, and do not move from the hope held out in the gospel. (Colossians 1:19–23)

Because of the cross we are so reconciled to God that we can stand before Him without any fear or accusation of wrongdoing. This kind of boldness before God seems impossible to those who have not known the real power of the gospel. To be offered such an unbelievable pardon from the highest court in the universe should create an urgency in us to fully receive this gift ourselves and then dedicate ourselves to telling others. It is to fully grasping this task that we now turn.

We Are Christ's Ambassadors

The task of telling others about the reality of this opportunity to be fully pardoned and reconciled to God has been given to us—those who have been reconciled. "We are therefore Christ's ambassadors, as though God were making his appeal through us. We implore you on Christ's behalf: Be reconciled to God" (2 Corinthians 5:20).

The role of an ambassador paints such an important picture because it carries with it the image of a gracious and compassionate representative of a government, not a prophet of doom and condemnation. The ministry of reconciliation has been given to people who have received mercy themselves so that they can in turn speak the truth in love. But beware: the messenger can be as important as the message; he can be a facilitator or a stumbling block for people deciding whether to receive the heavenly offer that is being made. What an incredible honor and responsibility we have been given.

God Is Making His Appeal Through Us

Here is one of the most extraordinary aspects of the ministry of reconciliation—God uses us to speak to others. This fact brings a simultaneous joy and fear when I ponder the implications of such a responsibility. If we aren't willing to speak to others, they may never hear. I know that no one likes to be pressured into sharing the gospel with others, but it is important that someone speak up. This, of course, takes on an even greater weight when we realize the gospel is the ultimate human right. It's time to embrace this calling to this ministry of reconciliation instead of running from it or denying that it has anything to do with us.

We can be at peace as we live our lives and simply watch for open doors into conversations with others. Through us God makes an appeal to others about being reconciled to Him through Christ. It isn't just a dialogue of ideas about God, in which spiritual things are tossed around like political debate. Eventually the question must be raised about making a commitment to believe the gospel. Many times I have simply asked people if they would be willing to believe in the gospel, and, if so, I've had them pray on the spot. For many of them, they hadn't said yes to the claims of Christ because no one ever urged them to do so.

We Must First Be Reconciled

To be a reconciler, you must first be reconciled to Christ. It isn't enough simply to be a church attender or to believe in God. You must first be born again and then transformed yourself. "Therefore, if anyone is in Christ, the new creation has come: The old is gone, the new is here!" (2 Corinthians 5:17). This kind of transformation is not easily forgotten.

In my third year at Mississippi State University, I was born again, and I became passionate about telling others about the gospel. My older brother Ben, a hardened skeptic in his third year of law school, attempted to talk me out of my newfound faith, studying the Bible to find as many contradictions as possible. The weekend he came home to convince me to forget about Christianity, I urged him instead to consider the claims of

Christ and put his trust in Him. To my shock, he responded to my challenge and was baptized that very weekend!

May I urge you to pause now and receive this miraculous offer of being reconciled to God. You can pray a simple prayer and acknowledge your need for a Savior and confess that you believe the gospel is true. Christ died on your behalf and was raised from the dead to prove He is the Son of God. Commit yourself this very day to be an authentic follower of Christ. All that you have read up to this point should answer the key questions that point to the truth of the gospel. It is time for you to act!

Forgiven Much—Love Much

The lives of countless people who have been reconciled to God bear witness to an irrepressible gratitude for His gracious gift. The best example is when Christ entered the house of a religious leader for dinner and the party was crashed by an unnamed woman, whom Luke simply calls "a sinner" (7:39). She proceeded to pour expensive perfume on His feet, and she was weeping so profusely that her tears fell on His feet and she wiped them with her hair. Her shocking public display of emotion was unnerving to all in attendance. The religious leaders never spoke out verbally against this upsetting spectacle but were visibly perturbed by the indignity of it all. Jesus, knowing they were troubled by the woman's actions, explained to the man who had invited Him to dinner, "Her many sins have been forgiven—as her great love has shown. But whoever has been forgiven little loves little" (v. 47).

For those who have lived lives of complete disregard for God and His commandments or have simply mocked the notion of any need of restraint or forgiveness, the revelation of God's mercy can be overwhelming, as it was for this woman. I am still not over the fact that Christ forgave me for all my sins and foolishness. Remembering things from my past before I knew the Lord and was reconciled to Him is painful. Every time I share my story with others, I feel as if I am transported back to the days when I first made that commitment and was baptized by Walter Walker in Oktibbeha Lake near Mississippi State University. The energy and grace from that moment drives me to this day to tell others about this amazing offer of reconciliation with God.

Entrusted with the Message of Reconciliation

The apostle Paul said that God has entrusted to us this ministry and message of reconciliation. It is our sacred duty to be faithful with such a great task and calling: "But as we have been approved by God to be entrusted with the gospel, even so we speak, not as pleasing men, but God who tests our hearts" (1 Thessalonians 2:4 NKJV).

One of the great missionary evangelists of this generation is David Shibley. For more than forty years he has labored in more than fifty nations of the world to faithfully bring the gospel to those who have never heard it. His remarkable efforts should inspire us to "attempt great things for God" and to "expect great things from God."[3] In his book *Entrusted*, Shibley makes the case for the gospel being a basic human right that we have been entrusted to communicate with the entire world:

> In an age of virulent belligerence against it, we have been given custody of the best news the world will ever hear. Its message gushes with light, life, and hope. This is our time. This is our call. We're entrusted with the gospel. Let's make it the anchor of our lives.[4]

This is the one of the most important traits we can possess—a sense of stewardship for the gospel. It isn't an option that we can take or leave. If we have been reconciled with God, then we must carry the message forward. It is indeed the most important news in all of history. It also carries the power to heal the wounds of division and hate in any situation.

Healing Hands: A Case Study in Reconciliation

One of the great privileges I've had is to lead a multisite church in the greater Nashville area, called Bethel World Outreach Church. Situated in a predominantly white area, it stands today as a testimony of racial reconciliation. The land where the original church building is located at one time had restrictions on the deed preventing the sale of the land to a black person. A few miles from the church is a statue of Nathan Bedford Forrest, the founder of the most infamous hate group in US history. It was this shameful residue of racism that provoked us to take a bold stand when I became pastor of Bethel in the year 2000.

Dr. Martin Luther King Jr. once said that the most segregated hour in America was the eleven o'clock worship hour on Sunday morning.[5] We determined to change that narrative by taking intentional steps to reach out to the African-American community and the more than one hundred nationalities represented in the greater Nashville metropolitan area. One of the most effective strategies we utilized was to advertise our church using the image of a black hand and a white hand, palm to palm, in an attitude of prayer. This multicolored set of hands was accompanied by our mission statement: "Reaching a city to touch the world."

We reserved space on several billboards around the city and placed the picture of the interracial praying hands with our mission statement. The message was clear for all to see. We were intentionally letting people of all ethnicities know that we welcomed them and were actively recruiting their participation. The church grew from several hundred to several thousand in just a few years. The real miracle was the transformation from a more than 95 percent white church to one that within four years was almost even in terms of black and white and had more than fifty nationalities attending.

Today the diversity is still a marvel for most visitors who attend. The ministry of reconciliation provides the answers for the issues that seem to perplex and confound our society. The issue of racial reconciliation is inextricably bound to being first reconciled with God. When Christ fully comes to live in your heart, racism is evicted. Here are a few of the key factors that produced this multiethnic congregation I've described.

Conviction That the Gospel Is for Everyone

Perhaps the most quoted Bible verse is John 3:16: "For God so loved the world that he gave his one and only Son, that whoever believes in him shall not perish but have eternal life." I often ask people to tell me, *what is the world Jesus died for?*

If you reduced the world of seven billion people to just ten, there would be a variety of representative ethnicities from around the world. One of the ten would be white, and one in ten would be black. It's important for me to stress that the overwhelming majority of the world's population is nonwhite. This reality should be reflected in our churches. For some it means understanding the call that comes with the gospel to reach all nations. The good news is not just for us as individuals but for the whole world. This conviction about the audience who deserves to hear the gospel can keep us from thinking church is only for those who look like us. Of course this applies to people of any color if they are followers of Christ.

At Bethel it was necessary to address what I would call "the theology of racism." This is the erroneous teaching that every ethnic group somehow was commanded to stay away from other ethnicities in the name of following the command to Israel not to mix with other nations. This was a call to purity of faith, not ethnicity. As believers today, we are not to marry unbelievers, but there is no mention of anything about ethnic separation. In fact, the apostle Paul taught, "From one man he made all the nations, that they should inhabit the whole earth; and he marked out their appointed times in history and the boundaries of their lands" (Acts 17:26). God made the variety of nations from "one man" (or "one blood," as translated in many Bible versions). The Greek word for "nations" used in this scripture is *ethnos*, or ethnicity. Every ethnic group is part of humanity. Just taking a simple DNA test will show you the remarkable genetic diversity in your own ethnic makeup and ancestral history.

A House of Prayer for All Nations

On one occasion in Scripture Jesus seemed to step out of character and get genuinely angry. This was when He entered the temple and saw that the house of worship had departed from its true purpose to be a place where people of all nations could come and seek God. He took a whip and literally began to clean house.

On reaching Jerusalem, Jesus entered the temple courts and began driving out those who were buying and selling there. He overturned the tables of the money changers and the benches of those selling doves, and would not allow anyone to carry merchandise through the temple courts. And as he taught them, he said, "Is it not written: 'My house will be called a house of prayer for *all nations*'? But you have made it 'a den of robbers.'" (Mark 11:15–17)

As we began to pray for the nations at Bethel, the nations began to come to us. As a result, many leaders from other nations helped us organize church plants back in their home nations, which has become a cycle of blessing for us. The more we pray for the nations, the more we find ourselves connecting with people in our own city who are from a variety of nations. The more we focus on becoming a people with a heart for the nations, the more outreach becomes a natural outflow from us. Time and time again, people from other nations who attend our church and hear of the more than seventy-five nations where we are currently teaching through the ministry of Every Nation (to which Bethel belongs) are overjoyed to see our concern and love for them.

The World at Our Doorstep

This points to one of the most important facts that energizes our outreach and fuels our consistent prayer for the nations: the world has literally come to us in the United States. Not only has there been an influx of immigrants and refugees, but there are more than one million international students studying in America.[6] Regardless of where you live, you will be stunned at the number of international students who come and study in your country. These students want more than anything else (besides their degrees) a friend from their host country.

Here in America, it is heartbreaking to hear the stories of those who came to our country and were ignored, mocked, or even attacked—simply out of fear in some cases. The word *hospitality* means "friend of the foreigner." This is what we are to be to those who are strangers among us. In fact, love and kindness to these international visitors can have an incredible effect on the advancement of the kingdom of God. By intentionally reaching out to these students, we have seen them come to Christ and return to their native countries to launch a campus outreach or church. If they returned to work in business or to teach, they were able to open doors for ministry that would not have been opened to traditional missionaries. This outreach to internationals has fundamentally changed the way we do missions. If someone has a burden for a particular nation, he or she doesn't have to travel around the world to visit them but can simply drive across town.

Modeling Reconciled Relationships

Perhaps the most important factor in our ethnically diverse congregation is the way we relate to one another as leaders. The leadership team is not only diverse; we are also friends who genuinely like one another and live out that friendship and partnership in front of the people. As our church grew to several locations, it became apparent that each congregation needed a senior leader. Our original and largest congregation is now led by James Lowe, an African American. My role transitioned to overseer of the various locations. My relationship with Pastor James is a source of great joy and encouragement for me, and I think it is a blessing to the people who attend our church. Many times people tell us that it wasn't the *teaching* about diversity that changed their hearts and minds but the authentic *relationships* they witnessed from the leadership.

In maintaining these relationships we must continue to be transparent with one another and have very frank dialogues about the challenges of bringing together such a variety of people from a wide range of cultures and nations. When Christ is Lord of every heart, this task is in no way a burden but a joy. We spend more time laughing at our differences in clothing styles, food preferences, and song selections than arguing or debating about them. We also address serious issues, including shootings that involve African American youth and the police as well as concerns about terrorism and its effects on attitudes toward foreigners and immigrants. It is in those times that our love for Christ and one another gives us the grace to deal with any issue rationally and with an astounding sense of peace and hope that, in the end, all things will work together for good because we love God and are called according to His purpose (Romans 8:28).

Summary

The world is in desperate need of reconciliation at virtually every level of human interaction. The brokenness is seen and felt in individuals, families, and nations. Into this crisis God has sent us with the ministry of reconciliation. Because we have been reconciled to God through Christ, we can now be the agent and voice of reconciliation to others. This is an awesome calling and responsibility for a follower of Christ. We must be willing to embrace this stewardship and bring the message and the demonstration of the reality of reconciliation through our own relationships and lifestyles.

As we live out this calling to reconciliation, we will begin to intentionally reach out to people from different backgrounds and ethnicities. The church must become what it is intended to be, a house of prayer for all nations (Mark 11:17). As we pray for the nations, the reality of a beautiful picture of true diversity will emerge, not coerced or contrived, but an atmosphere that begins to look like what we will see one day in eternity.

CHAPTER 10

THE MYSTERY OF GODLINESS

Experiencing True Freedom

Great indeed, we confess, is the mystery
of godliness:
He was manifested in the flesh,
vindicated by the Spirit,
seen by angels,
proclaimed among the nations,
believed on in the world,
taken up in glory.

—1 TIMOTHY 3:16 ESV

What does God expect of us? Our answers to this question reveal what our perceptions are about godliness. This seems like such an elusive term to define. We have an easier time defining what ungodliness is rather than godliness. Yet godliness is the end product of our beliefs about God and the result of our allegiance and obedience to Him. We examined the major religions of the world in chapter 7 and compared them to Christianity. Each of them offers a vision of humanity that showcases what ideal behavior should look like. The truth of a belief system is more than just its creeds, historical claims, and internal consistency. It is the fruit of those beliefs and their impact on the world.

Without a doubt, it is difficult to talk to others about Jesus Christ without having to field questions about the behavior of those who claim to follow Him. Hypocrisy can blind others to the truth claims of our faith. Islam faces a massive backlash as global terrorism is increasingly linked back to the explicit teaching of the Quran and the example of the life and actions of Muhammad.

The life of Christ, however, is unparalleled in history. There is no one who did the things He did or said the things He said. This is obvious to anyone who has taken the time to read the Gospels written about his life. Beyond His personal claims of being the divine Son of God is the call that He made to us to "be perfect, therefore, as your heavenly Father is perfect" (Matthew 5:48). He told the sanctimonious religious leaders of His day, "You belong to your father, the devil, and you want to carry out your father's desires" (John 8:44). He then proclaimed that those who followed Him would know the truth and the truth would set them free (John 8:32). He was speaking of the freedom that is the fruit of true godliness.

I remember as a teenager thinking that being a Christian meant giving up all the pleasures in this life and resigning myself to a life of misery and deprivation. For some reason, I bought into the false idea that godliness was the goal of only a few saints, martyrs, or missionaries. Little did I realize how wrong this picture is. To be holy is to be set apart for God. How could the Creator of our existence not be trusted to guide us into true joy and fulfill-ment? As King David extolled, "In Your presence is fullness of joy" (Psalm 16:11 NKJV). God's desire for our well-being is the ultimate motivation to warn us about sin and ungodliness, which is the chief enemy of our joy and happiness.

The Mystery of Godliness

Think of God's commandments as a sign in the road warning us of an impending hazard. Far from a capricious set of arbitrary restrictions, the Scripture is trying to guide us into the path of life, not death. However, being godly is not just following a set of rules. Every religion has plenty of rules and expectations of its adherents. The real issue is how we can be the kind of people who are "like God"—which is the simplest way to understand what godliness means. Unlocking this secret is why it is referred to as "the mystery of godliness." This means the answer isn't obvious. It requires us to look deeper and to seek to understand not just what God expects of us but how we can be like Him.

The good news is that the Scripture not only tells us it is a mystery, but 1 Timothy 3:16 (cited at the beginning of this chap-ter) also gives us six clues that unlock how we can become these kinds of people. This forms what scholars believe to be an *ancient creed*. In a world that is becoming increasingly perverse and spiri-tually dark, the essence of this creed may provide an antidote for this insidious and pervasive plague.

These are the clues that will help us unlock the age-old mys-tery of living the kind of life that is pleasing to the Lord, regardless of the challenges we face in our generation.

1. "Manifested in the flesh"

The first clue to this mystery is that God became man in Christ. He didn't just *appear to be* human; He became one of us. This would have been an unthinkable proposition to the Jewish people because God was the invisible Creator, and to become human would have meant lowering Himself or elevating the man Christ Jesus to the place of God. To the Greeks, it was scandalous to think that God, being conceived as pure spirit, could have comingled with flesh. The philosophy of Plato would have given them the perception that the flesh was something to transcend. Flesh was inherently and irreparably evil.

The fact remains: Jesus was God in human form. This means that God so desired humanity to be free from the power of sin and death that He not only died on a cross to pay the penalty for our sins, but He first lived a perfect life in the flesh, showing that it is possible. This is such a vital truth that the apostle John would warn that anyone denying that Jesus Christ had appeared in the flesh was the antichrist:

> This is how you can recognize the Spirit of God: Every spirit that acknowledges that Jesus Christ has come in the flesh is from God, but every spirit that does not acknowledge Jesus is not from God. This is the spirit of the antichrist, which you have heard is coming and even now is already in the world. (1 John 4:2–3)

Godliness Is Possible

Christ's deity is the center of the Christian faith. It is the essence of the central profession that makes us His followers: Jesus Christ is Lord. His deity means His words are true and His authority is ultimate. He is indeed King of kings and Lord of lords. It also means something very practical for us when it comes to grasping and unlocking the mystery of godliness. That truth is that *godliness is possible*. Christ overcame sin and the Devil as a human. If He never really became one of us, then all the trials and temptations were illusions or merely lessons to inspire us.

Scripture says He was "tempted in every way, just as we are—yet he did not sin" (Hebrews 4:15). The spirit of the antichrist is determined to keep us in bondage by deceiving us into thinking that we should be resigned to the fate of being permanent prisoners—captive to the lusts of the flesh. If Christ was never human, then the story of the human race is indeed one of utter failure to ever walk upright and holy before God. However, Christ modeled that this was possible and demonstrated how to do it.

In my mind this was a massive mountain to overcome. As a young person, I knew that the people who called themselves Christians were pretty much living as everyone else. There was little or no difference in their lives because they were Christian. This produced in me a mentality of defeat. Why would the commands of Jesus be so unreachable? Why would He ask us to do things that He knew we couldn't do?

This is one of the most insidious schemes the Enemy has ever foisted upon the human race.

Christ: Our Example

The artists in the Middle Ages painted pictures of Jesus with a halo of light around His head and gave the sense that He was otherworldly. This portrayal can lead us into dismissing Him as someone who could not possibly relate to our struggles, sufferings, and temptations. But nothing can be further from the truth.

We are called to imitate Christ. He walked in submission to the Father, was constantly in prayer, and used Scripture to battle the Enemy. These are the things we are called to do as well. In fact, we find out that Jesus humbled Himself, took the form of a servant, and did not use His divine nature to overcome but used only the spiritual weapons that are available to us. He demonstrated how to win over sin.

If you study how Jesus engaged in spiritual warfare, He used the power of the Word of God and answered every temptation with the phrase "It is written." We are called to put on the full armor of God (Ephesians 6:13). This means that this is the very armor Christ used in His earthly life. The only weapon He brandished is the same one we can use: "the sword of the Spirit" (v. 17).

As we fix our eyes on Christ, we find not only a compassionate and forgiving Savior but also a champion who will teach us to walk as He walked. If we say we are followers of Christ, this is exactly what we are called to do (1 John 2:5).

2. "Vindicated by the Spirit"

Just as the foundation of godliness starts with God reaching us through Christ, we must continually look for God's help through His Holy Spirit to access this power over "the sin that so easily entangles" (Hebrews 12:1). The Scriptures say that Jesus was declared to be the Son of God by the resurrection from the dead by the Spirit of holiness (Romans 1:4). Since Christ was without sin, "it was impossible for death to keep its hold on him," as Peter preached on the day of Pentecost (Acts 2:24).

Christ was crucified as a criminal in the eyes of man. He was put to death between two thieves as evidence of this public perception. Something greater was actually taking place. He was bearing the weight of the sins of the world. As the prophet Isaiah foretold hundreds of years before this event, "We all, like sheep, have gone astray, each of us has turned to our own way; and the LORD has laid on him the iniquity of us all" (Isaiah 53:6).

When He was raised from the dead, God vindicated Him and demonstrated His innocence. As the psalmist promised, "righteousness delivers from death" (Proverbs 11:4). The apostle Paul wrote that we receive the gift of righteousness through faith in Christ. We don't stand before God in our own righteousness but in the righteousness of Christ. He also wrote that "if the Spirit of him who raised Jesus from the dead is living in you, he who raised Christ from the dead will also give life to your mortal bodies" (Romans 8:11).

Christ's Spirit not only raises us up from death to life, but He can keep us from stumbling. Far greater than mere willpower is the power of the Spirit living within us that will help us escape from the gravitational orbit of the cycle of repeating the same sinful patterns again and again. This is the futility that is described in Romans when Paul cries out, "What a wretched man I am! Who will rescue me from this body that is subject to death?" (7:24).

In the fourth century, Augustine arrived in Carthage to devote himself to study and divulged the inward depravity he was dealing with in spite of being raised by a godly mother and having a knowledge of God and Christianity. His story is being repeated by thousands of young people who leave the homes of their youth for university and are ill-prepared for the intellectual challenges they will face as well as the moral assaults that await them: "Your mercy faithfully hovered over me from afar. In what iniquities was I wasting myself! I pursued a sacrilegious quest for knowledge, which led me, a deserter from you, down to faithless depths and the fraudulent service of devils."[1] We all experience this desperate condition apart from the Spirit's help.

The eighth chapter of Romans gives the details of this news that is too good to be true. We not only are set free from the law of sin and death but also are to be led by the Spirit to "put to death the misdeeds of the body" (v. 13).

Set Your Minds

Practically, we are told to set our minds on the things of the Spirit (Romans 8:5). The more we meditate on God's truth instead of on the failings of our past or the passing desires of temptations, the more we will see new habits of victory over sinful patterns. The Spirit will lead us into the truth of God's Word that promises victory. We are not under obligation to the flesh anymore to obey its desires (v. 12).

Grace Has Set Us Free

William Wilberforce, the English abolitionist, wrote about how our behavior is not excused by the grace of God, but altered: "Our natural condition is weak and fallen and our temptations are numerous; God is infinitely holy, yet He offers forgiveness, grace and enabling power to those who get honest with Him and are willing to repent."[2]

The grace of God is the reason we are saved and brought into the family of God. We must grasp the power of grace daily, even after yielding to Him. If we do, then we experience true freedom: "For sin shall no longer be your master, because you are not under the law, but under grace" (Romans 6:14).

It was this power that transformed Wilberforce's friend and mentor, John Newton, from a wicked, unjust slave trader to a champion of freedom. After his conversion, Newton would write the immortal words to a song known the world over: "Amazing Grace."

The Spirit Helps Our Weaknesses

The fact that we all struggle with temptation and a host of desires that are at odds with God's truth points to a remedy that must lie beyond ourselves. As we turn to God in prayer, the Holy Spirit strengthens us, fills us, to become "more than conquerors" (Romans 8:37 KJV). When we are filled with the Spirit, there is little room for other, competing desires (Galatians 5:16).

Think about how you feel after you have eaten a big meal. The offer of more food is rarely tempting. This is why the apostle Paul wrote, "I pray that out of his glorious riches he may strengthen you with power through his Spirit in your inner being, so that Christ may dwell in your hearts through faith" (Ephesians 3:16–17).

3. "Seen by angels"

This creed states that the God who became man in Christ was also seen by the angels. It was the angels who broke the news to Zechariah, Elizabeth, and Mary that a Savior would soon appear. They are the ones who heralded His birth to the shepherds and then lit up the night sky with a heavenly concert that defied imagination. Angels are heavenly beings that have appeared at critical moments and junctures in history. To see an angel is usually a sign of the Lord's nearness to us or to a situation of grave concern. The book of Hebrews states that they are ministering spirits sent to aid those who will inherit salvation (1:14).

Though these statements are true, they don't represent what

this passage is referring to. This isn't about people seeing angels but about what the angels saw. And then there is the question regarding what this has to do with us and our ability to live godly lives. I present my explanation of it with much humility and the recognition that my thoughts on this could be mere speculation. I will admit up front that there are possibly more credible interpretations of what this passage is speaking about.

To start with, we must go back to when angels rebelled against God, with more than one-third of them falling from heaven. It's mind-bending to consider a being who has lived in the presence of God and experienced the glory of God who then turns away and turns against the purposes of God on earth. What could have caused such a falling away?

A Closer Look at Angels

The book of Isaiah gives us important details about what angels look like:

> In the year that King Uzziah died I saw the Lord sitting upon a throne, high and lifted up; and the train of his robe filled the temple. Above him stood the seraphim. Each had six wings: with two he covered his face, and with two he covered his feet, and with two he flew. And one called to another and said:
>
> > "Holy, holy, holy is the LORD of hosts;
> > the whole earth is full of his glory!" (Isaiah 6:1–3 ESV)

The usual image of an angel shows only one pair of wings. In this passage they have *six* wings. One set was for covering their faces in the presence of God. Apparently the intensity of the brightness of the presence of God is too great for them. Because they are unable to look fully and completely at God, they must trust that God is good and His character is trustworthy. It is possible the angelic rebellion was instigated by someone making an accusation that was made in the garden of Eden: God cannot be trusted.

The angels who remained, therefore, would have rejected the accusation and stood firm in their trust of God. We know that when God became man in Jesus Christ, the angels saw that God was good. As Jesus said, "Anyone who has seen me has seen the Father" (John 14:9).

This devotion to God's truthfulness undoubtedly has something to do with great joy in heaven when a sinner repents. Repentance—turning away from sin and turning back to God—is the result of a deep conviction of wrongful behavior as well as a revelation of the kindness and goodness of God (Romans 2:4).

God Is Good

To live godly lives, we, too, must trust that God is good and has our best interest in all that He commands us. Time and time again I have watched people turn away from walking with God because of bitterness and disillusionment. They blame God (and those around them) for the failures and tragedies in their lives. In my countless interviews with skeptics, they have cited the existence of evil in the world as the chief reason they refuse to believe in God.

Just as the angels saw the goodness of God in the incarnation—God becoming man—it, too, is a reason for us to trust God's incomparable love. We must also trust Him by listening to His instructions about how to win over sin and evil. So many times

I hear people saying things like "All you need is the presence of God." That sounds very spiritual, but it is not the whole truth. Yes, it is encouraging and life-changing to worship God and sense His presence, but we must also have His Word in our hearts and in our mouths. We must put on the full armor of God so that we can stand strong against the schemes of the Devil (Ephesians 6:10–18). We are promised that, as a result, God is able to keep us from stumbling. The angels are standing by to aid us in this battle as well (Hebrews 1:14).

4. "Proclaimed among the nations"

The preaching of the gospel is the primary way that godliness spreads. As we preach Christ, lives are transformed, hearts are changed, and injustice is made right. The Bible describes this phenomenon again and again.

There is great debate in psychological circles as to whether people's nature and character can really change. This kind of change is the most common miracle of all. With humanity this is impossible, but with God all things are possible. This part of the creed spotlights how the mission of Christ affects us and our lives. I have found that within every command of Scripture is a blessing for us as we obey and fulfill it. Many times this takes place as we are warned to keep away from things that will hurt or destroy us and those we love. Like a road sign that alerts us of danger ahead or a label on a bottle of poison, God demonstrates His goodness and love for us in what He prohibits.

Then there is the blessing that comes from obeying the commands that call us to do something. One of the most challenging commands is to forgive others when they have wronged us. Though it feels so difficult, it is actually to our benefit to release others from their sins against us even as God has released us from our sins against Him. The reward for us is to be free from the cancer of bitterness and resentment. Over the years I have watched people become chained to the negative events of their past because of their failure to follow these instructions from the Lord.

When we proclaim the gospel to the nations, something happens to us as much as to those we speak to. Again, God's desire is to bless us as much as those who are unreached. First of all, racism is eradicated from our hearts as we demonstrate care and concern for other ethnicities different from our own. As we pray for the nations and then give them the gospel, we break down division and hate and show the world the power of Christ's love for all people. No one ethnicity can claim exclusive right to the love of God.

One of the most controversial moments in Jesus' ministry was when he spoke to a Samarian woman—whose ethnicity was looked down upon by Jews. Christ not only ministered to her, but she returned to her town with the message that He was the Messiah. The impact was stunning. When the twelve disciples brought food to Him, He refused and said, "I have food to eat that you do not know about" (John 4:32 ESV). He was giving them insight into something that I believe relates to the mystery of godliness. When we participate in God's mission to humanity, we are given strength from heaven. I have experienced this strength again and again over the years. Even though there is a sense of hearing, God's Word feeds my spirit in the way that physical food strengthens my body. Yet there is "food" that comes from obeying God's Word (not just hearing). This is what Jesus is explaining to His disciples in this encounter recorded in the gospel of John. He then says, "My food is to do the will of him who sent me and to accomplish his work" (v. 34 ESV).

We must grasp that God has an overall purpose for this planet. His mission is the most important cause that we could be involved in. Regardless of our vocation or sense of calling, we all can participate and make a difference. Another great promise from God that should be mentioned here is Romans 8:28: "And we know that for those who love God all things work together for good, for those who are called according to his purpose" (ESV).

As we dedicate ourselves to the purposes of God in our generation, we can have real hope that our steps will be ordered by the Lord. Good things will come to us. Certainly there are deep challenges as well, as we advance the cause of Christ into the nations of the world where it has historically been unwelcome or where it is currently illegal. We will need wisdom from heaven to know the best timing and strategy for our efforts. Even the apostle Paul was forbidden to go to various places by the Holy Spirit and later was able to have effective ministry in those very regions. May we not shrink back at this great opportunity to be poured out for God's kingdom in this critical hour.

5. "Believed on in the world"

One of the most fundamental principles of living the Christian life from start to finish involves our need to hear God's Word: "So faith comes from hearing, and hearing through the word of Christ" (Romans 10:17 ESV). This is an indispensable part of developing a deep trust in God's Word in the specific things He promises, not just in the general truthfulness and reliability of Scripture. This kind of faith, in the specific promises of God, is key if we are to unlock and experience the mystery of godliness. Having faith in God's promises results in us becoming children of God. It is that same faith we are to live by. This truth is very important to me because of how it radically changed my life in my junior year in college.

When I attended church services in my youth, I had a clear understanding that life on earth had a greater cause than itself. The existence of God was never in doubt in my mind. The challenge for me was the way I should live my life. From what I could tell, my life was no different than anyone else's who attended church.

My conclusion was that it didn't really matter how you lived as long as you broke no major laws. This mind-set gave me no power to withstand the growing sense of sickness in my own soul that something was wrong with the way I was living, in spite of feeling pretty normal compared to my peers. This is not the place for a confessional about my practices, but looking back, I was not a good person. I think this is why I was so fascinated with Augustine's *Confessions*. Written in the fourth century, it is the first real autobiographical work of its kind in history. Augustine bore his soul about the evil inside of him:

> The single desire that dominated my search for delight was simply to love and to be loved. But no restraint was imposed by the exchange of mind with mind, which marks the brightly lit pathway of friendship. Clouds of muddy carnal concupiscence filled the air. The bubbling impulses of puberty befogged and obscured my heart so that it could not see the difference between love's serenity and lust's darkness.[3]

Augustine justified his immoral actions as being normal behavior and gravitated toward philosophies and belief systems that supported his carnal desires. Hundreds of years later, this

deception is still rampant. It's usually not the truth that determines someone's moral code but his moral code that determines
his religious beliefs.

Augustine's mother, Monica, continued to pray for him. And
the faithful preaching of Ambrose, the bishop of Milan, continued to convict him that his behavior was wrong, in spite of the
culture's acceptance of his lifestyle. In the midst of his confusion
and depression, he related an unusual moment that turned his life
around. He heard the sound of a child reciting the lines of a song.
He interpreted the simple lyrics as God's instruction for him to
follow:

> For I felt my past to have a grip on me. It uttered wretched
> cries: "How long, how long is it to be?" "Tomorrow, tomor-
> row." "Why not now? Why not an end to my impure life in this
> very hour?"
>
> As I was saying this and weeping in the bitter agony of my
> heart, suddenly I heard a voice from the nearby house chanting
> as if it might be a boy or a girl (I do not know which), saying
> and repeating over and over again "Pick up and read, pick up
> and read."[4]

He went on to describe how one simple verse from the Bible
broke the chain that held him to his immoral practices. It is this
kind of faith in God's power that is critical for us to live the godly
lives we are called to live:

> So I hurried back to the place where Alypius was sitting. There
> I had put down the book of the apostle when I got up. I seized
> it, opened it and in silence read the first passage on which my

eyes lit: "Not in riots and drunken parties, not in eroticism and indecencies, not in strife and rivalry, but put on the Lord Jesus Christ and make no provision for the flesh in its lusts" (Rom. 13:13–14).

I neither wished nor needed to read further. At once, with the last words of this sentence, it was as if a light of relief from all anxiety flooded into my heart. All the shadows of doubt were dispelled.[5]

In the same way we can overcome the lusts of the flesh by hearing God's promise of victory and learning to fight the fight of faith. I have greatly benefited from the book of 1 John and its call for us as believers to walk as Christ walked. The secret to this life is to believe that we can overcome: "And this is the victory that has overcome the world—our faith" (5:4 ESV).

6. "Taken up in glory"

The final stage in the *mystery of godliness* is, following His resurrection, Christ ascended to the Father. The disciples witnessed this miraculous supernatural event and stood staring into the sky, dumbfounded. It was such a captivating scene that an angel had to speak to the astonished group of Christ's followers and admonish and remind them that there was work to be done:

"But you will receive power when the Holy Spirit has come upon you, and you will be my witnesses in Jerusalem and in all Judea and Samaria, and to the end of the earth." And when he had said these things, as they were looking on, he was lifted up, and a cloud took him out of their sight. And while they were gazing into heaven as he went, behold, two men stood by them in white robes, and said, "Men of Galilee, why do you stand looking into heaven? This Jesus, who was taken up from you into heaven, will come in the same way as you saw him go into heaven." (Acts 1:8–11 ESV)

Christ's ascension has many implications. All these things have a direct impact on our ability to live holy lives and to escape the corruption that is in the world (2 Peter 1:5). Here are a few of the most notable repercussions on our lives.

All authority is in His name. After His ascension, Jesus' place is now at the right hand of the Father. His name carries all authority in heaven and earth. As Christ's followers, we have been given the authorization to carry His message to the ends of the earth. We don't need anyone else's permission. In light of this we can be confident wherever we go. We have been given all we need to accomplish the task He has called us to.

He is alive. Christ's exit from this planet via His ascension makes it clear that He is alive. This means that He is still involved in the affairs of earth. As He promised, "Because I live, you will live also" (John 14:19 AMP). As we go, we do not go alone. This is why He told us, "For where two or three are gathered in my name, there am I among them" (Matthew 18:20 ESV).

Christ's personal involvement with us is real, not metaphorical. We must recognize that He is truly with us as well as inside of us through His Spirit. This changes our perspective on what we say and how we act. We can live godly lives because He is with us to help and encourage us.

The fear of the Lord. Because He is with us, He *is* aware of our deeds, both good and bad. We are told that we will stand before the judgment seat of Christ in the end. Being made aware of that, we should have one of the most important traits that produces godly lives: "For we must all appear before the judgment seat of Christ, so that each one may receive what is due for what he has done in the body, whether good or evil. Therefore, knowing the fear of the Lord, we persuade others" (2 Corinthians 5:10–11 ESV).

Like cholesterol, there are two kinds of fear: the good kind and the bad kind. We are told that "the Spirit God gave us does not make us timid, but gives us power, love and self-discipline" (2 Timothy 1:7). Being timid is the bad kind of fear. But the fear of the Lord is indeed good. It causes us to run from evil. When we realize that we will give an account for the things we do in our lives, it produces a restraint against evil. As the threat of a financial audit from the government helps restrain any potential misdeeds, facing accountability will bolster us against temptation and compromise.

The fear of the Lord helps strengthen our spiritual immune system. We are living in a culture of increasing darkness and impurity. No matter how hard we try to insulate ourselves from being exposed to sinful images and evil influences, we all face these indignities daily. Like righteous Lot, our souls are tormented by having to face depravity everywhere we turn. The fear of the Lord provides resolve to run from evil and to continue to seek the grace of God and the way of escape from every difficult challenge.

Summary

We are living in challenging times. When I think back on what I faced as a teenager, I realize how much more insidious and blatant temptation is today. Living godly has never been more difficult. I am so thankful that the work of Christ is greater than anything we can face. The mystery of godliness doesn't have to remain a mystery to us as Christ's followers. Paul gives Timothy the keys to unlocking the deliverance we need from the power of sin and death. The six statements in 1 Timothy 3:16 form a creed that we can memorize and utilize as a guide to remind us that victory is possible.

Godliness is possible because God became man in Christ. Religion tells us what we need to do to be accepted by God. Christianity begins with God reaching us, not us reaching Him through our efforts. Through the Spirit's help, we can be filled and empowered to live the way we are called to live. Like the angels who beheld the goodness of the incarnate Christ, we can be confident in God's love and care for us—regardless of the challenges before us. As we take the gospel to the nations, we partake of the strength that comes to us for working with Him in His purposes in the earth. Through faith in His promises, we can walk in the victory that He died and rose again to give us. And finally, because He is still alive, we can know that He is with us wherever we go.

"The fear of the LORD," we are told, "is the beginning of wisdom" (Psalm 111:10). Armed with the knowledge that we will stand before the judgment seat of Christ, we are motivated to shake off and steer clear of anything that might be displeasing to Him. Far from an oppressive kind of fear, which is destructive, in Psalm 19:9 this kind of fear is called "pure" and also "clean" (ESV). It will produce a purity and cleansing that will cause us to be filled with the joy of knowing that we are children of God.

CONCLUSION

The Fierce Urgency of Now

The *Washington Post* ran a story in 2016 in reference to a poll taken among young people in Iceland about their religious beliefs. The results of the poll were stunning: zero percent of the young people under twenty-five who were surveyed believed God created the world.[1]

When I read this, I immediately picked up the phone and called my publisher, Thomas Nelson, and asked about the possibility of releasing my book *God's Not Dead* in Icelandic. Thomas Nelson had published only one book in that language but said my enquiry would be forwarded to the man who had translated the book. He e-mailed me the next day. He and his wife happened to be in America on vacation, and within one week they were in my home in Nashville. Ágúst Ólafsson and his wife, Kolbrún, were deeply concerned about the lack of faith in their country as revealed in the poll.

God's Not Dead was translated into Icelandic and published, and at our first event—held in a movie theater next to the university campus in Reykjavík—more than three hundred people attended our two nights of teaching the truths of the gospel. Identifying himself as an "atheist," someone noted on his comment card, "I think the kindest thing a believer could do for an unbeliever is try to save their soul." This was a far cry from the belligerence and hostility usually associated with the clash between atheism and the Christian faith.

We are now embarking on a series of similar events in the coming months to continue to reach out to this nation. It is noteworthy, as a result of our initial event, that the news headline is now no longer true. Several Icelanders under twenty-five not only believe in the Creator but also believe in Jesus Christ, who died and rose again on their behalf. Believing that the young people of Iceland had a fundamental right to know the truth behind the Christian faith compelled us to action.

I started this book with the story of being in the midst of a revolution in the Philippines more than thirty years ago. By the start of the 1990s, the movement for freedom shook the Soviet Union and brought down barriers that divided countries and continents for more than a generation. Around the same time, protests swept across China to more than four hundred cities. The iconic image of a lone student blocking the path of an advancing tank in Tiananmen Square in Beijing represents the courage and conviction that the hunger for justice and truth can produce. In the twenty-first century, the Arab Spring sent shock waves across the Middle East and demonstrated the reality that oppressive governments and belief systems will eventually lose their stranglehold on the minds and hearts of people.

I believe I felt similar winds blowing in the United States when I walked the streets of Washington, DC, in January 2017.

I stood at the intersection of several movements of people with a wide range of political, social, and religious beliefs. The tension in the air was palpable. If you have ever been to a place where bodies of water converge, you know the turmoil can be dangerous for those trying to safely navigate their way through. Looking over the vast crowds that assembled over those few days when the American president would be inaugurated, followed by a march on Washington by thousands of women, I was taken back to the images of the summer of 1963, when massive crowds came to this same place in the midst of the civil rights movement and heard the "I Have a Dream" speech by Dr. Martin Luther King Jr.

Not only did he articulate the plight of the African American community and the injustices that needed to be stopped; he did so on the basis of a firm belief that these rights were real because they were bestowed by the Creator. He also framed the moment and pleaded with the country not to miss the fierce urgency of now: "We have also come to this hallowed spot to remind America of the *fierce urgency of now*. . . . Now is the time to make justice a reality for all of God's children."[2]

History records that America heeded the warning of Dr. King, and many changes were indeed made—yet today the clouds of racism and injustice still hover over our nation. We have come to an even greater moment of truth in terms of our need to recognize the crisis we are in and not dismiss the fierce urgency of now. This urgency isn't to align ourselves with a particular political party or social cause; it isn't about demanding the rights of a particular gender or ethnic group; it is actually about recognizing our duties and responsibilities to the One who bestows all rights—the Creator. Even a casual glance at the Scriptures reveals that nations stand or fall based on their faithfulness to God and His commands. If we reject God and His ways, we will forfeit His blessings and protection. If anyone has rights, the Creator has the right to determine the rules for His creation and to decide the fate of those who reject them.

The gospel of Jesus Christ is the message of peace and reconciliation between the Creator and His creation. It tells the story of how God Himself came to the planet He created and suffered on behalf of all people and bore the punishment for our acts of sin and injustice. It deals with injustice at its source. Jesus explicitly pointed to the source of the evil as not the things that are external in their influence but, in fact, that which comes from within us: "For it is from within, out of a person's heart, that evil thoughts come—sexual immorality, theft, murder, adultery, greed, malice, deceit, lewdness, envy, slander, arrogance and folly. All these evils come from inside and defile a person" (Mark 7:20–23).

He offers us not only forgiveness but also the promise of a new heart. This is the miracle that the message of Christ produces. It provides everyone who believes the power to overcome the sin and injustice that so easily beset us all and gives us real hope we can offer to others.

As followers of Christ, we are the ones who must not miss this urgent moment. We can no longer sit back and assume that the work of spreading the gospel is the responsibility of professional ministers or missionaries. We must awaken from the dangerous slumber of indifference and get prepared to give the reasons for the hope we have in the gospel, as 1 Peter 3:15 charges us. It is a daunting task before us, but not an impossible one. History tells us that moments like this, called *awakenings*, have taken place, and entire cities, regions, and nations have turned back to God.

It starts with us, who claim to follow Christ, embracing the mandate to make disciples of all nations as our highest priority. No other political cause or social agenda contains the power to make a lasting difference on the world that the gospel does. It is the message's truthfulness that elevates hearing it to the status of a human right. And because it has the power to stop injustice, it should be valued as the most important human right of all. Seeing the gospel in this new light, we all should reevaluate our lives, our priorities, and all the ways we spend our energy and resources. "Yet to all who did receive him, to those who believed in his name, he gave the right to become children of God" (John 1:12).

The message of *the human right* is to know Jesus Christ and make Him known. Christ died to give you the right to become His child. This doesn't mean that God owes salvation to anyone but that He has made this salvation possible for everyone. Regardless of your age, ethnicity, or social standing, you have a right to know what God has provided for you through the life, death, and resurrection of His Son. You are being offered freedom from the oppression and tyranny that hinder you from fulfilling the God-given purpose for your life. This freedom is not just for individuals but for nations as well. We have been given the awesome responsibility to give the message of this hope and liberation to the whole world. They have a right to know.

I am reminded of the work of the great champion for the abolition of slavery in England, William Wilberforce. His tireless efforts to rid his nation of the scourge of slavery demonstrated the power of the gospel to bring about change in the hearts of people and consequently achieve real justice for all:

So never forget that the main difference between authentic faith and the cultural Christianity that the majority of churchgoers in our country practice is primarily a result of faulty thinking about the core truths of the gospel. If understood at all, these truths are viewed by cultural Christians as unimportant to the actual practice of their faith. These truths have become mere curiosities often relegated to a time long gone that has nothing to do with the present. But to the men and women who possess authentic faith in Jesus Christ, these truths are the center of gravity toward which all of life is in motion. They are the sun of their solar system! They are the origin of all that is excellent and lovely and the source of light and life![3]

Theodore Parker, nineteenth-century abolitionist and minister, prefigured the words of Dr. Martin Luther King Jr.: "The arc of the moral universe is long, but it bends towards justice."[4] The gospel of Jesus Christ is both the center of gravity toward whom our lives are being pulled and the moral arc of the universe. When we align ourselves with heaven's agenda, we can expect heaven's help to accomplish the task.

ACKNOWLEDGMENTS

This is the third book in a series to help equip believers in sharing the truth of the Christian faith with unbelievers. The first book, *God's Not Dead*, inspired a series of movies by the same name. I am grateful to all the people involved who helped make this possible—especially Troy Duhon and Michael Scott. The goal of helping more people learn to defend their faith is being accomplished.

Thanks to the generosity of Bob and Candy Major and Danny and Diane McDaniel, we are able to film the multiple events taking place around the world on university campuses where the evidence for God and the truth of the Christian faith are presented. Remarkable things are happening in the least likely places (such as Iceland) where atheism and skepticism have become entrenched. We are excited about sharing these documentaries in the future.

The Human Right, the third book in this series, is by far the most challenging book I've ever written. My guess is that the focus on the importance of proclaiming the gospel added to the spiritual opposition I encountered. Besides being hit virtually head-on in a car collision, a variety of events have driven me to a heightened awareness of the need for greater prayer—not only on my part but also in soliciting the prayers of others. In fact, the night before I was in the car accident, Stormie Omartian, a godly woman of prayer and a prolific writer on the subject, was awakened in the night to pray for me. The next day she happened to be one of the first on the scene of the accident and was praying for me before the ambulance arrived. Thankfully, my broken bones healed, and this book was completed. Other incidents that I will not detail have reminded me that we are engaged in a great spiritual conflict for the hearts and minds of the more than seven billion people on this planet.

I am thankful beyond words for my wife of thirty-five years, Jody. Her constant quest to learn has had an enormous effect on me, as well as on our five children whom she homeschooled. She has brought many issues to my attention that have adjusted my opinions and deepened by understanding of history. The story about the Philippines that I used at the beginning of this book would not have been possible without her help. When I came to her in January 1984, and told her about my desire to begin a ministry in Manila, she was six months pregnant with our first child. She agreed to take a three-month-old child into the uncertainty of a nation in turmoil and against the advice of family and friends. I still marvel at her courage and determination to fulfill God's purposes. Her extraordinary faith was rooted in her love for the Scriptures and her devotion to reading about the lives of missionaries in previous centuries.

The inspiration for the gospel being framed as a human rights issue came from a group of people working at the Assemblies of God in Springfield, Missouri. I was invited to speak to their national ministry team and was affected by an initiative they had just launched called "The Human Right." The national youth leader at the time, Heath Adamson, and several of his colleagues devised a strategy to recast evangelism as the most urgent of all tasks. I committed immediately to partner with them to help develop tools and support material that would give greater clarity to the reality that the gospel was the ultimate human rights issue. I am grateful to them for releasing this entire project to me to steward and spread into the wider body of Christ. My hope is that believers in Jesus Christ in every church and denomination will recapture the passion for sharing the gospel.

I am thankful to so many people who have helped contribute in some way to this book. In a way, this is a result of a cumulative process over the last thirty-five years of my Christian ministry. I am indebted to my longtime friends at Every Nation Ministries and Bethel World Outreach Church in Nashville for encouraging me to write and standing with me through this and many other endeavors. I am thankful for the contribution of Dr. Brian Miller, who helped me in the initial stages of thinking through the topics that needed to be covered. Dr. Craig Keener reviewed the manuscript and continued to encourage me that this book would be helpful to many. Vishal Mangalwadi gave invaluable input in the chapter dealing with Hinduism and Buddhism. Fikri Youseff and Shaddy Soliman did the same in the portion dealing with Islam. Thanks also to Dr. Frank Turek and Dr. Richard Howe, who were very helpful in pointing out areas that needed attention and greater clarity. Dr. Dan Wallace, who has given input on other books I've written, again was gracious in looking over the chapter on the authority of Scripture.

My son Wyatt came up with the idea for the book's cover. I am thankful for his heart for the gospel. In fact, my project team includes three of my children: Louisa, who works as my executive assistant; William, who helps direct Engage Resources; and Charlie, who works in media. It is a blessing to have them at my side as we move forward in this campaign to spread the message that the gospel is *the human right.*

My good friends Ron and Lynette Lewis, James and Debbie Lowe, Dale and Joan Evrist, and Sol and Wini Arledge are continual personal sources of encouragement to me.

NOTES

Introduction: The Revolution We Need

1. This story is recounted in Rice Broocks, *Every Nation in Our Generation: Recovering the Apostolic Mandate* (Lake Mary, FL: Creation House, 2002).
2. Michael Lipka, "Why America's 'Nones' Left Religion Behind," *FactTank* (blog), Pew Research Center, August 24, 2016, http://www .pewresearch .org/fact-tank/2016/08/24 /why-americas-nones-left-religion-behind/.
3. *The gospel as public truth* is a term coined by theologian Lesslie Newbigin. See his book *Truth to Tell: The Gospel as Public Truth* (Grand Rapids: Wm. B. Eerdmans, 1991).
4. The *social gospel* reduces the Christian message to simply good works. It omits the need for transformation through the regeneration of the Holy Spirit by believing Jesus Christ is the Son of God and was raised from the dead.

Chapter 1: The Human Right

1. David Biello, "How Science Stopped BP's Gulf of Mexico Oil Spill," *Scientific American*, April 19, 2011, https://www.scientificamerican.com /article/how-science-stopped-bp-gulf-of-mexico-oil-spill/.
2. Javier E. David, "BP, Court Trade Barbs After Sharply Worded Oil Spill Ruling," CNBC, September 4, 2014, http://www.cnbc.com/2014/09/04 /bp-grossly-negligent-for-deepwater-horizon-oil-spill-conduct-was -reckless-court.html.
3. "Universal Declaration of Human Rights," downloadable document, United Nations, accessed May 2, 2017, www.un.org/en/universal -declaration-human-rights/.
4. "World War II," History.com, accessed July 20, 2017, http://www.history .com/topics/world-war-ii.
5. *Oxford Living Dictionaries*, s.v. "right," accessed July 20, 2017, https:// en.oxforddictionaries.com/definition/right.

6. Eric Posner, "The Case Against Human Rights," *Guardian*, December 4, 2014, https://www.theguardian.com/news/2014/dec/04 /-sp-case-against-human-rights.

7. Richard Rorty and Gianni Vattimo, *The Future of Religion* (New York: Columbia University Press, 2007), 72.

8. Michael J. Sandel, *Justice: What's the Right Thing to Do?* (New York: Farrar, Straus and Giroux, 2009), 102.

9. John Locke, *The Reasonableness of Christianity* (n.p.: Kypros Press, 2016), Kindle locations 246–49.

10. Vishal Mangalwadi, *The Book That Made Your World: How the Bible Created the Soul of Western Civilization* (Nashville: Thomas Nelson, 2012), 391.

11. Timothy Keller, *Making Sense of God: An Invitation to the Skeptical* (New York: Viking, 2016), 221.

12. Vindal Mangalwadi, "Truth Matters," YouTube video, 8:08, Reformation video #1, posted by Solid Rock TV, May 13, 2017, youtu. be/Rd6pk0a9hcE.

13. Lesslie Newbigin, *Foolishness to the Greeks: The Gospel and Western Culture* (Grand Rapids: Wm. B. Eerdmans, 1988), 26.

14. Friedrich Nietzsche, "The Madman," *The Gay Science*, trans. Walter Kaufmann (New York: Vintage, 1974), 181. (Originally published 1882.)

15. Penn Jillette, "Why Tolerance Is Condescending," YouTube video, 5:33, posted by Big Think, June 10, 2011, youtu.be/IpNRw7snmGM.

16. Robert M. Pirsig, quoted in Richard Dawkins, *The God Delusion* (Boston: Houghton Mifflin Harcourt, 2006), 28.

17. Keller, *Making Sense of God*, 12.

18. Zarathustra in Friedrich Nietzsche, *Thus Spoke Zarathustra: A Book for All and None*, trans. Walter Kauffman (New York: Modern Library, 1995), 13. (Originally published 1883–91.)

19. Lesslie Newbigin, *The Gospel in a Pluralist Society* (Grand Rapids: Wm. B. Eerdmans, 1989), Kindle locations 4106–8.

20. Timothy Keller, *Generous Justice: How God's Grace Makes Us Just* (New York: Penguin, 2010), 164–65.

21. Martin Luther King Jr., "I Have a Dream," speech, August 28, 1963, transcript, The Martin Luther King Jr. Research and Education Institute, Stanford University, https://kinginstitute.stanford.edu/king-papers /documents/i-have-dream-address-delivered-march-washington-jobs-and -freedom.

22. Elisabeth Rosenthal and Andrew Martin, "UN Says Solving Food Crisis Could Cost $30 Billion," *New York Times*, June 4, 2008, http://www .nytimes.com/2008/06/04/news/04iht-04food.13446176.html.

23. Zoe Shenton, "Stephen Fry's Furious Rant About God: 'He Is Utterly

Monstrous, Selfish and Deserves No Respect,'" *Mirror,* January 30, 2015, http://www.mirror.co.uk/3am/celebrity-news/stephen-frys-furious-rant-god-5072065.

24. Guy Hutton, "Global Costs and Benefits of Drinking-Water Supply and Sanitation Interventions to Reach the MDG Target and Universal Coverage," World Health Organization, 2012, http://www.who.int/water_sanitation_health/publications/2012/globalcosts.pdf.

25. Ibid.

26. Ibid.

27. Mangalwadi, *The Book That Made Your World,* 258.

Chapter 2: The Gospel as Public Truth

1. For a biographical sketch, see Paul Weston, *Lesslie Newbigin: Missionary Theologian: A Reader* (Grand Rapids: Wm. B. Eerdmans, 2006).

2. Lesslie Newbigin, *Truth to Tell: The Gospel as Public Truth* (Grand Rapids: Wm. B. Eerdmans, 1991), 2.

3. Lesslie Newbigin, quoted in Weston, *Lesslie Newbigin,* 149.

4. Christine D. Johnson, "Tell It Well," *Ministry Today* (March 2016), 18.

5. Weston, *Lesslie Newbigin,* 257.

6. John Williams, "The Gospel as Public Truth: A Critical Appreciation of the Theological Programme of Lesslie Newbigin," *Anvil* 10, no. 1 (1993): 11, https://biblicalstudies.org.uk/pdf/anvil/10-1_011.pdf.

7. Lesslie Newbigin, *The Gospel in a Pluralist Society* (Grand Rapids: Wm. B. Eerdmans, 1989), Kindle locations 4106–8.

8. Krish Kandiah, "The Gospel Is Bigger Than You Think," United Christian Broadcasters website, accessed July 20, 2017, http://www.ucb.co.uk/w4uasoarticle-Krish.

9. Newbigin, *Truth to Tell,* 5.

10. Gary R. Habermas and Michael R. Licona, *The Case for the Resurrection of Jesus* (Grand Rapids: Kregel, 2004), Kindle location 325.

11. Krish Kandiah, "Not Personal Spirituality, but Public Truth," *Thinking Matters* (blog), December 9, 2009, http://thinkingmatters.org.nz/2009/12/not-personal-spirituality-but-public-truth/.

12. Mark T. B. Laing, *Theology in Missionary Perspective: Lesslie Newbigin's Legacy* (Eugene, OR: Pickwick, 2013), 43.

13. Newbigin, *The Gospel in a Pluralist Society,* Kindle locations 4106–8.

14. Newbigin, *Truth to Tell,* 11.

15. Newbigin, *The Gospel in a Pluralist Society,* Kindle locations 231–36.

16. Ibid., Kindle locations 384–86.

17. Ibid., Kindle locations 110–11.

18. Ibid., Kindle locations 4490–92.

19. Ibid., Kindle locations 2402–6.

20. Newbigin, *Truth to Tell,* 34.

21. Augustine, *Nicene and Post-Nicene Fathers*, vol. 7 (Tractates on the Gospel of John), ed. Philip Schaff (Peabody, MA: Hendrickson, 1995), 184.

Chapter 3: The Cry for Justice

1. Martin Luther King Jr., "Letter from a Birmingham Jail," April 16, 1963, African Studies Center, University of Pennsylvania, www.africa.upenn .edu/Articles_Gen/Letter_Birmingham.html.

2. Mike Wooldridge, "Mandela Death: How He Survived 27 Years in Prison," BBC News, December 11, 2013, http://www.bbc.com/news /world-africa-23618727.

3. I have been strongly influenced in this area by Frank Turek and others.

4. Lesslie Newbigin, *Truth to Tell: The Gospel as Public Truth* (Grand Rapids: Wm. B. Eerdmans, 1991), 78.

5. Ibid.

6. King, "Letter from a Birmingham Jail," April 16, 1963.

7. "Hitchens vs. Blair, Roy Thomson Hall" (transcript), *Hitchens Debates* (blog), November 27, 2010, http://hitchensdebates.blogspot.com. au/2010/11/hitchens-vs-blair-roy-thomson-hall.html.

8. The Center for Public Policy Studies, "Texas Human Trafficking Fact Sheet," January 2013, http://www.htcourts.org/wp-content/uploads /TX-HT-Fact-Sheet-2.13.13.pdf?Factsheet=HT-TX.

9. "The United Nations Fourth World Conference on Women: Platform of Action" (September 1995), UN Women, http://www.un.org /womenwatch/daw/beijing/platform/armed.htm.

10. "Global Study on Homicide," UNODC, accessed July 20, 2017, https:// www.unodc.org/gsh/.

11. International Institutions and Global Governance Program, "The Global Regime for Armed Conflict," Council on Foreign Relations, February 15, 2013, https://www.cfr.org/report/ global-regime-armed-conflict.

12. Camilla Schippa, "Conflict Costs Us $13.6 Trillion a Year. And We Spend Next to Nothing on Peace," World Economic Forum, January 5, 2017, https://www.weforum.org/agenda/2017/01/how-much-does-violence -really-cost-our-global-economy/.

13. "The Numbers: Abortion in Numbers," LifeZone, accessed July 20, 2017, http://www.prolifeinfo.ie/abortion-facts/issues/the-numbers/.

14. Center for Strategic and International Studies, "Net Losses: Estimating the Global Cost of Cybercrime: Economic Impact of Cybercrime II," McAfee.com, June 2014 https://www.mcafee.com /de/resources/reports/rp-economic-impact-cybercrime2.pdf.

15. "Violent Crime," Crime in the United States 2013, FBI.gov, accessed July 20, 2017, https://ucr.fbi.gov/crime-in-the-u.s/2013/crime-in-the

-u.s.-2013/violent-crime/violent-crime-topic-page/violentcrimemain
_final.

16. Susan Jones, "11,774 Terror Attacks Worldwide in 2015; 28,328 Deaths
Due to Terror Attacks," cnsnews.com, June 3, 2016, http://www
.cnsnews.com/news/article/susan-jones/11774-number-terror
-attacks-worldwide-dropped-13-2015. Also see Sangwon Yoon and
Andre Tartar, "Paris Attacks: Global Economic Cost of Terrorism
Highest Since September 11, 2001," *Sydney Morning Herald*,
November 11, 2015, http://www.smh.com.au/business/the
-economy/paris-attacks-global-economic-cost-of-terrorism
-highest-since-september-11-2001-20151117-gl0vfk.html.

17. "The Global Economic Cost of Terrorism Is Now at Its Highest Since
9/11," Bloomberg, November 17, 2015, http://www bloomberg.com
/news/articles/2015-11-17/the-global-economic-cost-of-terrorism-is
-now-at-its-highest-since-9-11.

18. Statistics are taken from Anup Shaw, "Poverty Facts and Stats,"
Global Issues, updated January 7, 2013, http://www.globalissues
.org/article/26/poverty-facts-and-stats.

19. "Quotes for Faora-UI (Character)," IMDB, accessed May 5, 2017, http://
www.imdb.com/character/ch0246265/quotes.

20. Walter Kauffman (Translator's Notes, Thus Spoke Zarathustra: First
Part), Friedrich Nietzsche, *Thus Spoke Zarathustra: A Book for All and None*,
trans. Walter Kauffman (New York: Modern Library, 1995), 3.

21. Andrea Warren, *Charles Dickens and the Street Children of London* (Boston:
Houghton Mifflin Harcourt Books for Children, 2011), 3.

22. G. K. Chesterton, "Introduction," *Reprinted Pieces*, quoted in
Gary L. Colledge, *God and Charles Dickens: Recovering the
Christian Voice of a Classic Author* (Grand Rapids: Brazos Press,
2012), 1.

23. Charles Dickens, quoted in Colledge, *God and Charles Dickens*, 3.

24. Charles Dickens, *The Life of Our Lord* (New York: Simon & Schuster,
1999), 122.

25. Harriet Beecher Stowe, "1851 Letter to Gamaliel Bailey,"
electronic ed. (Charlottesville: Stephen Railton Institute for
Advanced Technology in the Humanities Electronic Text Center,
2006). This text is transcribed from the *Oxford Harriet Beecher Stowe
Reader*, ed. Joan D. Hedrick (New York: Oxford University Press,
1999, all rights reserved), 66.

26. Carl Sandburg, *Abraham Lincoln: The Prairie Years and the War Years* (New
York: Harcourt, 1954, 1982), 385.

27. See Stephen McDowell, "A Nation at Risk," Providence Foundation,
accessed July 21, 2017, http://providencefoundation.com
/?page_id=2530.

Chapter 4: The Search for Truth

1. *Oxford Living Dictionaries*, s.v. "post-truth," accessed May 5, 2017, https://en.oxforddictionaries.com/definition/post-truth.
2. See http://everynation.org.
3. Frank Turek, in discussion with the author, April 23, 2017.
4. Lesslie Newbigin, *The Gospel in a Pluralist Society* (Grand Rapids: Wm. B. Eerdmans, 1989), 170.
5. Marian David, "The Correspondence Theory of Truth," *Stanford Encyclopedia of Philosophy* (Fall 2016), ed. Edward N. Zalta, https://plato.stanford.edu/entries/truth-correspondence/.
6. "Difference Between Knowledge and Truth," Difference Between, accessed May 5, 2017, http://www.differencebetween.info/difference-between-knowledge-and-truth.
7. Ravi Zacharias, *Can Man Live Without God?* (Nashville: Thomas Nelson, 2004), 123–24.
8. See the Logical Fallacies website, accessed July 21, 2017, http://www.logicalfallacies.org.
9. David Hume, *An Enquiry Concerning Human Understanding*, 2nd ed. (Cambridge, MA: Hackett Classics, 2011), Kindle locations 2413–14. (Originally published 1748.)
10. Thomas Nagel, *Mind and Cosmos: Why the Materialist Neo-Darwinian Conception of Nature Is Almost Certainly False* (Oxford: Oxford University Press, 2012), 18.
11. Bertrand Russell, *Religion and Science* (Oxford: Oxford University Press, 1997), 243. (Originally published 1935.)
12. Michael Guillen, personal correspondence to author, June 5, 2017.
13. Eric Hedin, *The Boundaries of Science*, from an unpublished manuscript provided to the author.
14. Frank Turek, quoted in Nagel, *Mind and Cosmos*, 4. The author footnotes this quote with the following: "For a clear statement, see Steven Weinberg, *Dreams of a Final Theory* (New York: Pantheon Books, 1992), chapter 3."
15. Frank Turek, *Stealing from God: Why Atheists Need God to Make Their Case* (Colorado Springs: NavPress, 2014), 146.
16. See Mike Robbins, "Speak Your Truth," Oprah.com, accessed July 21, 2017, http://www.oprah.com/spirit/speak-your-truth_2.
17. Richard Rorty and Gianni Vattimo, *The Future of Religion* (New York: Columbia University Press, 2007), 71–72.
18. *Oxford Living Dictionaries*, s.v. "epistemology," accessed July 21, 2017, https://en.oxforddictionaries.com/definition/epistemology.
19. *Oxford Living Dictionaries*, s.v. "belief," accessed July 21, 2017, https://en.oxforddictionaries.com/definition/belief.

20. *Merriam-Webster*, s.v. "belief," accessed July 21, 2017, https://www .merriam-webster.com/dictionary/belief.

21. Peter Boghossian, *A Manual for Creating Atheists* (Charlottesville, VA: Pitchstone, 2013), 7.

22. Nagel, *Mind and Cosmos*, 10.

23. Boghossian, *Manual for Creating Atheists*, 181.

24. Tom Gilson, "Is Faith an Unreliable Epistemology?" *Thinking Christian* (blog), January 2, 2014, https://www.thinkingchristian.net /posts/2014/01/is-faith-an-unreliable-epistemology/.

25. Alvin Plantinga, *Where the Conflict Really Lies: Science, Religion, and Naturalism* (Oxford: Oxford University Press, 2011), 341.

26. Vishal Mangalwadi, *The Book That Made Your World: How the Bible Created the Soul of Western Civilization* (Nashville: Thomas Nelson, 2012), 392.

27. This thought was inspired from a discussion in Vishal Mangalwadi, *Truth and Transformation: A Manifesto for Ailing Nations* (Seattle: YWAM, 2012), Kindle locations 1468–69.

28. Lesslie Newbigin, *Truth to Tell: The Gospel as Public Truth* (Grand Rapids: Wm. B. Eerdmans, 1991), 5.

Chapter 5: The Reality of the Soul

1. J. P. Moreland, *The God Question: An Invitation to a Life of Meaning* (Eugene, OR: Harvest House, 2009), 11.

2. CBS/AP, "Outrage After Gorilla Killed at Cincinnati Zoo to Save Child," CBS News, May 29, 2016, http://www.cbsnews.com/news /outrage-after-gorilla-harambe-killed-at-cincinnati-zoo-to-save-child/.

3. Cristina Odone, "Let Us Pray for the Soul of Richard Dawkins," *Guardian*, May 13, 2007, https://www.theguardian.com/commentisfree/2007 /may/13/comment.religion1.

4. Sam Harris, *Letter to a Christian Nation* (New York: Alfred A. Knopf, 2006), 29–30.

5. William Lane Craig, *The Existence of God and the Beginning of the Universe* (Orlando: Here's Life Publishers, 1979), 3.

6. J. P. Moreland, *The Soul: How We Know It's Real and Why It Matters* (Grand Rapids: Moody Publishers, 2014), 15.

7. Charles Darwin, *The Descent of Man* (n.p.: CreateSpace, 2011), Kindle location 10994.

8. Plato, *The Collected Dialogues of Plato Including the Letters*, ed. E. Hamilton and H. Cairns (Princeton, NJ: Princeton University Press, 1961), 105d.

9. Raymond Martin and John Barresi, *The Rise and Fall of Soul and Self: An Intellectual History of Personal Identity* (New York: Columbia University Press, 2006), 13; and Hendrik Lorenz, "Ancient Theories of Soul,"

Stanford Encyclopedia of Philosophy (Summer 2009), ed. Edward N. Zalta, accessed May 8, 2017, https://plato.stanford.edu/entries/ancient-soul/.

10. Stewart Goetz and Charles Taliaferro, *A Brief History of the Soul* (Hoboken, NJ: Wiley-Blackwell, 2011), 12.

11. Edward Feser, *The Last Superstition: A Refutation of the New Atheism* (South Bend, IN: St. Augustine's Press, 2010), 51.

12. Ibid., 137.

13. This is a paraphrase of Feser's discussion in *The Last Superstition*.

14. Goetz and Taliaferro, *A Brief History of the Soul*, 34.

15. Augustine, *The Confessions*, trans. Henry Chadwick (Oxford, UK: Oxford World's Classics, 1998), 152.

16. Feser, *The Last Superstition*, 20.

17. Catherine O'Brien, *Transcription: The Afterlife Debate* (self-published, 2015), 38; see also "Is There an Afterlife?—Christopher Hitchens, Sam Harris, David Wolpe, Bradley Shavit Artson," YouTube video, 1:37:54, panel discussion, posted by theinfiniteyes, December 29, 2011, youtu.be /UjKJ92b9Y04.

18. Daniel Dennett, *Brainchildren: Essays on Designing Minds* (Cambridge, MA: MIT Press, 1998), as quoted in Mario Beauregard and Denyse O'Leary, *The Spiritual Brain: A Neuroscientist's Case for the Existence of the Soul* (New York: HarperOne, 2009), 4.

19. "Sam Harris: The Self Is an Illusion," YouTube video, 6:52, Harris discussing the properties of consciousness, posted by Big Think, September 16, 2014, youtu.be/fajfkO_X0l0.

20. Moreland, *The Soul*, 35.

21. David Chalmers, "How Do You Explain Consciousness?" (transcript), TED Talks, March 2014, https://www.ted.com/talks/david _chalmers_how_do_you_explain_consciousness/transcript ?language=en.

22. David Chalmers, quoted in Oliver Burkeman, "Why Can't the World's Greatest Minds Solve the Mystery of Consciousness?" *Guardian*, January 21, 2015, https://www.theguardian.com/science/2015/jan/21 /-sp-why-cant-worlds-greatest-minds-solve-mystery-consciousness.

23. Chalmers, "How Do You Explain Consciousness?"

24. Susan Greenfield, "The Neuroscience of Consciousness," YouTube video, 1:34:17, posted by the University of Melbourne, November 28, 2012, youtu.be/k_ZTNmkIiBc. Transcribed by the author.

25. Ibid.

26. Christof Koch, "Is Consciousness Universal?" *Scientific American*, January 1, 2014, https://www.scientificamerican.com/article/is -consciousness-universal/.

27. Moreland, *The Soul*, 38.

28. Daniel Dennett, in Goetz and Taliaferro, *A Brief History of the Soul*, 1.

29. Moreland, *The Soul*, 79–80.

30. Ibid., 398–401.

31. C. S. Lewis, *Mere Christianity* (New York: HarperOne, 2009), 25–26.

32. Marcus Conyers and Donna Wilson, "Metacognition: The Gift That Keeps Giving," *Edutopia* (blog), October 7, 2014, https://www.edutopia .org/blog/metacognition-gift-that-keeps-giving-donna-wilson-marcus -conyers.

33. Eben Alexander, "Proof of Heaven: A Doctor's Experience with the Afterlife," *Newsweek*, October 8, 2012, http://www.newsweek.com /proof-heaven-doctors-experience-afterlife-65327.

34. Ibid.

35. Gary Habermas, in discussion with author, March 15, 2017.

36. Moreland, *The Soul*, 36.

37. Sharon Begley, "Better Brains: The Revolution in Brain Science," *Scientific American* (podcast and transcript), August 8, 2007, https:// www.scientificamerican.com/podcast/episode/465b1677-e7f2-99df -36e1378b1640d492/.

38. Lewis, *Mere Christianity*, 9–10.

39. Stephen Hawking, *The Grand Design* (New York: Bantam, 2012), 32.

40. Sam Harris, *Free Will* (New York: Simon & Schuster, 2012), 64.

41. "John Searle—What Is Free Will?" YouTube video, 9:02, interview, posted by Closer to Truth, January 8, 2013, youtu.be/_rZfSTpjGl8.

Chapter 6: God Has Spoken to Us

1. Bart D. Ehrman, *Jesus, Interrupted: Revealing the Hidden Contradictions in the Bible (and Why We Don't Know About Them)* (New York: HarperCollins, 2009), xi.

2. Frank Turek, *Stealing from God: Why Atheists Need God to Make Their Case* Colorado Springs: NavPress, 2014), xxv.

3. Bart D. Ehrman, *Misquoting Jesus* (New York: HarperOne, 2007), 9.

4. See Bill Pratt, "Is There a Mistake in Mark 2:26?" Tough Questions Answered (blog), September 27, 2009, http://www.toughquestions answered.org/2009/09/27/is-there-a-mistake-in-mark-226/.

5. Dan Wallace, in discussion with author, c. March 2015.

6. Jonathan Peterson, "How the Bible Created the Soul of Western Civilization: An Interview with Vishal Mangalwadi," *BibleGateway Blog*, July 27, 2015, https://www.biblegateway.com/ blog/2015/07/how-the-bible-created-the-soul-of-western-civilization -an-interview-with-vishal-mangalwadi/.

7. See "Lawrence Krauss, The Colbert Report" (video clip), Comedy Central, June 21, 2012, http://www.cc.com/video-clips/e6ik9l/the -colbert-report-lawrence-krauss.

8. J. Ed Komoszewski, M. James Sawyer, and Daniel B. Wallace, *Reinventing Jesus* (Grand Rapids: Kregel, 2006), 17.

9. In personal correspondence with author in May 2017, New Testament scholar Craig Keener raised the issue that some consider the account of the seventy to be "legend." However, Keener wrote, "No one disputes the existence of the Septuagint. Instead, say something like this: after the first century, the OT was *independently* preserved by Jews and Christians, so Islamic claims of corruption of the OT are for all practical purposes impossible; no one cognizant of the history of the period can suspect Jews and Christians of collusion!"

10. Bruce M. Metzger, "Important Early Translations of the Bible," W. H. Griffith Thomas Lectures, Dallas Theological Seminary, 1993, https://faculty.gordon.edu/hu/bi/ted_hildebrandt/new_testament_greek/text/metzger-earlytranslations01-bs.pdf.

11. "The Old Testament in Greek," History of Bible Translations, History World, http://www.historyworld.net/wrldhis/PlainTextHistories.asp?historyid=ac66.

12. Vishal Mangalwadi, *The Book That Made Your World* (Nashville Thomas Nelson, 2012), 91.

13. Timothy Keller's Facebook page, April 1, 2015, https://www.facebook.com/TimKellerNYC/posts/930042907035596.

14. Mangalwadi, *The Book That Made Your World*, xxi.

15. Vishal Mangalwadi, *Truth and Transformation: A Manifesto for Ailing Nations* (Seattle: YWAM, 2012), Kindle locations 314–15.

16. Richard Dawkins, *The God Delusion* (Boston: Houghton Mifflin Harcourt, 2006), 51.

17. Frank Turek made this point in a classic Q & A session with a student. See "Frank Turek Answers Atheist's 3 Objections to Christianity," YouTube video, 6:10, posted by Frank Turek, April 16, 2013, youtu.be/XjHhtWL_3Og.

18. "U.S. Senate Chaplain Dr. Barry Black Full Remarks at National Prayer Breakfast (C-SPAN)," YouTube video, 26:36, posted by C-SPAN, February 2, 2017, youtu.be/zyvNg1kk9tQ.

19. "Chicago Statement on Biblical Inerrancy with Exposition," Bible Research website, accessed July 24, 2017, http://www.bible-researcher.com/chicago1.html.

Chapter 7: Jesus Versus the World Religions

1. Lesslie Newbigin, *The Open Secret: An Introduction to the Theology of Mission* (Grand Rapids: Wm. B. Eerdmans, 1995), Kindle location 2225.

2. Drew Desilver and David Masci, "World's Muslim Population More Widespread Than You Might Think," *FactTank* (blog), Pew Research Center, January 31, 2017, http://www.pewresearch.org/fact-tank/2017/01/31/worlds-muslim-population-more-widespread-than-you-might-think/.

3. For additional details see the Political Islam website, at https://www
   .politicalislam.com/shop/.
4. "The Five Pillars of Islam," Religions, BBC, September 8, 2009, bbc
   .co.uk/religion/religions/islam/practices/fivepillars.shtml.
5. Encyclopedia of Islam, 2nd ed., s.v. "al-Kur'an," "Hadith," accessed July 24,
   2017, http://referenceworks.brillonline.com/browse/encyclopaedia-of
   -islam-2; the Hadith, Bukari 33:23.
6. David Garrison, A Wind in the House of Islam: How God Is Drawing Muslims
   Around the World to Faith in Jesus Christ (Monument, CO: WIGTake
   Resources, 2014).
7. I am indebted to Vishal Mangalwadi for his input in the sections on
   Hinduism and Buddhism. Many of the terms and definitions describing
   key aspects of the respective belief systems came directly from our
   in-depth dialogues.
8. Acharya Rajneesh, Beyond and Beyond (Bombay: Jeevan Jagruti Kendra,
   1970), 12.
9. Ibid., 12–14.
10. See Alf Hiltebeitel ed., Criminal Gods and Demon Devotees: Essays on the
    Guardians of Popular Hinduism (Albany: State University of New York
    Press, 1989).
11. A recent study by Transparency International says that India is the most
    corrupt country in Asia Pacific. Sixty-nine percent of Indians polled
    confessed to having to pay a bribe to get public services. See http://www
    .indiatimes.com/news/india/india-is-the-most-corrupt-country-in-asia
    -pacific-two-third of all indians-have-to-pay-bribe-says-transparency
    -international-272923.html.
12. AP, "Millions of Hindus Plunge into Ganges River in India to Wash Away
    Their Sins," Telegraph, January 14, 2013, http://www.telegraph.co.uk
    /news/worldnews/asia/india/9799882/Millions-of-Hindus-plunge-into
    -Ganges-River-in-India-to-wash-away-their-sins.html.
13. Vishal Mangalwadi, The Book That Made Your World: How the Bible Created
    the Soul of Western Civilization (Nashville: Thomas Nelson, 2012), 23.
14. Third Mundaka, Second Khanda, verse 3.
15. Senaka Weeraratna, "57th Anniversary of Historic Step to Revive
    Buddhism in India," The Buddhist Channel, October 13, 2013,
    http://www.buddhistchannel.tv/index.php?id=9,11641,0,0,1,0#.
    WVFknMaZPMU.
16. "The Four Noble Truths," BBC, Religions, last updated November 17,
    2009, http://www.bbc.co.uk/religion/religions/buddhism/beliefs
    /fournobletruths_1.shtml.
17. Lewis Richmond, "The Buddha's Teachings About the Soul," HuffPost:
    The Blog, updated July 27, 2011, http://www.huffingtonpost.com/lewis
    -richmond/buddhas-teachings-about-t_b_866474.html.

18. *Encyclopedia Britannica*, s.v. "Vihara," accessed July 24, 2017, https://www.britannica.com/topic/vihara.

19. *Oxford Living Dictionaries*, s.v. "buddhu," accessed July 24, 2017, https://en.oxforddictionaries.com/definition/buddhu.

20. Katherine J. Wolfenden, "Hobbes' *Leviathan* and Views on the Origins of Civil Government: Conservatism by Covenant," *Inquiries* 2, no. 12 (2010): 1–2, http://www.inquiriesjournal.com/articles/349/hobbes-leviathan -and-views-on-the-origins-of-civil-government-conservatism-by-covenant.

21. "Christ, My Bodhisattva," Ram Gidoomal interview by Andy Crouch, *Christianity Today*, April 27, 2007, http://www.christianitytoday.com/ct /2007/may/17.34.html?start=2.

22. George Dvorsky, "Why the Dalai Lama Is Hinting That He Could Be the Very Last One," *i09* (blog), December 22, 2014, https://io9.gizmodo.com /why-the-dalai-lama-is-hinting-that-he-could-be-the-very-1674077042.

23. MeiMei Fox, "10 Ways 10 Days of Silence Will Blow Your Mind," *HuffPost: The Blog*, May 5, 2012, updated July 5, 2012, http://www.huffingtonpost .com/meimei-fox/meditation-retreat_b_1474445.html.

Chapter 8: Open Their Eyes

1. Ming Wang's story is told in his book *From Darkness to Sight: How One Man Turned Hardship into Healing* (n.p.: Dunham Books, 2016).

2. Ming Wang, in discussion with the author, April 25, 2017.

3. "A 30-Year History of the Future: Nicholas Negroponte," YouTube video, 19:43, a journey through the last thirty years of technology, posted by TED, July 8, 2014, youtu.be/5b5BDoddOLA.

4. Mark Galli, "Speak the Gospel," *Christianity Today*, May 21, 2009, http:// www.christianitytoday.com/ct/2009/mayweb-only/120-42.0.html.

5. Ed Stetzer, "Preach the Gospel, and Since It's Necessary, Use Words," *The Exchange* (CT blog), June 25, 2012, http://www.christianitytoday.com /edstetzer/2012/june/preach-gospel-and-since-its-necessary-use-words .html.

6. When Paul talked about the Jews, he was speaking of the religious authorities, not broad-brushing the ethnic group of which he was a part. All of the apostles were Jewish, as was the Lord Jesus Himself.

7. Stetzer, "Preach the Gospel, and Since It's Necessary, Use Words."

Chapter 9: The Ministry of Reconciliation

1. David Remnick, "The Seventh Day," *New Yorker*, May 28, 2007, http:// www.newyorker.com/magazine/2007/05/28/the-seventh-day.

2. IMEMC Agencies, "What Do Israelis Say About the Arabs?" IMEMC News, November 3, 2005, http://imemc.org/article/14776/.

3. William Carey, as quoted in *The Baptist Herald and Friend of Africa* (October 1842) and "The Missionary Herald" in *Baptist Magazine*, January 1843, 41.

4. David Shibley, *Entrusted: Anchoring Your Life in the Gospel* (Bedford, TX: Burkhart Books, 2016), 8.

5. "The Most Segregated Hour in America—Martin Luther King Jr.," YouTube video, 0:52, King speaking on *Meet the Press*, April 17, 1960, posted by Jason Tripp, April 29, 2014, youtu.be/1q881g1L_d8.

6. Tara John, "International Students in U.S. Colleges and Universities Top 1 Million," *Time*, November 14, 2016, http://time.com/4569564/international-us-students/.

Chapter 10: The Mystery of Godliness

1. Augustine, *The Confessions*, trans. Henry Chadwick (Oxford, UK: Oxford World's Classics, 1998), 38.

2. William Wilberforce, *Real Christianity*, ed. Bob Beltz (Grand Rapids: Regal Books, 2006), 39. (Originally published 1797.)

3. Augustine, *The Confessions*, 25.

4. Ibid., 152.

5. Ibid., 153.

Conclusion: The Fierce Urgency of Now

1. "0.0% of Icelanders 25 years or younger believe God created the world, new poll reveals," Iceland Magazine, January 14, 2016, http://icelandmag.visir.is/article/00-icelanders-25-years-or-younger-believe-god-created-world-new-poll-reveals; Rick Noack, "In This Country, Literally No Young Christians Believe that God Created the Earth," *Washington Post*, January 23, 2016, https://www.washingtonpost.com/news/worldviews/wp/2016/01/23/in-this-country-literally-no-young-christians-believe-that-god-created-the-earth/?utm_term=.959a44a71bdf.

2. Martin Luther King Jr., "I Have a Dream" speech, August 28, 1963, Washington, DC, available online at American Rhetoric, http://www.americanrhetoric.com/speeches/mlkihaveadream.htm.

3. William Wilberforce, *Real Christianity*, ed. Bob Beltz (Grand Rapids: Regal Books, 2006), 128.

4. "Theodore Parker and the 'Moral Universe,'" transcript, Clayborne Carson interviewed by Melissa Block, September 2, 2010, *All Things Considered*, NPR, https://www.npr.org/templates/story/story.php?storyId=129609461.

INDEX

U

U-Belt (Manila), xiii–xiv, xxi–xxii
United Nations, 4, 58
United States Constitution, 5, 97
Universal Declaration of Human
 Rights, 4
University of Cape Town and
 University of Stellenbosch, 51
University College London, 123
University of North Carolina–Chapel
 Hill, 134
Uthman ('Uthmān ibn Affān, third
 caliph), 169

V

Vattimo, Gianni (coauthor, *The
 Future of Religion*), 89
Vedas, 84, 176
victims of human trafficking,
 estimated number of, 58
Victory (Manila church), xiv, xv
violence, 26, 58, 60, 157, 164, 196
 and genocide in the Old
  Testament, 147–49
 total cost of global, 58
Vipassana, 183
Vulgate, 138–39

W–X

Wallace, Dan (Bible scholar), 135,
 137, 267
Wallace, J. Warner (author, *Cold Case
 Christianity*), 81
Wang, Ming (Wang Vision Institute),
 187–88, 189, 280ch8n1
Washington, George, 142–43

Washington Post, 159
Warren, Andrea (Dickens
 biographer), 70
water, number of people with
 inadequate access to, 59
Westminster Confession, 25
Weston, Paul, 27
Wheaton College, 133
Wilberforce, William, 72, 246,
 263–64
William the Silent (William of
 Orange I), 292
Williams, Dr. John (Anglican
 clergyman), 28
women, oppression of, 2, 58, 170
World Health Organization, 16, 17
World War II, 4, 25–26, 63
Wycliffe, John, 138

Y–Z

yoga, 171, 174, 183
Yuccas, Jamie (CBS News), 104

ABOUT THE AUTHOR

Rice Broocks is cofounder of the Every Nation family of churches, which currently has churches and campus ministries in more than seventy nations. He is also the senior minister of Bethel World Outreach Church in Nashville, Tennessee, a multiethnic, multisite church. Rice is a graduate of Mississippi State University and holds a master's degree from Reformed Theological Seminary, Jackson, Mississippi, as well as a doctorate from Fuller Theological Seminary, Pasadena, California. He is the author of several books, including *God's Not Dead*; *Man, Myth, Messiah*; *The Purple Book: Biblical Foundations for Building Strong Disciples*; and *Every Nation in Our Generation*.

For more information, please visit RiceBroocks.com.

Become an ADVOCATE
THEHUMANRIGHT.ORG

God's Not Dead

Evidence for God in an Age of Uncertainty

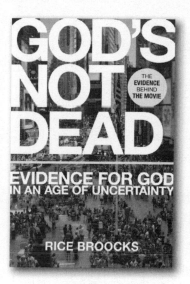

Faith in God is rising, yet so is skepticism. The evidence for the existence of God must be grasped and clearly articulated to answer this challenge. Drawing from the areas of philosophy, science, history, and theology, we can form persuasive arguments for God's existence and His presence in our lives. *God's Not Dead* equips us with the tools, providing clear, easy-to-follow explanations of the key concepts and controversies. *God's Not Dead* is apologetics for the twenty-first century.

"This is quite simply the most concise, punchiest, and wide-ranging argument for the existence of God and the truth of Christianity that has been written in recent years."

—David Aikerman
Former senior correspondent, *Time,*
and author, *One Nation Without God?*

"*God's Not Dead* answers the thin case of the New Atheists, stirs Christians to confidence in their gospel, and empowers believers for both the spiritual and intellectual battles of our times."

—Stephen Mansfield
New York Times bestselling author

Man, Myth, Messiah

Answering History's Greatest Question

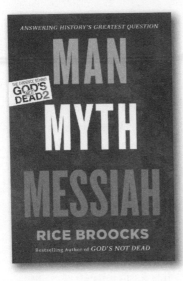

In his follow-up to the bestselling *God's Not Dead*, Rice Broocks looks at the evidence for the historical Jesus and exposes the notions of skeptics that Jesus was a contrived figure of ancient mythology. *Man, Myth, Messiah* also establishes the reliability of the Gospels as evidence for the resurrection, validating Jesus' identity as the promised Messiah.

"I highly recommend this volume to you as a way to answer tough questions, ground the proclamation of the gospel message, and be prepared to share these truths with others, all from one text. Dr. Broocks is a capable guide to bring us safely to our destination."

—Gary R. Haberman, PhD
Distinguished Professor and Chair, Department of Philosophy and Theology, Liberty University

"In *Man, Myth, Messiah* Rice Broocks takes a massive amount of historical research on Jesus and makes it accessible, interesting, and relevant for today. This book will both strengthen the belief of Christians and challenge the unbelief of skeptics. . . . Isn't it worth wrestling with the question Jesus said matters most: *Who do you say I am?*"

—Sean McDowell, PhD
Biola University professor, internationally recognized speaker, and bestselling author, *The Fate of the Apostles*